SLIPPERY PATHS *in the* DARKNESS

Titles in The Missiology of Alan R. Tippett Series

The Jesus Documents (2012)

The Ways of the People: A Reader in Missionary Anthropology (2013)

The Road to Bau and *The Autobiography of Joeli Bulu* (2013)

No Continuing City (2013)

Fullness of Time (2014)

SLIPPERY PATHS *in the* DARKNESS
PAPERS ON SYNCRETISM: 1965-1988

THE MISSIOLOGY OF ALAN R. TIPPETT SERIES
DOUG PRIEST, SERIES EDITOR
DOUG PRIEST, EDITOR

WILLIAM CAREY
LIBRARY

Slippery Paths in the Darkness: Papers on Syncretism: 1965-1988
Copyright © 2014 by Fuller Theological Seminary
All rights reserved.

No part of this book may be reproduced, stored in a retrieval system, or transmitted in any form or by any means—electronic, mechanical, photocopy, recording, or otherwise—without prior written permission of the publisher, except brief quotations used in connection with reviews in magazines or newspapers.

All scripture quotations, unless otherwise indicated, have been paraphrased by the author or are from an unknown translation.

Scripture quotations marked NEB are taken from the New English Bible, copyright © Cambridge University Press and Oxford University Press 1961, 1970. All rights reserved.

Published by William Carey Library, an imprint of William Carey Publishing
10 W. Dry Creek Circle
Littleton, CO 80120 | www.missionbooks.org

Mel Hughes, editor
Pourio Lee, cover concept
Rose Lee-Norman, indexer
Josie Leung, designer
Wisnu Sasongko, cover art, courtesy of Overseas Ministries Study Center

William Carey Library is a ministry of Frontier Ventures
Pasadena, CA 91104 | www.frontierventures.org

23 22 21 20 19 Printed for Worldwide Distribution

Cover Photo: "The Heart of the Village" by Wisnu Sasongko, 2004.

Library of Congress Cataloging-in-Publication Data

Tippett, Alan R. (Alan Richard), 1911-1988.
  [Works. Selections. 2014.]
  Slippery paths in the darkness : papers on syncretism: 1965-1988 / Doug Priest, editor.
      pages cm. -- (The missiology of Alan R. Tippett series)
  "Papers by A.R. Tippett, researched between 1965-1988, for specific encounters."
  Includes bibliographical references and indexes.
  ISBN13: 978-0-87808-479-1 -- ISBN10: 0-87808-479-7 1. Christianity and other religions. 2.
Missions--Anthropological aspects. 3. Missions--Theory. 4. Syncretism (Religion) I. Title.

BR127.T5725 2014
266--dc23

2014016580

CONTENTS

Series Foreword vii
Foreword ix
Slippery Paths in the Darkness xvii
Preface xix

CHAPTER 1: The Encounter of Communions 1
CHAPTER 2: Christopaganism or Indigenous Christianity? 9
CHAPTER 3: Formal Transformation and Faith Distortion 25
CHAPTER 4: The Meaning of Meaning 41
CHAPTER 5: The Dynamics of Syncretism in the Mission of the Church 61
CHAPTER 6: Star-gazing 79
CHAPTER 7: The Ethnotheology of the People of God and Their Covenant Relationship . 85
CHAPTER 8: Toward a Typology of Contemporary Idolatries Invading the Koinonia and Causing Syncretism, in Biblical Perspective 101
CHAPTER 9: A Survey of the New Shape of Syncretism in Postcolonial Mission and Ministry at Home and Abroad: Contemporary Confrontations 171

Afterthought and Declaration 191
References 193
Index 205

SERIES FOREWORD

Always the creative thinker, Alan Tippett, transplanted to the United States from Australia (never really integrated), is the originator of the concept of cultural fatigue which continues after culture shock has passed. One afternoon he walked the entire midtown business district of Pasadena seeking "a reel of cotton." Returning in despair, what was he asking for? Well, of course, a spool of thread. However, in the field of anthropology, he didn't miss a thing and had a compendious knowledge, especially of the Southern Pacific sphere.

His alert mind took him in many directions, some complete surprises, and from volume to volume in this series you will find very little overlap and much that is rich for contemplation. Thanks to Doug Priest as well as Darrell Whiteman, Charles Kraft, and Greg Parsons for making sure these gems of thought are still available.

Ralph D. Winter
Pasadena, California
May 2009

FOREWORD

R. Daniel Shaw

I was invited to the School of World Mission faculty at Fuller Theological Seminary in 1981. Despite having retired in 1977, Alan R. Tippett was still coming from his beloved Australia to teach an occasional course. This gave us time to interact, and I recall leisurely conversations about the state of mission in the Pacific and around the globe; there was nothing "retiring" about his mind or his interests. A glimpse of his motivation for mission and his strong desire for people to experience God's transforming power gave me a perception of both his anthropological concerns as well as his passion for quality research. He combined these academic pursuits in order to produce findings that could be put to missiological use. To that end, I am honored to write this foreword to these articles highlighting Tippett's perspective on syncretism—a topic that has dominated mission studies since William Carey set out for India.

This volume chronicles Tippett's lifetime of concern for the relationship between enabling the church to be Christ's representation in a place (a cultural context or society) and the potential for "uncritically" combining local beliefs and values with Christian thinking—what he calls "syncretism." Two things dominate these essays written over a twenty-five year span: Tippett's commitment to scholarship and his deep understanding of and appeal to Scripture. Every page brings mission concerns to the Bible as Tippett applied his considerable anthropological insights to practical problems plaguing missionaries, while seeking to ascertain God's perspective and intent for the biblical context in which these issues were also relevant. It is clear there is "nothing new under the sun" (Eccl 1:9), and we can apply old answers to new circumstances. References to his "paradigm" in the preface reflect this interface between scholarship and Scripture. In the final segment, "Afterthought and Declaration" (which is really a lament and final words), he strongly connects cultural elements with Scripture, maintaining a theme throughout the volume. Together these inspire anyone who takes the time to read through this documentation of a scholar's "research into the subject" for the purpose of avoiding "Slippery Paths" that lead to darkness. What is clear is Tippett's desire to emphasize God's intention for us to enjoy the light of Christ's glorious presence in the here and now, as well as in the future promised to all who, by faith, believe that Jesus is the only name leading to salvation (Acts 4:12).

As Tippett makes clear in his introduction to chapter 5, syncretism is the interface between what was there when missionaries arrived and what remains when they depart. He asks: What kind of Christianity do they manifest? Is it really Christian, or still largely quite animist? Is it just a new kind of animism? This has been debated right through the period of colonial missions. Missionaries in the midst of the action have disagreed, largely because as westerners they have not understood the dynamics of the process that is cross-cultural and, therefore, by definition, not from the West. Rare was the missionary who appreciated that "religious and magical change do not take place at the same rate" (62)[1], thus creating a time lag that juxtaposed traditional religion with the influx of Christian beliefs and values. I have often presented syncretism as an "incompatible mixture of Christianity and local beliefs and traditions." The question is, "incompatible with what?" Too often culture rather than the Bible has been the focus—incompatible with the missionaries' culturally conditioned sensibilities rather than God's intent. Scripture must be the standard by which we measure local beliefs and behaviors based on those beliefs. And, we must let God be the judge, not us. This suggests Paul Hiebert's[2] perspective on critical contextualization as a local project, one in which people must determine before God and their understanding of Scripture what their position must be and then work to make a difference in their context. Too often it has been missionaries attempting to make a difference and local people not understanding and therefore "reverting" to their customary practice, or worse, a dual religion which kept their traditions at arm's length from Christianity. Syncretism can only be avoided by applying biblical knowledge to cultural understanding. Doing so ensures people have the freedom to process the gospel through their own cultural grid. It also encourages missionaries to provide the supportive encouragement necessary to develop a "rule of faith and practice" commensurate with cultural expectations—people need to make the gospel theirs. "That, of course, is what the Christian message and mission are all about. Though we are not of these worlds, we are sent forth into them as He was sent into ours (John 17:14-18; 20:21-22)" (63).

"[H]ow to avoid syncretism and to achieve an indigenous Christianity?" (9). This is the key question of the volume. It demonstrates the contrast between what Tippett called "Christopaganism"[3] borrowed from the Latin American literature (Visser't Hooft 1963) and its alternative, "Indigeneity," a term Kraft adopted. Syncretism and Indigenous Christian-

---

[1] Page numbers given without an author or date refer to the page numbers of this book.
[2] Hiebert and Tippett were colleagues, along with Charles Kraft—all on the same faculty at the same time. It was a marvelous commixture of anthropological acumen and missiological insight as each, in his own genius, sharpened the others during faculty lunches, read the others' work, and applied his individual research to the cause of world mission. This was the context I entered—oh the bliss!
[3] For a definition of his terms, be sure to look at 17ff.

ity "found their common drive in a 'striving for meaning' with institutions and terms that were relevant for specific historical cultural situations" (25). "A cultural cohesive complex is a notion embodied in a cultural form with a regular behaviour pattern" (72). Today, we would call this a "religious schema," but as Tippett understood, "The practise continues and the set of ideas survives with it" (72). It is these practices that must be dedicated anew to honoring Christ, making him Lord above all else, and in turn transforming people's understanding of who they are before God. Without the transformation, no amount of religious understanding will bring them in line with God's expectations. But as people become aware of God's presence through His word, incarnation changes people's awareness through the power of the Holy Spirit. A Trinitarian perspective brings people into an awareness of who they are before God. To outsiders this may appear syncretistic, but rather than replace their beliefs and values with a contrastive set they do not understand, it is best to allow Christ to incarnate in that cultural environment and allow the Holy Spirit to do a work of transformation using the life and issues people understand, thus moving them "beyond contextualization" (Shaw 2010).

> "On the mission field, there are problems that rise with attempted contextualization, as we strive to plant congregations that are culturally meaningful. Christ will come to them in garments with which we may be unfamiliar; but He will come in communion, and they will know the spiritual belongingness of their kind of Κοινωνια (*Koinonia*)" (6-7).

"On the one hand we try to preserve 'a pure faith and an essential gospel' and on the other, we seek to give it 'an indigenous garment'" (10). Tippett draws a stark contrast between "contextualization" which he characterizes as "syncretism that is formal—cultural modes of expression," and "Christopaganism" which he considers "theological, ethical and philosophical conceptualization which can be heretical and unchristian" (66). Both are syncretism, but one focuses on experience within a cultural context, while the other imposes an outside perspective resulting in misunderstanding and misappropriation of that which is of God.

> The common misunderstanding in both these errors relates to the problem of meaning. In one the meaning is not Christian. In the other it is not culturally relevant. And in my opinion, one is as sad a distortion of faith as the other. The greatest methodological issue faced by the Christian mission in our day is how to carry out the Great Commission in a multi-cultural world, with a gospel that is both truly Christian in content and culturally significant in form" (40).

The focus must be on honoring God. The concern is not on the "forms" of worship but rather the intent of the worship in which those forms are consecrated to giving honor and glory to Christ as Lord. Biblical teaching is the counterpoint, allowing people to process God's word in their own linguistic and cultural environment where their understanding of spiritual reality is an expression of their beliefs and values. God's word in the hands of people transforms their understanding into an awareness of God's presence in their midst, the "word among us," and enables them to determine how best to worship in a God-honoring way that shifts their animism and pagan understanding to the truths of the God of creation, to the one who created them in His own image (Shaw 1988, 12ff).

Syncretism is not only something that happens "out there" in the world, it is also widely manifest in the "urban West" through astrology, divination, and a fascination with the occult that generates a myriad of religious expressions. These beliefs and practices leave the door "wide open for entry into the demonic world" (79). They are largely unchallenged by Christians because of the concern for dialogue and upsetting beliefs and values that go against biblical truth. Thus we see Tippett dealing with issues not much different than the contemporary environment where secular issues mitigate against Christian influence. And yet, they emanate from religious longing, a deep desire to know why a person is here and what their destiny is.

Recurring themes from symbolic anthropology (the cup, the cross, the virgin Mary, the saints, and so much more), mythology (which Tippett calls a people's "faith formulation" [16]) the dialogue between the individual and the communal (what Erikson calls "small places" in contrast to "big ideas" [Eriksen 2010]), repeated references to Bible translation (Ulfilas, early manuscripts and versions, as well as key translators such as Wycliffe, Tyndale, and Nida[4]), and his familiarity with the role of communication[5] all inform a vibrant narrative.

A reading of this collection of papers provides a history of mission as Tippett uses case studies from across the ages, from Irenaeus, a Celtic pastor dealing with Gnosticism, to examples from his experiences as a Methodist missionary in Fiji and as a professor in Pasadena. His love-hate relationship with Los Angeles took him to the streets where he was frequently seen visiting alternative bookshops, interviewing shop owners and patrons, and taking in the sights and sounds of Los Angeles sprawl: Hollywood, ethnic neighborhoods and the specific religious expressions encased within them—voodoo and cultic shops selling potions of all kinds, tattoo parlors, masseurs. Tippett took in the life of communities wherever he found himself, interwove it with his vast anthropological reading, and the resultant mixture made him a rare combination of explorer, anthropologist, and theologian. His text is heavily footnoted with asides reflecting interaction with students in the context of Fuller Theological Seminary and the School of World Mission where students from around the world landed in his classes.

---

4   Tippett knew and understood the importance of Bible translation and its role in making Christ known in his day.
5   "Communication is a two way process. God may be omniscient, but I am not. He may speak to me, but I must hear and understand. The limitations in the process are with me. He is supracultural, but I am culture-bound. Therefore there must be an incarnation" (22).

He writes in a dynamic narrative style punctuated with missionary stories from the Australian outback (where two streams converge in a "tempestuous meeting" that symbolizes "the 'history of religion' and the 'history of mission,' which, when they meet, create a whirlpool" at the vortex of which we find missiology [25]). "The history of schism, syncretism, and nativistic movements in the church show how long we have taken to learn the lessons of the whirlpool at the meeting of the waters" (36). Interspersed with voluminous references to the anthropological literature of his day, Tippett masterfully connects anthropology and his own research and wide ranging interests with biblical concerns. It is all woven together in a near spell-binding litany of ideas focusing, in this volume, on his concern for syncretism and its impact on the mission of the worldwide church.

In chapter 7, Tippett connects ethnotheology and ethnohistory, both of which he helped conceptualize (Tippett 1973). Ethnohistory enables others to appreciate the historical development of a community based on the eras of cultural development people themselves identify. For example, in the era before Christ, the Israelites reflected on the Egypt experience, the exodus, the wilderness, the judges, the kings, the prophets, the exile, the post-exile, and the intertestamental eras. Critical to the method is the identification of boundaries delineating transition from one era to another. Tippett uses this approach to show God's covenant relationship with the people of Israel and how departures from God's intention for the relationship lead to syncretism. Once the concept is clear, he shows how the approach leads to an "ethnotheological" development of themes reflective of people he researched and demonstrates that "theological awareness that syncretism shatters a covenant relationship" affects how people interact with God today. This is a powerful juxtaposition of biblical theology and culture which has often distorted biblical truth for religious responses that were syncretistic, and Tippett minces no words in showing his contempt.

In chapter 8, Tippett utilizes his "Phenomenology of Religion" course to develop a typology of practices—complete with a myriad of illustrations—that can assist researchers in identifying the nature of religious expressions they encounter almost anywhere on earth. From identifying deities to understanding all manner of shamanic expression, sorcery, witchcraft, satanism, and a multiplicity of spiritual manifestations including ghosts, personality cults, and Scientology (demonstrating the maladies of the West in distorting God's intentions). He writes to enlighten the church to the impact of these religious manifestations that he views as making insidious inroads to the Western church in America, Australia, and even in Europe which had long since shifted from reformation to secularization and syncretism. Tippett anticipates the late twentieth century interest in "power ministries" when he notes:

> Possibly the most widespread encounters of syncretism in our present world scene (certainly the most pernicious in their threat to human happiness and

stability) are demonic or satanic. These may be either organized, corporate satanism or individually demonic, and prosper because the Christian rank and file refuse to take them seriously" (168).

Tippett's protégé, Charles Kraft, as well as his colleague Peter Wagner took these matters to heart following Tippett's death and sensitized a whole generation of students to insights from renewed spiritual awareness of principalities and powers and their impact on doing mission (Kraft 1989; Wagner and Pennoyer 1990).

Tippett concludes the volume by comparing colonial and postcolonial (remember, this was written before the current focus on "Post Modernity"), showing how the shift is represented by multiculturalism, migration, and religious dialogue—this clearly anticipates the current fixation on "globalization." But through it all, he holds to his thesis that what we see in the world is already reflected in the Bible and generates a heightened awareness of the human condition both in its generality as having been created by God, and in its particularity in the context of each culture. Tippett sums up the value of his work by noting,

> The human situation under postcolonial multiculturalism may have changed dramatically; but the human predicament is the same. The testing tools remain the same. The frame of reference and the fixed centre stand firm. The people of God must still stand true in the covenant relationship (189).

In short, people are able to avoid syncretism by remaining true to God's word. They must be faithful to the truths of their encounter with Jesus, and manifest that truth in the context of a lifestyle consistent with their cultural identity. Doing so will help avoid *slippery paths in the darkness*, and "allow for the cohesion of the first commandment and the Great Commission" (191). This is what Donald McGavran had in mind when he said, "We yoke these sciences to the missionary passion and use them in the service of the Great Commission" (McGavran 1965, 239). Each supports the other, and together they generate the essence of missiology, a multi-disciplinary approach to enabling the development of the gospel through biblical principles that mitigate against uncritical combinations of local beliefs and values with biblical concerns—syncretism.

Pasadena, CA
November, 2013

References

Eriksen, Thomas Hylland. *Small Places, Large Issues: An Introduction to Social and Cultural Anthropology*. 3rd ed. London, UK: Pluto Press, 2010.

Kraft, Charles H. *Christianity with Power: Your Worldview and Your Experience of the Supernatural*. Ann Arbor, MI: Servant Publications, 1989.

McGavran, Donald A., ed. *Church Growth and Christian Mission*. New York, NY: Harper and Row, 1965.

Shaw, R. Daniel. *Transculturation: The Cultural Factor in Translation and other Communication Tasks*. Pasadena, CA: William Carey Library, 1988.

———. "Beyond Contextualization: Toward a Twenty-first-Century Model for Enabling Mission." *International Bulletin of Missionary Research* 34, no. 4 (2010):208-15.

Tippett, Allen R. *Aspects of Pacific Ethnohistory*. Pasadena, CA: William Carey Library, 1973.

Visser't Hooft, W. A. *No Other Name: The Choice Between Syncretism and Christian Universalism*. Philadelphia, PA: Westminster Press, 1963.

Wagner, C. Peter, and F. Douglas Pennoyer. *Wrestling with Dark Angels: Toward a Deeper Understanding of the Supernatural Forces in Spiritual Warfare*. Ventura, CA: Regal Books, 1990.

SLIPPERY PATHS IN THE DARKNESS

Papers by A. R. Tippett, Researched Between 1965–1988
For Specific Encounters.

There is a phrase used by the prophet Jeremiah, who was lamenting the attitude of the religious leaders of his day, who "broke the heart" of the Lord by their failure to discern the questionable elements that had been introduced even "into His House." He described their ways in terms of *slippery paths in the darkness*.

It seems to me an apt term for describing our own frequent irresponsibility in the church today with respect to our consent to so many questionable practises and religious disloyalties; whereby we threaten to fracture the *covenant relationship* itself. We have one conference after another, commissions and consultations on all kinds of phenomena—occultism, astrology, and syncretism. This is all pretty well exactly what the prophet was disturbed about in his day. We dialogue. We rationalize. Ultimately we do little about it and the covenant relationship of the people of God is surely fractured thereby.

The salvation of the remnant was eventually possible only by means of a *new covenant, a better covenant* written on their hearts. The two important pronouncements of the prophet were the tragedy of the fracture of the covenant relationship, by disregard to the first commandment and disloyalty to God by His people; and His continuing purpose to restore the world if His people would only repent and return to Him again. He assured them and pleaded with them at this continuing purpose.

The point of this collection of papers is to investigate the very sad slipperiness of these paths in the darkness; both through Scripture and in our own day, and the nature of the repentance required for the covenant restoration. Having been fractured "from our side" it can only be renewed "from the divine side." We cannot write the terms. We can only respond "Yes" or "No" to His offer, and give sincere thanks to Him for His abundant grace.

PREFACE

This collection of papers was not written for publication. It was not compiled with a single audience in view. It was certainly not written for the interfaith dialogue, which would require a quite different basis for discussion. I trust the reader understands that as he reads.

The writer's paradigm is the scriptural view of the Κοινωνια (*Koinonia*) as the people of God in the covenant relationship; a relationship which requires loyalty to God in Christ and recognizes no other gods.

The writer's paradigm is that the Bible itself is accepted as the rule for faith and practise. It is not on trial, but accepted as the revelation of God over a long historic time period and over numerous cultural situations, to be evaluated contextually rather than literally; that it is to be regarded as the measuring tool as it comes down to us.

The writer's paradigm is that the covenant relationship of the people of God applies through time and culture unto "the end of the age," and thus should speak to us in our ethnohistorical contexts of today.

It is assumed that the reader will place himself or herself in the situation required for the correct audience, cultural situation, and occasion to which I am speaking: that is, that "he will sit where I sat" as he reads.

"The Encounter of Communions" was a sermon delivered to an evangelical college audience training for mission in a syncretistic world.

The three studies presented at Milligan College, Chapters 2–4, were part of a symposium presented to an audience of missiologists when the contours of postcolonial missiology were being formulated. The four participants came from different nationalities, different denominations, and different disciplines. If we had a common basis for discussion, it was that the day of mission was not dead.

The paper on "The Dynamic of Syncretism in the Mission of the Church" was for an Anglican commission on the subject. I was asked to share my experiences and open the aspects of the subject I felt they might want to discuss. I had no authority but was merely asked to share. Unfortunately a couple of the participants were incapable (or unwilling) to even consider the subject from the point of view of my paradigm. They could not separate it from the interfaith dialogue. Of course, I was dealing with the inner life of the church, not the interfaith dialogue for which I should have used a different paradigm as our basis for discussion.

The two papers on the ethnotheology of my paradigm and the search for a typology were written for no purpose other than my own further research into the subject, and my investigation of the Bible as a valid testing tool for the situations overloaded with syncretism. I found it stimulating to research and hope you find it the same to read.

The star-gazing article was for a popular religious paper, with a Bible-believing readership.

1

THE ENCOUNTER OF COMMUNIONS

(1 Cor 10)

The problem of coming to grips with pagan religion emerged on a new and practical level at Corinth, in the Graeco-Roman world. Corinth represented a cosmopolitan centre with many features of urban life akin to those now emerging in the urbanization of the third world in our own day. The threat of syncretism and coexistence were real problems. First Corinthians 10 is not merely a passage of teaching within the church, it bears on the nature of her life and witness to this day. We confront a practical, down-to-earth situation of the church's involvement and encounter with the world.

It had been the intention of Jesus to establish a community of persons in a fellowship relationship, a church dedicated to the task of performing His ministry and mission in the world. Christians bore witness in order that others might be won out of the world and brought into the fellowship (1 John 1:3) and strengthened by it to go back into the world again. Thus the Lord was able to differentiate between their being in the world but not of the world (John 17:15–18), sent into the world, yet given to Him out of the world to be kept in His word and strengthened in the fellowship, and to remain in the world after His physical departure, as His community (vv. 6–11).

As time went on, His original called community increased in numbers, and in the book of Acts, we see how the church emerged with a specific program of church-planting. These congregations differed in character, in form, and in composition, according to the situations within which they were planted, but many of the same problems of temptation and testing occur in various contexts. One of these problems related to the nature of the fellowship itself and who was to be regarded as a true participant in it. How indigenous is the young church to be? If we grant that the forms of the new community should be culturally appropriate, what about their basic belief within which their communion was held together? The Christian mission is engaged in the task of bringing about real religious and social change. Its primary task is to change pagans into Christians. Its business is to see that the old gods die. Its duty to its Lord is to bring Him converts who are indeed "new creations."

It seems to me that there are two points where the Christian mission can become ineffective if we are not careful. First, our witness itself may be indistinct or defective. Second, the actual encounter may be ineffective so that new converts actually bring aspects of their old paganism into the church. It was this second problem which Paul found confronting the church at Corinth.

This study presupposes the uniqueness of the way to God in Christ, but we are considering here the definiteness of Christian commitment, the demand for a clear-cut break with the old way, which is a specific act—both an act of rejection and an act of acceptance. A failure to recognize the exclusiveness of Christ leads to universalism. The failure to demand a definite decision from an individual or congregation to cut off from the old allegiance leads to a conflict of loyalties, which becomes disruptive to the fellowship and destructive to its witness.

It is for this reason that Paul confronts the Christians in fellowship at Corinth with this dogmatic statement—"You cannot drink both the cup of the Lord and the cup of devils" (1 Cor 10:21). Let us probe into this a little more deeply.

Let Us Consider the Symbolism of the Cup

In both the Old and the New Testaments, the cup is a symbol, although this is not peculiar to Scripture, which makes it a good figure for comparison. Many societies use the cup as a symbol of various levels of interaction and fellowship—for welcome and farewell, for agreement and reconciliation between individuals and peoples. It may be social or political, or commercial or religious. I would think the cup is almost a universal symbol. In pre-Christian times, it is often found as a symbol or means of intercourse with the spirits. This is true of most of the primal societies I know. It is a symbol of fellowship, whatever the level.

In all the forms of interaction and agreement I have met, the cup is first something offered, and second something received or accepted, and third something which creates an understanding, agreement, or reconciliation. It seals a pact, a relationship. It is a confirmation of a decision made, a pledge of mutual loyalty and sincerity.

A whole book could be written on this, for there are many types of fellowship and agreement, but the cup is always a two-way action, offered and received within a bond of loyalties. The decision on my part to share in fellowship with one community may exclude me from a similar relationship with another if those two are incompatible, for that would involve me in duplicity and reflect on my sincerity and loyalty. You cannot bind yourself in loyalty to one army and fraternize with the enemy. This was just exactly the problem in the young Corinthian church, and Paul had to challenge them directly on the matter. "You cannot drink the cup of the Lord and the cup of devils! To which κοινωνία (koinōnia) do you belong in Corinth? Whose κοινωνία (koinōnia) are you?"

Let Us Reconstruct the Corinthian Way of Life

Corinth was not a completely typical Greek city. It differed somewhat in its traditions and its accomplishments with respect to the arts and literature. It did not have the same reputation for virtue as some cities. Some have noted Italian characteristics about it. In any case Corinth projected a specific image before the world. It was a cosmopolitan city where philosophies, religions, and values intermingled. It was an important junction city on an isthmus with harbours facing in opposite directions to Italy and to Asia, where shipping and trade came from east or west. It was a roadway bottleneck where the southern and northern routes met. We can understand how it became commercially important and concerned with the business of making money.

To this we may add a word about its materialism, humanism, and dedication to the glorification of man. This humanism was manifest in the better sense in the famous Corinthian games from which Paul borrowed some of his imagery. On the other hand, it had a less savory aspect in its sensualism. Its dominant religious life was the deification of these things—the worship of Bacchus, the god of wine, and of Venus, the goddess of sexual love. In point of fact, if you refer back to Liddell and Scott (1929), you'll find that classical Greek had a derogatory word, "to Corinthianize" κορινθιάζομαι (korinthiazomai), which was used by Aristophanes to suggest an overemphasis on whoredom. So Corinth had created for herself this kind of an image among the more moral Greek cities.

Christian converts had to live beside this kind of sensualism, and temptation confronted them in the following way: instead of asking themselves how they reacted against this lifestyle by having Christ "living in them," they asked, "How far may we participate in these things?" It was a bad shift, and Paul would not let them get away with it. He came to the heart of the "fellowship" ideal, stating things in terms of communion relationship. These are two quite different communions, he pointed out, and they are incompatible. "Whose Κοινωνια (Koinonia) are you? You cannot drink the cup of the Lord and the cup of devils." Jesus had faced the same issue in terms of master and servant—"No man can serve two masters!" or again "You cannot serve God and mammon."

Now let us consider the context and note Paul's argument. He takes the Jews as an example. They were called to be God's people. They drank of that spiritual following (v. 4), yet many of them failed, and God was not pleased with them (v. 5). Paul enumerates the reasons why—they craved for evil things and worshipped false gods (v. 7), they became highly sexed (v. 8), they exploited the goodness of God (v. 9), and they were discontent with their lot (v. 10), which were all parallels to the Corinthian problems who were thereby warned of the peril of being satisfied with legal self-justification: "Whereby let him that thinks he stands take heed lest he fall" (v. 12). The only answer, says Paul, is to be whole-heartedly within the κοινωνία (koinōnia) as fully participant κοινωνία (koinōnia). The cup is offered and accepted. The sincere fellowship between two parties is sealed. "You cannot drink the cup of the Lord and the cup of devils," which would be insincere and disloyal. That is the exegesis of the passage as I see it.

How Did This Work Out in the Church?

Back in the fifth century a body of Christians fell away from the church, in exactly the same way as we find neo-pagan resurgences in some communities today and semi-secular cults in Western lands. The movement I have in mind here was known as the Tanit Cult. These Corinthian Christians worshipped the Queen of Heaven, and did so on Sunday mornings before going to church. They thought they could do both. An apologist named Salvian rose up in that day in Corinth just as Paul had done in his, and expounded again this very Pauline passage to challenge the error.

This Corinthian error is not as rare as we might suppose. In Fiji I have met professional school teachers in Christian schools who declared themselves to be both Christian and Hindu depending on which group they chanced to be fraternizing with at the time. In Mexico I have done research in several places where I found so-called Christian communities worshipping Mezo-American Indian deities and seeing no incompatibility.

I once spent a Saturday afternoon watching a great open-air play, which dramatized the experiences of a tribe of Indians. It purported to be their true experience, and the whole village took part in the spectacle and derived considerable revenue from it. It was set on a Roman Catholic rancho, and the tribe was declared to be Christian. They venerated the statue of the Virgin Mary in accord with one well-known pattern, and the drama featured the celebration of a Christian baptism. However, as the play moved to its climax, it became quite apparent that in reality they were sun-worshippers. As this episode "stole the show" and became the grand finale, were they not really trying to take both the cup of the Lord and the cup of devils?

Over a number of years, as I have travelled in many lands trying to help young churches, time after time I have been made aware of this kind of duplicity. It may usually be accounted for by one of two causes. Either the "cut-off point" from the old faith has been inadequate; or the instruction given to the young converts moving into the fellowship has been deficient. In either case a clear-cut decision is called for. For both individuals and groups, there should be a definite verdict for Christ; otherwise the church which emerges will be syncretistic and manifest a conflict of loyalties.

What Does This Say to Us in Our Own Context Today?

The legalism of Corinth was its basic weakness. You could indulge in this or that as long as you did it within the law. You could make as much money as you could, or drink as much as you liked, or indulge as much in free love, and glory in the flesh, as long as you could say: "Why, what is wrong with it? I am not breaking the law" ("being baptised into Moses" as Paul put it) and went on, "Corinthians, this is not good enough: your criterion is the fellowship not the law."

To get beyond this legalism (in which we ourselves are adept) and come into the communion fellowship relationship involves first a personal experience and then a choice or commitment.

Here in this city of Corinth, Aphrodite (the Roman Venus) was widely worshipped. She was the embodiment of physical desire and superbly represented in a famous statue, which some have declared to have been the most perfect human form created by man, crafted by a skilled artisan with her arms outstretched in sensual invitation. Thus was she known over the ancient world, and especially so in Corinth.

Over against this figure, there stands Another, also with arms outstretched, with another kind of love that says "Come unto me!" Let me use this as a sustained metaphor. The ravages of time have left the voluptuous goddess without her arms, and now the world knows her only as an excavated artifact. Her invitation is seen as temporary and unsatisfying. Yet never a week goes by without those other outstretched hands in a communion group somewhere with the invitation, "Take, eat . . . Take, drink . . . in remembrance of me." The symbolic cup is offered and received again and again, and will be "until He come." Here is an abiding complex: His invitation and the Christian response, both individual and collective in the entity which is His fellowship of participants. This is the criterion of communion. It was right for the Corinthians to be confronted with the choice involved. Nor is this the only example of this in the New Testament. And it has been repeated over and over again in the history of the Christian church: The offer of two cups at the same time, and the clear understanding that the acceptance of one means the rejection of the other. The Communion requires it.

One is reminded of this same imagery of the cup in the Song of Omar Khayam:

> Indeed the idols I have loved so long
> Have drowned my glory in a shallow cup
> And sold my reputation for a song.

> And much as wine has played the infidel
> And robbed me of my robe of honour.

> Alas that Spring should vanish with the rose
> Ah! Whence and whither flown again, who knows?

> (And then to what end? . . .)

> I . . . turn down an empty glass.

Against that unsatisfying temporal fellowship, once again we hear the eternal words, "Drink this in remembrance of me!" and moreover the assurance that this would continue until He drink again the fruit of the vine with us in the Kingdom (Luke 22:18). This is the Communion test—one the satisfaction for a moment and then an empty glass turned down; the other an abiding continuation of experience, even unto the messianic banquet as Bonar's communion hymn puts it:

> Feast after feast thus comes and passes by;
> Yet, passing, points to that glad feast above;
> Giving sweet foretaste of the festal joy,
> The Lamb's great bridal feast of bliss and love.

I have asked the question, what does this say to us today? It speaks to us on two levels—the individual and the communal. Although communion is a corporate act, it is nevertheless an interrelationship of individuals. The communion test comes to each individual as a person. Then it comes to each Κοινωνια (Koinonia), the multi-individual unit in church growth theology. The temptation to syncretize comes at both the individual and corporate levels.

The communion criterion helps the individual to make his acceptances and rejections wisely. One is always confronted with the question, "With respect to this decision, will it impair my fellowship with Christ?" One does not ask "Can I do this or that within the law? How far can I go and still be a Christian? What is wrong with it?" If you think this way, which is legalistic and pre-Christian in any case, your criterion for decision-making will be in your own mind, a pure rationalization, which you can bend to your own desire, I can go that far without the Bible and without Christ, and that is certainly just not good enough.

The only law to be kept in mind is that the cup of the Lord and the cup of devils cannot go together. Ultimately nothing in life is worthwhile if it jeopardises one's fellowship relationship with Christ. This, for individual and Κοινωνια (Koinonia), is the supreme value. Whether one is involved in witness in the urban scene, the university, the school, or the commercial world, at home or overseas, we set this value above all others—to preserve, cultivate, and enrich the covenant relationship with Christ.

We are ever being confronted by the need for making choices. There is some encounter before me at every corner of the road. Always there are incompatible cups held out to me. Whatever I decide, whatever it cost, my prayer is "Lord Jesus preserve our communion. May the only satisfaction I seek be in Thee." I say with Bernard of Clairvaux,

> Jesus, Thou Joy of Loving Hearts;
> Thou Fount of Life, Thou Light of Men;
> From the best bliss that earth imparts
> We turn unfilled to Thee again.

And when syncretism would creep in on the congregational level we may consider again that same communion hymn. On the mission field, there are problems that rise with attempted contextualization, as we strive to plant congregations that are culturally meaningful. Christ will come to them in garments with which we may be unfamiliar; but He will come in communion, and they will know the spiritual belongingness of their kind of Κοινωνια (Koinonia). But let us not be too self-satisfied about ourselves. Our commitment to Christ was not merely a single act that stands as effective for all time. Of course we did make such a commitment, but it didn't end there. Every step of the way I need Him beside me. Satan never lets up on me. He is always thrusting an alternative cup before me. Sometimes it is obvious. Sometimes it is subtle. Sometimes it is rational. Whenever anyone in discussion of the faith challenges me with "Why, what is wrong with it?," my temperature drops and I sense danger. Whenever a Christian group begins to rationalize about something—the harmlessness of astrology, tarot cards, ouija boards, yoga, or the like, I shudder, because I know the communion criterion is on the line somehow.

"What is wrong with it?" This is a bad question, because it has no point of reference. Ultimately it depends on rationalization in your mind or mine. We must agree to differ, or put the discussion (and decision) off for a time. A communion relationship with a Person is known and felt. It can be fractured when a wrong decision is made. Christ Himself is the point of reference. This is good for individuals or fellowship groups. This is not to denigrate human reason or dialogue. It is rather to say they are not the ultimate reference point; which is rather where, and how, we stand in fellowship with Christ.

The very question "What is wrong with it?" suggests disagreement and division. The communion relationship suggests unity.

> Joined in one spirit to our Head,
> Where He appoints we go;
> And still in Jesus' footsteps tread,
> And show His praise below.
>
> Partakers of the Saviour's grace,
> The same in mind and heart,
> Nor joy, nor grief, nor time nor place,
> Nor life, nor death can part (Charles Wesley).

2
CHRISTOPAGANISM OR INDIGENOUS CHRISTIANITY?

When Dr. [Tetsunao] Yamamori supplied us with the "terms of reference" for this series of lectures, he spoke of the adjustments required in the spread of Christianity from one human culture to another as it takes root, and raised the question: What are the limits of such adjustments?

We agreed that the first lecture of the series should prepare the stage for our exchange, taking up a position in such a way that the other speakers could react either positively or negatively, either by developing the argument further or by turning it in another direction. In any case the first presentation, it was felt, should pinpoint the missionary problem which underlies the whole series—namely, how to avoid syncretism and to achieve an indigenous Christianity. So often the search for the latter leaves us with the former instead. The purpose of this presentation, then, after delineating the scope of the series and defining the terms, will be to demonstrate the character of the alternatives—Christopaganism or indigeneity.

The Scope of the Lecture Series

In popular missiological literature, the theme of our lecture series has been discussed under a number of terms. From the negative aspect it is spoken of as syncretism or as Christopaganism. Writers on the old Spanish Catholic colonies in particular have used the latter term. In both the Old and New Testaments, the people of God were warned about the mixture of pagan religion with their own.[1] For this reason, it is inevitable that any mis-

---

1   This is one of the basic themes of the whole Bible. The people of God are to be the people of One God, who will not tolerate any polytheism or syncretism. In the revelation through Moses we have it in the first law of the Decalogue (Ex 20:2-6) and again in the last long message of Moses to Israel, "Then he tells them to "go in and possess the land," he warns them to have no traffic with the idols or fertility cults of Canaan (Deut 4:14-19; 5:6-9; 6:12-15; 13:29-30, etc.). For the prophets also—"I am the Lord thy God, there is none else, there is no God beside me" (Isa 45:5, 22 etc.), and for failing to observe this warning there is judgement (Jer 7:17-31).

In the New Testament church again the people of God are tempted; but as there is to be only one God, so there is to be only one way of access to Him (John 14:6; Acts 4:12). Yet in the Corinthian church, for example, the congregation has to be told they cannot take both the cup of the Lord and the cup of devils (1 Cor 10:21). See Tippett (1973d, 25-33). This is not the only warning against syncretism Paul gave to that congregation. See also Visser't Hooft (1963, 50-82).

sionary whose roots are in Scripture will be predisposed to resist anything in the churches he plants which could lead to syncretism.

Yet the basic principles of anthropology and communication theory, indeed also of what we call incarnational theology, tell us that the churches we plant (and by churches, here I mean the Christian fellowship groups, however simple) in cultures other than our own must be relevantly part of those cultures. We are continually (and quite rightly) warned of the danger of planting foreign Western Christianity on what we have for so long called "the mission field."

Thus, on the one hand, we try to preserve "a pure faith and an essential gospel," and on the other, we seek to give it "an indigenous garment." For example, the moment we translate a portion of Scripture into a language, which has hitherto only built its vocabulary for a pagan worldview and belief, we are confronted with the problem not only of translation but of reception. Yet, unless the written word of God can be incarnated in the linguistic flesh of the receptor people, the saving experience is not likely to be transmitted.

The basic problem, therefore, would seem to be how to communicate the essential supracultural[2] core of the gospel to new believers in other cultures without having it contaminated by the non-Christian forms with which it must be communicated and shared. This contamination may be manifested in any aspect of Christian ministry—apostolate, proclamation, fellowship, service, or teaching, all of which in the last analysis, are culturally conditioned.

It was partly the fear of this which hindered early missionary efforts in the fourth century. Ulfilas, for instance, had little support for his translation proposals, as it was thought the pure gospel could not be transmitted in the impure tongue of the Goths.[3]

This raises a whole nest of problems and questions that are within the orbit of these presentations. Perhaps the first of them is: What exactly is the essential core of the gospel which has to be transmitted? As we look at the Scriptures within their Hebrew and Greek garments, just what is supracultural, and what is cultural? The history of the translation

---

2   The term *supracultural* in this sense comes from the linguistic ethnotheologians. The earlier form, *supercultural*, (Smalley 1955, 58–71), has been abandoned because of possible ambiguity. The recent writings of Charles H. Kraft (1973a, 118–20) have distinguished between the cultural and supracultural. "God," says Kraft, "is supracultural. He stands outside of culture, and is not bound by culture unless he chooses to be bound by it. Man, however, is immersed in culture and unable to escape his culture-boundness."

3   Ulfilas (c311–388) worked as a pastor and leader among the Visigoths, and for thirty-three years as Bishop of the Trans-Danubian Goths. His great achievement was the translation of the Bible for which purpose he had to create a written form of the language. According to Möeller (1893, 32) this was "the foundation of the Christian civilization of the Goths, the foundation stone of German literature." Christianity had spread among the Goths through Christian prisoners captured from Cappadocia (Fisher 1945, 92); (Kidd 1922, 2:364–65). Ulfilas was familiar with Latin, Greek, and Gothic, and served as a go-between. "He was completely one with the Goths, both in language and sympathy" (Cross and Livingstone 1974). Many historians have been so concerned with his Arianism that they have failed to appreciate Ulfilas's methods and skill as a cross-cultural communicator. For further sources on Ulfilas see Ayer (1952) and Wand (1954, 181–82).

of the English Bible is a story of the struggle for cultural relevance in communication, a struggle for meaning, not only across cultures (Hebrew and Greek to English)[4] but across generations of semantic change (Elizabethan, Victorian, and Modern). Likewise, in every mission field over the last century, Scripture translation reminds us that the gospel, which is above culture, nevertheless has to be presented in a meaningful cultural form.

If the mission of God was achieved by the incarnation of His Son—culture-bound as a Jew, and a Jew of Galilee, and a speaker probably of Galilean Aramaic, and by occupation a carpenter in the tradition of his earthly father—and he in turn said, "As the Father hath sent me into the world so send I you into the world," thereby giving us a model for mission (Tippett 1970a, 64–65), I think we may assume that we are bound to work within the limitations of the cultural forms of the people to whom we are sent.

On the other hand, as we examine the churches of the nineteenth and twentieth century mission fields, we frequently find one of two situations. First, it is thoroughly Western in form, teaching, and values and quite unrelated to the cultural ethos, so that people live a borrowed, foreign kind of existence, or a dichotomous one which compartmentalizes the religious and secular. Or, second, we have the tragic manifestation of syncretistic worship, Christopagan—more another form of animism than Christian, because the thinking is animistic and the ritual magical. In all these manifestations, Christian missions have been sorely criticised by the anthropologists; and although this has been grossly generalized, one cannot dispute that we have frequently deserved the criticism.

Destructive or cynical criticism is both unkind and useless; but criticisms may be valuable if they lead us to take a hard look at our methods and correct our mistakes. No secular anthropologist has yet proved his ability to sit where we sit, and therefore has little right to speak. Given the biblical mandate of the Christian mission and the scientific principles and methodological anthropology and communication technique (without which no one should go to Christian missions today), how do we plant Christian communities that are at the same time both truly indigenous and truly Christian? Or as our frame of reference puts it: "What are the cultural limits to the adjustments" that have to be made with the passage of the supracultural message from one culture to another?

This is a missiological subject. It has a theological dimension, but is not confined to theology. It has a historical dimension, but is not confined to history. It has an anthropological dimension, but is not confined to anthropology. It has a strategic dimension, but is not confined to strategy. For this reason, we participants will approach the subject, each

---

4   Work in this area is proceeding under the name of *Ethnolinguistics*, in which the missionary is involved in biblical translation and interpretation, as Kraft points out, not in two, but three or four cultural frameworks. He says, "The Bible records God's revelation as it was perceived in Hebrew, Aramaic, and Greek language and culture. Our own perception of this revelation, however, is pervasively affected by our Euro-American culture. We translate and interpret the revelation into appropriate linguistic and cultural forms of still another culture" (1973b, 233). He goes on to relate this to planting churches which are conceptually indigenous (ibid., 234).

from one of these four dimensions, but the common bond between us is missiology. We stand now at a formative period in "the history of the expansion of Christianity," as Latourette spoke of it. An old era of mission has passed, and we are suffering the birth pangs of a new one. We look into Scripture and ask what are our basic underpinnings and our divine directions. We look into the past and ask what history has to say to us today. We examine the new insights and dimensions of anthropology and linguistics and try to analyse the transition we seek to achieve. We explore missionary strategies and relate methods to results—acceptance or rejection, growth or non-growth, understanding or misunderstanding, foreignness or indigeneity. Although we approach our basic problem from four quite different angles, nevertheless we each trespass on the others' ground at some point or other. We may well tangle with each other at times. But we begin from a common base—the task of bringing Christ cross-culturally to the nations.

I would hope that each of us would bring the perspectives of his particular discipline to bear on the general subject in a way which forces the others to take alignments with his information and opinion, not that we need necessarily be led into heated debate, but that we may relate to each other in a symbiotic rather than a reactive manner.

Definition of Terms

In current popular missiology, apart from the writing of members of our panel, several standard works for the missionary deal with our subject. The first of these is a translation from Dutch—Bavinck's Introduction to the Science of Mission (1964) in which he devotes Chapter 9 to this topic. The second is Luzbetak's The Church and Cultures (1963) in which Chapter 13 has the same title as the book. From the linguistic point of view, Nida (1959, 1960), Smalley (1955, 58–71), Reyburn (1957,194), Kraft (1973a, 109–26), and others have written on the ethnotheological problems in communication. A number of anthropological analyses of Christopaganism are in existence—perhaps the best of them Madsen's Christopaganism (1957), and there are biblical studies like Visser't Hooft's No Other Name (1963) which describe an identical problem as Paul met it in the first century church.[5]

All these writers have written independently of each other. Apparently there never has been any attempt to coordinate these various researches, and to formulate a common terminology as a basis for discussion. In the same way, we who will exchange our ideas during these sessions have come to the subject, not only from different perspectives and experiences, but with different preferences in terminology. Even the word syncretism, which has long been in use in all disciplines, may give us trouble.

---

5   Visser't Hooft has a whole chapter on the struggle of the New Testament church with syncretism. He deals with Antioch, Ephesus, Corinth, Rome, Samaria, Lystra, Athens, Colossae, and Pergamos.

Syncretism may be defined as the union of two opposite forces, beliefs, systems, or tenets so that the united form is a new thing, neither one nor the other.[6]

With critical consideration however, we observe that either a distortion of Christian theology by mixing it with pagan myth to form a new kind of teaching on the one hand, or the singing of, say, a Western Calvinist theology in an unfamiliar chant to a drumbeat previously used only for pagan dances, on the other, may both be defined as syncretism. Yet at this point I wish to make a distinction between them. In the former we are dealing with a basic concept, a matter of thought and belief. In the latter we are dealing with the cultural forms in which they are expressed. Until this differentiation is clearly recognized we will never be able to draw a line between these quite different processes. This is implied in our opening question about the "limits of our adjustments."

It seems necessary therefore, that we find a new term for the second of these. We thus retain syncretism or Christopaganism for the essential content, the metaphysical, the theological, the fusion of belief systems so that the supracultural gospel is contaminated—leaving us with a new kind of animism. The second, which covers the cultural adjustments that have to be made to achieve the indigeneity of the newly planted Christianity, we may consider briefly now.

Luzbetak's term is accommodation, which he defines as, "the respectful, prudent, scientifically and theologically sound adjustment of the church to the native culture in attitude, outward behaviour and practical apostolic approach" (1963, 341). Bavinck (1964) starts his discussion with the use of "accommodation" and "adaptation" as alternatives, and before long is involved in a lengthy discussion on various types of accommodation—external, aesthetic, social and juridical, intellectual, religious, and ethical (following Thauren). He also points out that accommodation is one thing to a missionary and quite another set of problems to the people of the recipient culture. He also differentiates between the Catholic and Reformation viewpoints. After eleven pages of discussion (169–79), he rejects the term accommodation, saying, "the Christian life does not accommodate or adapt itself to heathen forms of life, but takes the latter in possession and thereby makes them new." He prefers the term possessio, "to take possession." For the next twelve pages (179–90), he discusses the practical problems of "possessing" a culture, or the entire life, so that a young church, living close to Christ and the Scriptures, may hope for fresh dynamics. He grants the need for expressing faith in forms of the old cultural heritage, but demands it be achieved without denying Christ (190).

The linguists with their incarnational theology, prefer the term transformation, maintaining the constancy of the supracultural and the variability of the cultural forms with

---

6 I believe the etymological derivation of the word takes us back to political events in early Crete where two parties coalesced, συγκρητίζω (synkretizo) thus giving birth to a noun meaning the union of opposites (two Cretan parties united against a third, forming a new unit—συγκρητισμος (synkrestismos) hence "syncretism" as defined above.

each society. They see God "starting with people where they are," and guiding man in the process of culture change "the People of God in partnership with God," using "culture to serve as a vehicle for Divine-human interaction." Kraft comes to grips with Bavinck and argues that possessio suggests the capture of a culture by force from without, rather than a possession from within. As an observer, I see in Bavinck and Kraft the Calvinist and Arminian views of the sovereignty of God.[7]

I would hope that we can avoid devoting too much of our time to semantic discussion at the expense of practical confrontation with the missiological problems themselves. Whether we speak of adaptation, accommodation, possessio, or transformation, we are using the term over against that of syncretism or Christopaganism—and to this extent I think the issue is clear. It is this basic dichotomy we seek to illuminate in order to draw a line somewhere between the supracultural and cultural, the gospel and the form.

As our discussion continues and we look at concrete situations, undoubtedly two questions will continually arise: Is the gospel influencing the cultural form? Or, is the cultural form influencing the gospel? As we strive to employ a factual missiological data base for our arguments, we shall not only operate within the values and criteria of our respective disciplines, but we shall draw our data from different geographical regions and cultural systems—incorporating our different areas of experience—India, Indonesia, Europe, and Oceania. Because we have no representative from Latin America, I shall commence in this lecture with a case study of syncretism from that continental region.

Syncretism or Christopaganism

Perhaps it would be appropriate in an introductory study like this to analyse a specific case of syncretism and to delineate some of its anthropological ingredients. I seek a locality where Christianity has been established long enough for the existing structures to have crystallized in a form stable enough for objective analysis. That is, I am not seeking so much a case of religious formulation whereby syncretism is currently emerging, but rather a stabilized and functioning religious form in which the process of syncretization is more or less complete and has resulted in a currently operating pattern of faith and practise.

My data base is the case study of a real character, one Juan, a small peasant village official, who considered himself a Christian and left his autobiographical record (Pozas 1962), from which I borrow at length. Even where length has necessitated abbreviation, I have retained Juan's own terminology, to reduce the possibility of my being a misinterpretive middle-man. Many years ago Spaniards invaded his homeland and forced their

---

7   These phrases are cited from the typescript draft of a manuscript now awaiting publication, from a section entitled "Transformational Culture Change." [Later published, Kraft 1979, 345ff.] Kraft has written elsewhere of conceptual transformation in language in missionary situations (1973b, 237–47).

well-known form of Christianity on his forebears. But Spanish Christianity suffered a considerable degree of modification in the process of transmission, and at the time when the autobiography was written, Juan considered himself a normal Christian, and as a village leader, his life was pretty well what the "Christian" villagers expected it to be. In point of fact it was so thoroughly Christopagan as to be hardly Christian at all.

On a basis of Juan's autobiographical statements, I shall enumerate a few anthropological elements, which throw light on the character of this syncretism, and raise some questions about their origin; for they certainly have both theological and missiological (strategic) significance. Time will confine me to four ideas, and these I can only pinpoint: (1) the capacity of cohesive cultural complexes for survival, (2) the orientation of mythical thinking and belief, (3) the demand for a therapeutic system, and (4) the notion of the living dead. In discussing the character of this specific case of Latin American Christopaganism from each of these points of view, I want to point out that none of these is confined to Latin America or to the present day. These experiences must have been shared by those taken into Christianity in the movements of the first century and the Middle Ages. I have often wondered whether historians should not re-examine these great movements with a new interpretive analytical tool based on the known dynamics of present day movements both into and out of the church.[8]

The Capacity of Cohesive Cultural Complexes for Survival

A cohesive cultural complex is here a notion embodied in a cultural form with its regular behaviour pattern—a practise which continues and a set of ideas which survives with the practise. Thus in a descriptive passage Juan tells us:

> Three hours later the sky grew bright and the sun came up behind the mountains. My mother put some coals into the clay incense burner and went out to greet the first rays of the sun. She dropped some pieces of copal into the burner, knelt down to kiss the ground, and begged the sun to protect us and give us health. (Pozas 1962, 47).

---

8   Latourette calls the period from 500 A.D. onwards "The Thousand Years of Uncertainty." I doubt if he really explores the cultural dynamics of the period. True, he allows for the "inward vitality" of expanding faiths, and he comes back to the "hidden springs of conduct" of the conquering faith with a self-protective sentence or two that this may "carry us far beyond the domain to which the historian is supposed to be restricted. At the most he can only recognize the possible existence of realms into which the canons of his craft forbid him to venture" (1966, 14). This fine historical study which ethnohistorians could have given further depth is incomplete. Men like Wallace and Barnett, who have pondered the dynamics of the innovative process and stress situations in historical reconstructions, have improved our tools. My contention is that we should turn the information we have of the dynamics of contemporary religious movements and the diffusion of Christianity onto the documents of the Middle Ages, which so often have been interpreted in the light of the heresies or the politics of Graeco-Roman Christendom. I disagree that these "hidden springs of conduct" are "beyond the domain of the historian" and think that our missiological insights of modern people movements should be brought to bear on the experiences of Boniface and Patrick.

This is sheer nature worship, both in its faith and practise—an offering to the sun at the point of appearance of morning light. The sun is greeted. The earth is kissed. The act of prayer for human protection is directed to the sun whose warmth and light give healing and health. Yet this man considers himself a Christian. Yet he worships the creation not the Creator.

The point I wish to make in this particular instance is that this is not a corruption of his Christianity but a survival of a discrete cultural unit, an animistic cohesive cluster of both faith and practise which co-exists with his so-called Christianity, and represents a compartment of this pagan life he never surrendered to Christ. He sees no contradiction in it. It has persisted for several centuries. It has resisted disintegration. It has rejected absorption. And Christian education has failed to communicate a doctrine of God the Creator, which would have corrected it. So the first point I want to make about Christopaganism is that it is not always a fusion or intermingling of Christian and pagan ideas. It is often an agglomerate with cohesive animistic units embedded in it. A number of these units may coexist, in spite of the fact that they represent flat contradictions to one another. They are cohesive and they change or survive cohesively as units like a phonetic pattern in linguistic change (Sapir 1949, 186–87).[9] It should not be impossible to deal with them.

The Orientation of Mythical Thinking and Belief

No part of the religion of a people shows up its basic animism more quickly than its mythology—in other words, its faith formulation. We return again to Juan for a case study.

> He tells us that the Savior watches over people on the road. He died on a cross to save the wayfarer from the Jews, whom he equates with devils, and who were supposedly cannibalistic. Originally the sun was as cold as the moon, but it grew warmer when the Holy Child was born. He was the son of a virgin among the Jews, who sent her away because they knew the Child would bring light. St. Joseph took her to Bethlehem where the Child was born. The sun grew warmer and the day brighter. The demons ran away and hid in the mountain ravines. Their activity is confined to night because the Savior watches over the day, for the sun is the eye of God. After three days the Holy Child started work as a carpenter. He made a door from a log. The

---

9   The linguist Edward Sapir who laid many of the foundations of ethnolinguistics demonstrated the cohesion of phonetic clusters. A single consonant—p, t, or k—will resist change until the whole cluster p-t-k will change as one thing. He shows how the English series

        $p\ t\ k$ $b\ d\ g$ $f\ th\ h$

corresponds point for point with the Sanskrit

        $b\ d\ g$ $bh\ dh\ gh$ $p\ t\ k$

The analogy serves to illustrate how cultural clusters survive in Christopaganism. The whole complex of faith and practise is a discrete unit, and has to be confronted as such in Christian education, with a Christian doctrine of creation and a worship pattern which expresses it for the convert.

log was too short so he stretched it out like a rope to the required length. Fearing him the people determined to kill him and the family fled from village to village across the mountains. In one village he planted a cornfield. The people were bitten by a swarm of flies. The Savior said—"Don't eat them, eat me instead." He visited the afterworld and then they nailed him to a cross so the people would remember that demons would be punished and would stop eating people (Pozas 1962, 94–96 [summarized]).

Let us backtrack briefly over this completely confused but supposedly Christian account of the life of our Lord. It covers the journey to Bethlehem, the nativity, the flight into Egypt, the carpenter of Nazareth, the vicarious death on the cross. There is a suggestion of the sacramental partaking of the body of Christ and his descent into hell.

Within this structure is woven a number of animistic features—the role of the sun and moon, the cannibal demons, their residence in the mountains, traditions of the origin of the cornfield, and the swarm of flies.

There is no coherent relation between the details of the story; but there are clear equations—the biting flies, demons and Jews, the light and warmth of the sun with the light of Christ, the conflict of light and darkness, of Christ and demons, the vicarious character of being bitten by flies and being nailed to the cross.

We could not ask for a better (or more appalling) example of syncretism than this; or anything which cries out more pathetically to the strategy of mission. The educational follow-up of conversion was so defective as to permit this fusion of the gospel narrative with ancient traditions of the origin of the cornfield (their main subsistence staff of life) and some ancient epidemic of biting flies (diptera). The fear of cannibalistic demons (equated with the role of the Jews as the enemies of our Lord in the last days of his flesh on earth) is obviously an example of the problem of meaning in cross-cultural gospel communication. This reminds us that the meaning ascribed to the message by the receptor may be quite different from that ascribed by the advocate.[10]

Moreover, an anthropological principle is involved here. Behind this strange belief structure inherited by Juan from his Christian forbears lies a mythical orientation, a preference for the narrative or pictorial faith-formulation. It should have provided no problem to the pastors of the first converts. The simple biblical narrative would have delighted them and would have served as a perfect functional substitute to their mythology. One can only assume that the Spanish teachers of the early converts failed to do this, with the

---

10   Barnett points out that when the advocate (novelty introducer [evangelist in our case]) or an observer conceptualizes acceptance [conversion] in terms of his own thought processes instead of those of the acceptor (or rejector), it can only lead to "confusion and artificiality"—the observer's fallacy (1953, 339). On my recent trip to New Guinea, I found many cases of native converts who had accepted Christianity because they thought that thereby they would acquire the prosperity and power of the white man whose religion it was. Now they are passing through a stage of disillusionment—as also are the missionaries who had assumed they understood the gospel.

result that the converts who cherished the narrative form, tried to weave together the old and the new, grasping at the points which were open for equation. This is a basic principle of innovation. People will accept readily new ideas which reinforce or coalesce with existing ideas, and in many cases the meaning ascribed to the new is derived from the old in the same way that (in a completely different context) many Greek words in the New Testament have Hebrew, rather than Greek, meanings.

Once again this facet of syncretism reminds us of the fundamental importance of the teaching program in the follow up of conversion. The Great Commission, after all said both: "make disciples" and "teach them."

The Demand for a Therapeutic System

Another area of cultural analysis which exposes any inherent syncretism is the whole field of belief regarding sickness and healing. When I find myself within an animist community for a few days I usually try to ascertain their basic theories of sickness.

After the burial of his father, Juan was sick of *komel* (a sickness caused by fear) and called an *ilol* to diagnose it. The *ilol* demanded candles, copal resin, aguardiente, a rooster, and flowers, and returned the next day for a healing ritual. Juan explains the theory of sickness (greatly abbreviated) thus:

> Each person has a chulel (a representative animal in the mountains) which shares his fortunes—health, sickness, fatness, hunger, and so on. Some hostile chulels prey on those of ordinary people, so that the latter sicken. If a demon ties up a chulel, the person whose chulel it is sickens. The *ilol* has to sacrifice a rooster to untie the chulel and set him free. The flowers had to be picked before sunrise and put on a small altar, the rooster hung up by its feet, the candles lit, the resin put on hot coals in the incense-burner, and a prayer had to be offered to the demon concerned to appease his feelings against the victim. The aguardiente drink would be spilled on the ground and the following prayer offered, "Holy Earth, Holy Heaven; Lord God, God the Son, . . . take charge of me and represent me; see my work, see my struggles, see my sufferings. I place the tribute in your hands. In return for my incense and ray candles, spirit of the Moon, virgin mother of Heaven, virgin mother of Earth, in the name of your first Son, your first glory, see your child oppressed in his spirit, in his chulel."

During this prayer the *ilol* killed the rooster by twisting his neck and Juan records—"Suddenly I felt free!" He knew that, his chulel having been seriously mistreated, he himself was not yet well, but that he would recover now (Pozas 1962, 88–91).

The therapy, belief structure, and psychology are all thoroughly shamanistic. The only traces of Christian borrowing are the references to the Virgin and the Son, and this was probably a case of protective borrowing. The divinatory diagnosis, the sympathy of patient and forest creature, the shamanistic process of curing, the psychological moment of release, the libation of liquor—all these are animistic survivals from the pre-Christian society. In no way whatever has Christianity changed or "possessed" this therapeutic configuration or its philosophical base.

Whatever Christianity brought to Juan's people, it completely bypassed this aspect of life. It raises one of the basic questions of missionary failure. If religion is to fulfill the role that has been ascribed to it in a communal society as "integrator" (Radin 1937, 15; Malinowski 1948, 53), "governor" (Wallace 1966, 4), the "universal feature" (Lowie 1952, xiv–xvi), the "sanctioner of the mores" or "the part of the mores which rules" (Sumner and Keller 1927), etc., it must both recognize and provide ways of dealing with the basic felt needs of the society. The animist has a confidence in the shaman and regards him as a benefactor and an essential person. When a new religion neglects its therapeutic ministry in a communal community, that society will inevitably retain its shamanic configuration. Either religion and healing will become compartmentalized and religion will lose its function as integrator of society, or the configuration of animistic diagnosis and healing, with its philosophical underpinnings, will be incorporated into its new religion. This is another way in which Christianity has often become syncretistic—by failing to meet the basic felt needs of the society. These long-standing needs often arise from the environment or physical condition of the converts and continue after conversion, and Christianity is effective only as it meets the needs of its adherents. Neglect of these physical, environmental, and cultural needs, forces the newly converted community to seek solutions elsewhere. When these solutions have pagan overtones, the Christianity becomes syncretistic.

The Notion of the Living Dead

"Everything is the same as when I was little," says Juan, "When I die and my spirit comes back here, it will find the same paths I walked when I was alive, and it will recognize my house" (Pozas 1962, 7).

Then there is the ritual of the Day of the Dead, when special bowls are taken from a chest for offerings of food to the souls of the dead, which Juan describes in the following way:

> One of my brothers went to the village to ring the bell . . . to call the souls. I went to the graveyard with my father, to clear the weeds from our family graves and to mark a little path in the direction of our house so the souls wouldn't get lost when they went for their offerings. . . ."My parents died here in this house," my father said, "and my father's parents also. The souls of your mother's parents will go over to the other house, because they lived and died there."

Here we are confronting the animistic concept of the living dead, which is the basis of ancestor worship. The conceptual structure is based on kinship and inheritance, and the dead are still recognized as part of the life of those who continue to live in the traditional place of abode and work the lands of the lineage. They still must eat the produce of the land and receive the services of the present occupants of their lands.

"In every house there is a table set with food for souls," says Juan, and goes on to add that theirs "was spread with pine needles and wild orchids." These are protective taboos against the mysterious power (cf. mana in Melanesia) associated with the things of the dead. The souls were offered tamales with beans and a gourd of cornmeal beverage. Juan's mother prepared the meal and set it out on the table. They thought of the souls as those who left an inheritance and the mother called,

> Come and eat!
> Come and taste the flavor of the food!
> Come and enjoy the fragrance of what you eat!

They burned candles in all the houses that night. Juan is certain the souls do come and partake of the food left for them.

The conversation this night concerns the sun and moon and ties in to the ancient pre-Christian worldview and origin myths (ibid., 48–51).

When Juan's father died, the symbolism of the burial was based on the notion of his departure on a journey across a lake infested with frogs. He takes food with him—chicken, tortillas, and salt. Every time he rests, the living dead share some of his food. He also had clothes and money to buy fruit on the journey, and when the ceremony is over the mourners wash in proper animistic fashion (ibid., 87–88).

What does Christianity, the new religion, say with respect to death and the life after death? Was the Christian eschatology credible to Juan's forebears when they became Christian? Are the dead still living and continually concerned with the cohesion and perpetuity of the tribe which they founded? How does Christianity preserve the entity of the lineage, the strength and stability of the family, the continuity and security of tribal lands—all part of what Sir Henry Maine called the concept of perpetuity. In communal society, it is the faith-formulation of the living dead and the cycle of associated ritual practises which preserve this.

If Christianity does not provide a vital eschatology (by "vital" I mean a living one that is actually believed and is the base of actual religious performance) he runs the risk of perpetuating the animistic notion of the living dead—which leads, of course, to Christopaganism or the co-existence of polytheism.[11]

---

[11] Some attempt has been made recently by the African theologian John S. Mbiti to relate traditional and Christian eschatology (1969, 159–84 and 1971), but theologians have not yet had much exchange on the subject, which certainly bears on the issue of syncretism and indigenous Christianity.

Summary

I have pinpointed four anthropological notions which show how syncretism may impose itself on Christian missionary effort. They are not exhaustive or confined to Latin America. On the surface, Spanish Christianity defeated animism and imposed its Western Christian structure on the defeated, leaving the animists no option of rejecting it. In the main, they found Spanish Christianity incredible. This forced acceptance was not a meaningful one, and therefore they preserved their old values and faith-formation at the heart. The continued morning worship of the sun, the shamanistic ritual of healing and the theory of sickness on which it stood, and the ritual of the Day of the Dead all demonstrate that the conqueror was, in point of fact, the conquered.

Examination of case histories like that of Juan also shows how anthropological or ethnohistorical investigations raise important questions for missionary strategy, and demand theological evaluation of missionary effort. So I feed these illustrations "into the hopper" in the expectation that we will want to discuss some of the points I raise.

To this point I have been taking a hard look at the negative aspect of our subject: namely, what must be avoided in cross-cultural missionary activity. But there is another side to which I must refer briefly.

The Alternative: Indigenous Christianity

It would be a tragedy to see cross-cultural church planting as merely a negative thing. After all, the gospel is positive, not negative—an experience to be entered into and shared. Somehow the supracultural core of truth, in both the written and the living word of God has to be incarnated in the culturally-bound churches or fellowships. We seek an assurance of salvation, when worshippers may say as individuals that they know him whom they have believed and are persuaded of his ability to keep what they have committed unto him against that day, and as communities they share the experience. We need in each cultural unit a written word of God in the vernacular language, for public and private use (reading, hearing, or memorizing). The gospel has to come through in indigenous rhythm and speak its message to the heart. For the man from the forest, the worship must have the capacity to vibrate with the beat of the drum. The arts and crafts of the group must be employed to absorb the energy, skills, and dedication of the artists and craftsmen of the group, that their manual and mental competencies may be expressive of spirituality, and help the group to worship the Lord in what, to their eyes and ears, may be described as "the beauty of holiness," even though discordant or grotesque to the westerner. We need a meaningful faith which holds together the daily life within the cultural structures, however strange may seem their modes of tilling the soil and plowing the deep. The universal human problems—finding one's way in the darkness, comforting the bereaved, encouraging the discouraged, preserving the family, solving the personal disagreements—will all have their peculiar formations in any culture different from our own. No religion can be indigenous unless it comes to grips with these universal problems in their culture-bound forms. When the laughing and crying, the feasting and mourning, the instructing and singing are truly culturally patterned, then we are looking at indigenous Christianity—here the gospel is at work in an experience of incarnation. And this is a far cry from syncretism.

Communication is a two way process. God may be omniscient, but I am not. He may speak to me, but I must hear and understand. The limitations in the process are with me. He is supracultural but I am culture-bound. Therefore there must be an incarnation. The space about me is alive with vibrations and impulses of which I am completely ignorant. I touch a button on my television, and in a few moments, these vibrations are transformed into sounds and pictures. They are immediately meaningful because the sounds are in my own language, and the pictures are of things I recognize. The problem of communication is one of meaning. That is why if the gospel is to be meaningful in any given culture it must be expressed and experienced in the forms of that culture. Syncretism is frequently due to what Barnett calls "the subliminal striving for meaning" (1953, 117),[12] the meaning the convert ascribes to the new religion being an expansion only of his old frame of reference. The expansion may be one of two kinds. Either he will innovate with new (foreign) religious forms retaining the conceptual framework, or with the Christian gospel using meaningful cultural forms for expressing it. The former I have called syncretism, and the latter I am calling indigenous Christianity.

Now, lest you imagine that I have been unfair to Latin America in my exposure of its Christopaganism, let me give you an example of indigenous Christianity which I witnessed myself in the same part of the world. Juan lived in Mexico. This account comes from Guatemala, but the people in it are from another sub-group of the same great Maya tribe as Juan. I merely transcribe here a passage from my own field notes:

> Somewhere about mid-day, after an hour of very dusty driving, we arrived at the market town for the area, and after cleaning up we went down to the church. It was a long and commodious building with a narrow frontage on a cobblestone street, which led onto the plaza, where a huge Catholic structure dominated the skyline. The street was alive with people with every kind of merchandise with tables, carts, and music, for the fiesta was in full swing. The Evangelical church boasted an upper room and a backyard. The local women's

---

12 Barnett says that this subliminal striving for meaning is "a central need of the ego system" and is drawn from an individual's "unconscious struggle to understand his universe in terms of what he already knows." As he configurates it, he ascribes meaning only on a basis of "the frames of reference available to him, namely, those provided by his past experiences" (1953, 117–18). This is why the follow-up of conversion requires a careful period of Christian instruction. Without this, the convert ascribes meanings predetermined by his pagan preconceptions of what religion is.

group had prepared food in the yard and stood behind their pots and containers. Each visitor took a plate and passed along the line for a serving of tamales, tortillas, and baked sweet bread. One concoction was said to be a culinary peculiarity to that locality alone—which made it a social talking-point. There was meat in the tamales, and this was wrapped in banana leaves. All the members of the congregation were involved, and we all ate together as a community.

After the meal, we observed the Sunday school in session. I went to the adult men's class in the upper room, which was crammed to the door. I sat with the others on the floor and nobody seemed to notice I was a foreigner. The class was mostly illiterate, but the peasant teacher used the blackboard and demonstrated pictorially the story of Cornelius from Acts. The class participation was good, and sometimes the leader was asked to read a point from the Bible. The singing was hearty. The prayers were multi-individual—everyone talking to the Lord at once regardless of his neighbor. Subsequently the groups went into church for the united worship service. The building was already full. I counted a sample of ten seats and figured there were about a thousand people present. Normally the congregation was about three hundred, but this was fiesta week and the country groups were in town. Special Christian services serve as a functional substitute for the old festival, the best values of which are preserved, the gathering at the market center, the joyful celebration, the fellowship that is wider than the town itself. The seating of the congregation reflected sex and age-grade grouping rather than regions. The presence of extended-families was apparent. Annually they change their officiating elders during fiesta week, as was done in their old pre-Christian priesthood.

The opening of the service was dramatic—guitars, bass, small organ, and rattles. The singing was lively and in the vernacular. They borrowed Western artifacts but used them in their own way. They amplified the music and preaching in the street outside so that it mingled with the jingles of the market as a witness. The ceiling was decorated with streamers of all colors and the walls with epiphytes, which must have required a lot of congregational preparation and participation. There was a table of vernacular literature at the door for any who could read.

The service was led by one of the elders, appointed by his colleagues for the day. He does not preach, but calls on one of the congregation. This reflected the local pattern of social organization. That day he happened to call on an old man, who not having the preaching skills of the young preachers, preferred to give his testimony. He had been the first convert in the locality, and narrated how the evangelical religion came to the district and how the church grew there. [After this follows a description of how the pattern of leadership reflected the social structure.]

> The meeting was now open for testimony, and folk from the small rural groups shared their experiences. This made me aware of a widespread Christian movement in the area, and a people excited about what the Lord was doing in their midst. For the duration of the fiesta, a different kind of church meeting was planned for each evening—praise and testimony one night, a baptismal service on another, appointment of officials, and so on. Their turning away from the secular festival had left no cultural void here: their own program was a real functional substitute.
>
> To me the most exciting episode of the worship service was the introduction of five men, who had determined to become evangelicals. They were already receiving Christian instruction, and would be baptised before the fiesta finished, I saw each of these men in turn hand over his personal fetish. To this week it had been a fearful and powerful thing. Now, before the congregation of people who had known him all his life, he "cast it from him" as a mere thing, a "not-god" as the prophet Isaiah might have said. One of these I noticed was an old Mesoamerican female figurine, an ancient fertility fetish—face, head, and breasts—whose creator lived long before the Spanish had come.

The description goes on for four more pages, but I must leave it and make the point I wish to emphasize. Not at any point was there a foreigner in charge. Everything was done by the people in their own way. This differed from the ways I was myself familiar with, but I saw no one there who seemed to be bored or out of touch. The whole thing was obviously exciting and meaningful, intensely cultural and indigenous. It was as far removed from the faith-formulations of Juan as it could possibly have been.

In my second lecture, I shall probe more deeply into the dynamics of this kind of indigenous Christianity which I have set up as over against Christopaganism. Before you hear that lecture, you will have heard from each of my colleagues, who are quite free, of course, either to build on what I have suggested or to draw our discussions out into some other dimension he might wish to discuss.

3
FORMAL TRANSFORMATION AND FAITH DISTORTION

In my first presentation, I considered syncretism as over against indigenous Christianity and found their common drive in a "striving for meaning" with institutions and terms that were relevant for specific historical cultural situations. Looking at syncretism anthropologically, we found that it was frequently activated and held together by any one or more of a number of identifiable forces—the persistence of cohesive clusters of ideas, an orientation to mythological thinking and belief, the demand for a therapeutic system, or the notion of the living dead. Very briefly I described indigenous Christianity only enough for it to be recognizable as a viable alternative to syncretism as a "culturally relevant striving for meaning." In other words, my focus was rather on the nature of syncretism rather than on indigenous Christianity.

In the second presentation, which I am calling "Formal Transformation and Faith Distortion," I shall dig more deeply into the subject from the position of the indigenous church confronting syncretism, and the dynamics of the experience of the Christian fellowship group (church) in its encounter with the world and with its culture. Let me begin with an analogy.

Religion or Gospel

I once lived near a place called Wangaratta. That is an Australian Aboriginal name meaning "The meeting of the waters." For the Aborigines it must have been a most exciting place as the flood waters spread out across a great swamp that teemed with wildlife, and through the centre, two significant rivers ploughed deep courses and came together in a tempestuous meeting. As far back as the Aborigines could remember, it had been the same, and the meeting of the waters figured in their myths from the dreamtime. Every generation of Aborigines as far back as their history went knew those streams, the meeting of the waters, the flooding, as I have known in my own day.

Let me use this as an allegory, of the confluence of those two streams of intellectual endeavor known as the "history of religion" and the "history of mission," which, when they meet, create a whirlpool. No missionary who navigates these waters can escape that whirlpool. It is a timeless hazard, and every missionary must navigate it for himself, and likewise every generation of missionaries. The missionary will focus on either the universals and commonalities of religion, per se, or on the uniqueness of the gospel.

I am using the terms religion-man and apostolic-man as descriptors of missionary attitudes to cross-cultural evangelism, because I believe that most missionaries (including mission executives) do, in point of fact, navigate one of these two streams. This is manifest when they bring their respective crafts near the whirlpool. The vortex of the whirlpool, of course, is precisely the same as McGavran calls "the eye of the storm" (1972): we are dealing with the very nature of the Christian mission, bringing the pagan to his "moment of truth," helping his faith re-formulation, and setting him on the Christian way without destroying his cultural lifestyle. It is in these matters that a missionary reveals whether he is a religion-man or an apostolic-man. The former may opt for some form of coexistence between Christianity and the non-Christian faiths—say, a kind of non-persuasive dialogue; or the notion that Christ is already there as a Presence, and all we need to do is to be there and to be faithful, leaving everything else to Him; or he may even settle for some kind of syncretism with the hope that the second or third generation, with more Christian education behind them, will be more truly Christian. On the other hand, the apostolic-man, operating on the traditional definition of mission in terms of the Great Commission and other utterances of our Lord, will call for a definite and demonstrated change of faith—a conversion experience. In one sense, the recent debates about the definition of mission are beside the point: down through history, these two categories may be found, and they have continuously demonstrated the disagreement, both inside and outside the church.

The notion of the whirlpool has something ominous about it. It rather suggests the possibility of being sucked in and destroyed. In my studies on power encounter, I have used a model for demonstrating the nature of the conversion process and have stressed a number of these danger points. In that process the ocular demonstration of an animist's faith-change is followed by his incorporation into the fellowship group; or if enough persons are involved at the same time, a young church is planted.[13] In this paper I want to focus on that point of time in the process and take a look at the whirlpool caused by the meeting of the waters.

To do this I shall have to distinguish between formal cultural transformation and faith distortion. The former is a qualitative change within continuing cultural forms due to the acceptance of the Christian faith. The latter is a compromise of the core of the Christian faith for personal, economic, or religio-universalistic advantages. The former leads to a

---

13 The dynamics of the cross-cultural conversion experience was presented by the writer to the annual meeting of the American Scientific Affiliation in 1967 and discussed. The paper was circulated in a multi-graphed form as a "Research in Progress Paper" (Tippett 1967a). Subsequently a smaller additional paper developed the topic further. The reader may also refer to Tippett (1973d, 122–27), and for further discussion on the concept of power encounter, see (Tippett 1967b, 100–10).

new set of values without seriously disrupting the cultural lifestyle. The latter leads, via syncretism perhaps, to another kind of paganism. Once the Jerusalem Council agreed that Greeks could become Christians without first becoming Jews (Acts 15), this problem arose; but it was a risk that the church had to take if it was to evangelize the world—on the human level, it was the same kind of risk which God took in creating man in his own image, and which Christ took with the incarnation to the cross.[14]

To show the continuity of this problem through Christian history, I shall now discuss the concepts of formal cultural transformation and faith distortion as Irenaeus encountered them in his congregation of Celts at Lyons in the second century. Subsequent to this, I shall come down to modern times and try to show the similarities between the two periods of history. To return to my sustained metaphor—the meeting of the waters and the whirlpool are always there, and the dangers for our navigation are the same as faced by Paul in the first century and Irenaeus in the second.

A Second Century Encounter: Irenaeus and the Gnostics

The name of Irenaeus has gone down in history as a Christian apologist and writer. His writing is significant as a contribution to ecclesiology, theology, church history, and biblical criticism. Yet to leave the name of Irenaeus there, is to miss the whole point of his life and work. Irenaeus was no armchair theologian. He was a pastor of the church in a precise situation. The purpose of his writing was to strengthen his flock in the belief in one God and in their faith in the redemption of man through Christ, the Son of God alone. His claim to our consideration is not that he was an early Christian scholar, but that in the cultural complex of a second century Christian community, he found the forces of Gnosticism impinging on and penetrating his pastorate and upsetting his young converts. Irenaeus is at once a concerned pastor in a precise situation. *Against Heresies* (1953) is not a theologico-philosophical treatise but the reflection of a dynamic situation and the struggles of a shepherd caring for his flock.

The Gnosticism of both Valentinus and Marcion invaded his pastorate and ramified through the life and thought of his parishioners. He was dealing with a practical, not a philosophical matter, which threatened the faith of his people. *Against Heresies* does not stand as a theological thesis per se. It is merely the contemporary and culturally relevant means he chose to handle a practical problem. The important thing is not that Irenaeus wrote such a work in five books, but that he confronted a threatening situation in the

---

14 The conference at Jerusalem, stimulated by certain Pharisees who had become Christian and insisted on the forms laid down by the Law of Moses being applied to Gentile converts (Acts 15:1), determined that the Gentiles should be Christians in their own way, being merely warned of the dangers of idolatry, religious prostitution, and heathen sacrifices (vv. 19–20), which might well lead to syncretism. This was a significant step—not only because it gave a Greek Christian the right to remain a Greek, but also because it recognized the element of risk—the risk to faith, as it were.

church. That threat was to basic Christian doctrines—the incarnation, the resurrection, the sacraments, the Person and work of Christ among them.

The fact that he explored critical and exegetical method and thereby established an approach to Christian scholarship which became a tradition is, for the moment, beside the point. He was not to see the course of church history in the centuries that followed. He was dealing with a threat within the church at his own point of time in history—as first John and then Ignatius, in whose tradition he stood, had done before him. The fact that *Against Heresies* was received by the church at large suggests, not so much its brilliance, but that the situation he was combating was widespread and not confined to his pastorate. Thus his writing became a bridge between the Johannine/Ignatius tradition before him and the work of the later apologists. No doubt, in the longtime purposes of God this was good and important for "the church through time;" but the real significance of this work is within a cultural complex at a specific point of time in history, and if that speaks to us at all, it surely says that as His servants and stewards we are concerned with dynamic confrontations in the life and culture of our own day, and with the mental, technological, and spiritual equipment we have at our disposal.

Against Heresies begins with a brief description of the situation in which certain men "by skillful language" are introducing "impious views" which the "hearers cannot always distinguish from the truth," because they are "decked out in attractive dress." The argument of Irenaeus stands on the restatement of a biblical creedal statement and the claim that the Christian faith remains firm as one cohesive thing, even across the barriers of geography, culture, and language.

Against this straightforward faith statement, he outlines the views of several patterns of Gnosticism—themselves by no means one. The Gnostics used the names Father, Son, Holy Spirit, and other Christian terms, but attributed non-Christian meanings to them. Thus, for example, "the Holy Spirit was produced by the Truth (identified as one of the second Dyad, offspring of Ineffable and Silence, in the first Ogdoad) to inspect and fructify the Aeons, entering into them invisibly, through whom the Aeons produced the plants of truth" (*Against Heresies* Vol 1. 11). Again the Logos is one with Zoe, Anthropos, and Ecclesia, as coming from the Tetrad of the first and second Dyads. And again, Christ was conceived by the Mother, who was outside the Pleroma with a shadow; Christ cast off the shadow and returned to the Pleroma, leaving the Mother with the shadow outside. Thus they assembled all manner of strange notions and peddled them by giving them biblical names and therefore biblical status.

Had it not been for apologists like Irenaeus, the Gnostics might well have taken over the church and made it merely another form of paganism by faith distortion.

How could the church ever have been tempted to accept such doctrine? We ask this question every time a nativistic prophet leads a breakaway from a modern mission field church. Let me put up a few feasible reasons for the success of the Gnostics, that occur to me as I read *Against Heresies* and put myself back into that second century situation.

(1) The written Word was not then in the hands of every believer, as it is today. Their knowledge of Scripture depended on what their leaders read or expounded. Therefore they had no personal criteria for judging a heresy.

(2) There were many formal similarities between Gnosticism and Christianity. Gnostics met regularly for congregational worship, used preaching from a supposedly sacred book, on which they had commentaries, and they sang hymns.

(3) They struggled with similar ideas—the redemption from evil, and reunion with the supernatural, for instance.

(4) They engaged in missionary programs to win people to their faith.

(5) They used similar terminology in pressing their theological ideas, and appropriated, not only scriptural names, but episodes for allegorical reinterpretation—the baptism of Christ, the request of the mother of the sons of Zebedee, the experiences of Eve and Mary, and so forth. The young Christians recognized these as biblical.

Thus was Irenaeus much exercised because his Christian flock was unable to discriminate clearly what was the truth, because it was skillfully presented and "decked out in attractive dress." Apparently the second century saw Greek nativistic movements, which claimed to be genuine reinterpretations of Christian Scriptures. This has very close similarities with the Hauhau Movement of the Maori Wars, the John Frum Movement of the New Hebrides, and other nativistic movements in Oceania and Africa.[15]

The Continuity of Encounter

In my allegory of the meeting of the waters and the whirlpool, I made the point that each generation in its turn passes by this way. This pressure on young Christians for faith distortion is ever with us. Every Christian community with a sense of mission must inevitably come into encounter with non-Christian faiths. Sometimes it is another faith that just enters the scene like the Hare Krishna in Los Angeles today, or the Sōka Gakkai, each of them using Christian missionary and witness techniques on the streets and from door to door[16] and like the followers of Valentinus who worried Irenaeus, with carefully honed emotional jargon and attractive trimmings, we cannot escape this kind of engagement—not unless we shut ourselves off from the world in isolation, which, unhappily, some churches have

---

15 Hauhauism and its offshoots have been discussed at greater length in a study of the obstructive factors which cut across the Maori people movements into Christianity (Tippett 1971b, 59–73, 181, and footnotes 93–106, pp. 246–48). The notion of the people movement and nativistic movement as positive and negative polarity is discussed in the same book (214–16). For further factual information on Hauhauism, see Babbage's book on the subject (1937), and for the John Frum Movement, see the book by the French anthropologist, Jean Guiart (1956).

16 The Hare Krishna have headquarters in forty major cities of the U.S.A. In the 1960s Sōka Gakkai was claiming growth of thirty-five thousand a year, and another Japanese sect was winning two thousand converts a month, only five percent of them Japanese.

done, and for which they must someday surely give answer to Him who sent them into the world as He was sent into the world.

If we suppose that the cultural structures themselves are amoral, there are only two feasible directions for young converts and new congregations to move. First, using the structural and formal similarities of the religions—prayer, worship, art, music, liturgy, etc.—as stepping stones, the church may strive to win them for Christ, what Bavinck calls possessio[17] and the ethnolinguists call transformation (Kraft 1973b, 237–48), to transform the cultural forms by making them Christocentric. Formal cultural transformation is thus a faith reformulation.

Second, over against this is the possibility of faith distortion, which is often the easy way out. One accepts the presence of Gnosticism (or paganism or animism) on the basis of formal similarities regardless of the faith content. This may be an unintentional acceptance—maybe a mere resignation to coexistence or rationalization about it. It may be accepted in the hope that with time and Christian education, the faith will come. In any case, it is bound to lead to syncretism and eventually to another form of paganism. In the case of Irenaeus, he recognized the subtlety of using biblical incidents and the names of the three Persons and the Trinity as "validation" for a spurious doctrine. He accused the Gnostics of using the name of Christ "as a kind of decoy," misguiding the people and "spreading their evil poison of the Serpent, the prince of apostasy" (*Against Heresies* Vol 1. 27:4).

The apostle Paul had felt the same dangers in the first generation church, and dealt with it firmly in his letters, which, like *Against Heresies*, are not merely literary documents, but products of dynamic situations—"Ye cannot drink the cup of the Lord and the cup of devils" (1 Cor 10:21), he asserts. And yet Paul drew on many of the cultural forms and values of the Greek colonial world—enough to serve as a data base for a textbook in anthropology.[18] Nevertheless, the one thing on which neither Paul nor Irenaeus would budge one inch was the nature and work of God the Father, Son, and Holy Spirit, and the way of salvation they opened to the believer. And of course they had the authority of Jesus for this (John 14:6).

Thus, in our own day, Visser't Hooft resists the notion of Christianity as a "species of the genus religion," just one other expression of the universal religion. He argues it is

---

17   Bavinck says, "The Christian life does not accommodate or adapt itself to heathen forms of life, but it takes the latter in possession and thereby makes them new" (1964, 178–79).
18   He draws his imagery from the social configurations of military life, architecture, agriculture, and athletics, to name a few of the more important. To take athletics, for example, one might refer to V. C. Pfitzner (1967), a major scholarly work. It also receives good coverage in Howson (1872, 65–91). It also has a place in many works on biblical customs, e.g., Chapter 31, in F. H. Wright (1953). The same may be done for the other configurations mentioned. But the point made here is that although Paul was not ignorant of the world scene in which the Christian encounter was taking place, was living in the world and not an isolationist, and was talking to farmers, athletes, and townsmen in real life situations, he was, nevertheless, quite intolerant of syncretism in their Christian faith.

an "adequate and definitive revelation of God in history," that classifying Christianity as one expression of "a general phenomenon called religion is to set it in a framework which is foreign to its nature" (1963, 94–95).[19] This of course is just what the religion-man does, when he permits co-existence or syncretism in the hope that Christian education will correct the matter in a generation or so; or when he allows Christ to be regarded as on a par with the Indian holy people,[20] for example.

Christ can break into a cross-cultural situation and possess or transform a social structure, an institutional complex, or a language, but the transformed form must be Christian: there must be no tampering with the Persons of the Trinity or the saving work of God for mankind—the basic core of the gospel, the supracultural, must stand. Formal cultural transformation by all means—but faith distortion, certainly not. There is no place in Christian mission for any theological Walt Whitmans:

> I respect Assyria, China, Teutonia and the Hebrews,
> I adopt each theory, myth, god and demi-god,
> I see that the old accounts, bibles, genealogies, are true, without exception.

or again,

> Thee in thy all-supplying, all-enclosing worship
> Thee in no single bible saviour, merely,
> Thy saviours, countless, latent within thyself,
> Thy bibles incessant within thyself, equal to any, divine as any. . . .[21]

Despite its cultural dissimilarities, our day is not very different from the day of the Christian conflict with Gnosticism. Many of our would-be policy makers are indeed "Gnostics." They would engage in faith distortion by removing Christ's place as only Saviour,

---

19 In differentiating the world religions from the world of revelation, Jean Daniélou says, "The worst misunderstanding of Christianity or of Judaism is to make them religions among other religions—the very error of syncretism" (1964, 17–18).

20 This is the attitude, for instance, of the members of the Navaho peyote-eating cult when they seek a corporate religious experience "in the Peyote Spirit, rather than in Christ, for Christ is but the culture hero of the white man."

21 The first lines cited come from "Birds of Passage," and the second from "Thou Mother with Thy Equal Brood." These are typical of Whitman's pantheism, of which many other passages might have been cited, for example:

> My faith is the greatest of faiths and the least of faiths,
> Enclosing worship ancient and modern and all between ancient and modern,
> Believing I shall come again upon the earth after 5000 years, Waiting responses from oracles, honoring the gods, saluting the sun,
> Making a fetish of the first rock or stump, powwowing with sticks in the circle of obis,
> Dancing yet through the streets in a phallic procession, rapt and austere in the woods a gymnosophist,
> Drinking mead from the skull-cup, to Shastas and Vedas admirant, minding the Koran,
> Walking the teokallis, spotted with gore from the stone and knife, beating the serpent-skin drum,
> Accepting the Gospels, accepting him that was crucified,
> Knowing assuredly that he is divine, . . ."
> (Poem 43 in *Song of Myself*)

Apparently it does not occur to Whitman that many of these religious patterns are incompatible. His pantheism can be no more than an abstraction. Such syncretism is impossible if one accepts the gospels as John indicates (*Leaves of Grass*).

and the biblical emphasis of persuasion for decision in Christian witness to the nations. They compromise with the religions by seeking a universal religion, which supposedly finds Christ or the Spirit in all the religions. These are the "Gnostics" within our ranks. Out in the streets the missionaries of the religions buttonhole people with enticing words of self-realization, calling on Christians in their homes, striving for a faith distortion. Our worship patterns are borrowed and people sing—"Buddha loves me this I know." Our theological terminology is used to their ends and the meanings are manipulated.

Christ and the Spirit are sweet and beautiful names that become decoys, offering instead a bitter poison from the prince of apostasy. One has to ask if we are with Irenaeus in Lyons or in the Christian West. The only difference is that all our lives we have had the written word of God in our hands—and therefore surely we are more responsible for the preservation of the faith.

Manifestly we are dealing with an aspect of the Christian encounter with the world that runs through history, and will continue to do so as long as we are called to Christian mission. If this be so, then maybe we should take a hard look at a few cases of formal cultural transformation and faith distortion, so that we may understand it better as we meet it in cross-cultural mission today. We are not hard pressed for examples.

Cross-Cultural Encounters

The case of the Chamula Indian, who supposed himself to be a Christian, we have already discussed at length. The supposedly Christian features of his faith touched on the Virgin Mary, the symbol of the cross, the Trinitarian formula, and the patronage of the saints—all appropriated somewhat magically. His attitude to the spirits of the dead, his communion with his ancestors, worship of the sun, his totemistic and shamanic beliefs and practises were all thoroughly animistic. The festival performances and mythical worldview were syncretistic. His anchor in Christianity was rooted in the names of the Godhead, the saints, biblical characters, and events—all wrenched from their true context. What purported to be the life of our Lord—the nativity, flight into Egypt, death on the cross, etc.—was interwoven with sun and moon worship, animistic pukujes and chulels, demons on the mountains, a Maya myth of the cornfield, a legend of biting flies (equated with the Jews), and so on. The Virgin Mary was confused with a local fertility goddess and also with the moon divinity. The Trinitarian formula was a magical chant. The Father was beyond the reach and knowledge of man in the place of the dead. The Son of God was equated with the sun, who goes to visit the absent Father by night and returns for the day. The moon was his mother.

Each time I dip into Irenaeus' *Against Heresies* and consider the Gnosticism that troubled him, I am reminded of Juan, the Christopagan Chamula. The similarities between the two syncretisms are remarkable, and the fallacies on which the respective faith-formulations were accepted are identical. The distortion is due to the acceptance of biblical characters, places, names, and events as truth, purely for their own name's sake; the words being biblical but the myths pinned on to them being quite false.[22]

This is why the post-conversion instruction is so important when new believers are being incorporated into the Christian fellowship group. It also shows why the Christian pastor or teacher must be quite clear in his own mind about the difference between the transformation of forms and the faith-formulation which goes with it. Let me develop this a little by comparing formal transformation and faith distortion, first, in the field of, say, indigenous art and crafts, and then in the rhythms of a people whose social regulations are preserved by oral tradition, art and rhythm being the mechanisms of communication.

Formal Transformation and Faith Distortion in Art

A converted Navaho Indian woman, an expert rug maker by pre-Christian profession, who had always hitherto depicted such things as the activity of the corn spirits in the rug design, now worked out a Christian design based on symbols like the cross and Scripture references. She presented the rug to the church for use in the worship service—a most appropriate gift. In another nearby congregation, the church is ornamented with Navaho paintings. They feature the corn but not the corn spirits. They rather point to the Lord of the harvest. In the case of the rug, the materials, the Navaho vegetable dyes, and the technology are indigenous. In the painting, although the paint medium is introduced, the style of indigenous sand-painting is preserved. In both cases, the skills and psychological satisfactions are all preserved both for the craftsmen and the audience, who knows and understands the meaning of these forms of communication. They recognize that the message and not the form has changed. This formal cultural transformation speaks to them to the effect that Christ is glorified, and not the corn spirits.

By way of contrast, let me comment on a beautiful book I received the other day—an anthropologist's delight. It is a well-written account of the origin myths of a community of Australian Aborigines, hitherto nomadic but now transhumant, with their central location under missionary patronage. The book is beautifully illustrated from a series of panels painted with the indigenous pigments in native style by Aboriginal artists. These panels depict the spirit people and fauna of the tribal origin stories. I am certainly pleased that this tremendously interesting folklore is to be preserved both in art and narrative. However, I would expect it to be done in a museum or a culture centre. One is certainly surprised to find the panels arranged as a background to the communion table in a Christian church;

---

22   Another form of the same fallacy I have met in the Solomon Islands and in the United States, where people calling themselves Jehovah's Witnesses exploit the same persuasive device. They cite Scripture—one passage after another—each time getting a nod of approval from the listener, in spite of the fact that they are quite unrelated and all extracted from their context. Thus, the bare fact that Scripture was cited elicits a belief in a non-scriptural position.

not because aboriginal art should not be there—I believe it should—but because the display is a record of what they are supposed to have left behind them. It will undoubtedly force the converts who worship in that church to so dwell on the dreamtime that their worship will be a coexistence and probably in time highly syncretistic—for the panel and the altar cross symbolize two incompatible belief systems. Over against the empty Christian cross which symbolizes the death and resurrection of our Lord, the Christian hymnbooks in the pews, and the lectern with the Bible on it (i.e. the pull towards the gospel) is set the record of spirits with an eschatology and origin of the dreamtime, the totemism, the ritual bag, the animism of Thunderman, the totemic tree of life linking earth with the spirit world, and its totemic animal messengers going to and fro between the two with communications (i.e. the pull towards the ritual song cycles and Australian totemism).

The two represent quite different theologies and confront the congregation with two different focal points for today's and tomorrow's religion. The placing of the two conflicting views before the congregation at every worship service is bound to be confusing. In an historical culture centre, the presentation might have been preserved with historical respect and treasured as tradition, but it is not the kind of thing to put before young converts when they enter the place where they specifically want to worship the Lord. In that church, they must find the supports they need for a religion which will stand by them today and tomorrow. For the Australian aborigine, this is a day of acculturation. It is anthropologically unsound to build in the archaic features of totemism, which will only let them down in more ways than one. More important still, if they have really become Christian, they need a worldview that is relevantly Christian. One is surprised that the missionary invitation to the Aboriginal artists should have been in terms of "whatever they would like to paint" and not to use their art forms to paint something Christian. This suggests a "religion-attitude" rather than an apostolic one. In that it has set a "bone of contention" before the young converts, it is regrettable. In that it fails to provide for the problems of today and tomorrow, it is again regrettable. In that it fails to present the Christ in a Christian church it is, in my opinion, misguided and irresponsible, and will be seen as such even by anthropologists who rejoice that the folklore is preserved. It was the anthropologist Malinowski who pointed out what a missionary was bound to be and do if he was to be true to himself (1965, xv).[23] What I can only speculate on is why it was put there. Was it an attempt to make a Western church building more indigenous? Was it to reduce the culture shock of rapid culture change by letting the converts see that the missionary was not anti-cultural? Was it to help the converts retain their sense of ethnic entity? Was it to impress upon the Aboriginal converts that it was their church, not that of the westerners?

---

23 He says of the missionary: "He would not be true to his vocation if he ever agreed to act on the principle that Christianity is as 'any other form of cult.' As a matter of fact, his brief is to regard . . . Christianity as entirely different, the only true religion to be implanted . . ." (1965: xv [1938]).

Was it the "religion-attitude" which claimed that we should look at totemism and find Christ already there? Many of these would have been valid reasons for setting an Aboriginal panel there in the central place in that church. But the fault lies in the fact that it is a totemistic panel, a belief system which by profession they have left. Anthropologically it does not relate to their current profession. Theologically there is nothing Christocentric about it. Both anthropologically and theologically it offers nothing for today or tomorrow in a rapidly changing world: it offers nothing but a conflict of values. Furthermore, the fact that the Aboriginal artists elected, with the approval of the people, to depict the dreamtime as the subject for the panel, shows something sad or disillusioning about the depth of their conversion and their need for Christian instruction.

For a non-literate people like this, with whom symbolic communication is by art instead of letters, it is essential for their art to be won for the purpose of communicating the Christian faith and ethic. For semi-nomadic people like this, the notion of the journey is a key image for the preservation of their faith and the establishment of ethical and procedural reference points in the traditions of the people. This is one reason for the tremendous value of Pilgrim's Progress in so many societies for reinforcing and applying biblical values.[24] Furthermore it is narrative in form. In the light of this, what can be done to correct the problem panel in the church, short of removing it and offending the tribes concerned?

Anthropologically and historically, it is incomplete. It could be completed in the same art style so that the last panel depicts the conversion of the people to Christianity. This would bring it into line with their present belief. A Christocentric panel as the end of the journey would change a faith distortion to a formal transformation, and remove the perilous dichotomy of the panel over against the altar cross. As things are at present, this dichotomy can lead only to unnecessary conflict, a phony coexistence, or syncretism. If the panels show the journey from totemism to Christ, there is harmony in the belief system and considerable teaching value; as there was when Ratu Cakobau, the cannibal Fijian had the killing stone at Bau transformed into a baptismal font and set it before the congregation as "a reminder of the greatness of their salvation."

To build in the conflict between totemism and Christianity, for whatever motivation, is to misunderstand the whole nature and function of these cultural art forms and tribal storytelling. These things are never static. The whole idea is that they represent the ongoing process of tribal history. The events of the journey depict the characters who have molded history, and the significant innovations at their historic points of time. They tell the living

---

24 Possibly no Christian book has been more influential in the spread of Christian values than Bunyan's Pilgrim's Progress, which was translated into scores of languages during the last century. It had its cross-cultural appeal, not only in the notion of the pilgrimage, but also in its literary form and the use of the "name with a meaning," a common device in pre-literate societies.

how things came to be as they are. Therefore if the art and storytelling techniques are to be genuinely preserved, the total art or story complex must tell the Christian congregation how they came to be what they now are. Thus, the most recent panel will show the foreigners bringing the good news, the people accepting it, the discovery of the Bible from which they read at worship, the building of their church—all in the same artistic medium. Thus would the art and narrative show the people how they became what they currently are. Unless something like this is added, the totemic panel will not be credible in a Christian church, or it will injure the Christianity by faith distortion. The road is perilous but it has to be followed if the church is to be indigenous, and the passage from animism to Christianity is to be meaningful and smooth. The history of schism, syncretism, and nativistic movements in the church show how long we have taken to learn the lessons of the whirlpool at the meeting of the waters.

Formal Transformation and Faith Distortion in Rhythmic Transmission

Much of what I have said of the Aboriginal panel series of paintings may also be said of oral traditions—stories, songs, dances, dirges, and rhythmic history. The people are brought along the road to their present state. If that is a state of Christian experience, at least for the first generation of Christians, that must be reflected in their songs and sagas. What happens fifty years thereafter is the business of the church of fifty years after—and that is a different matter, which we are not discussing at the moment.

The question of what is to be done with pagan dances and chants when a people becomes Christian has long been a bone of contention among missionaries and missionary supporters—but it is a foreign and Western problem. The fear of syncretism has led many missionaries to reject the dance and chant as a communication form, lest the people continue to cling to their pagan associations, but the argument is not rational. The fallacy of the reasoning is that all these media of rhythmic transmission are bundled together under one judgement of the form rather than the content. Would it be reasonable, for example, to deny ourselves the use of language itself because it can be used for communicating profanity?

Yet many missionary supporters have advocated this with dances and chants among their converts, equating a native dance with the sex associations of its Western prototype. And many anthropologists have grouped all missionaries under the condemnatory generalization for prohibiting and destroying these art forms. The charge is not fair. Where it has been true, the converts have usually felt a cultural void, social needs have been unmet, and sooner or later there have been reactions. But all missionaries have not been like this.

The British missionaries in Fiji, for example, prohibited certain dances, like the wate and dele, which were associated with victorious return from war and sexual abuse of the bodies of the victims, to be followed by cannibal festivities. They demanded that their converts reject any dances or entertainments which were vulgar and sexy; but they did not prohibit the dance and chant per se. In this way, they taught their converts to discriminate between appropriate and inappropriate dances and songs. Dances were retained for social entertainment, even for church festivals. They still preserved and dramatized their sagas. They composed new chants to cover their unfolding history in Christian times. They commemorated their church building instead of pagan temples. They created dirges in their bereavements, and, in their lighter moments, opened the door to satire and hilarity. I have seen all these dances, and have the accompanying chants of many of them. One of them covers the history of a century of the expansion of the church in their islands. With their own peculiar cultural rhythmic media, they did exactly what we in the West have done with radio, television, and the printed book—used them for communicating the gospel. Indeed one of the most dramatic dances I have ever seen was an old Fijian war dance resurrected for a precise instructional purpose, years after the acceptance of Christianity. It ended with a declaration of the coming of the gospel at the climax of the dance, whereupon every dancer gave a shout (an honourific act) and broke his beautifully carved spear across his knee. A white man in the audience bewailed this destruction of native artifacts. What he failed to realize was the dramatic symbolism of this act in the chant and dance, which the Fijian spectators understood full well—the gospel had broken the spear. The dance was the talk of the countryside for weeks. This was a true indigenous creation in the best form of oral tradition. It brought the audience out of the past and left them in the present. It demonstrated that Christianity did not destroy the indigenous creativity in chant and dance, and distinguished again between "formal transformation and faith distortion"—for in this case, however old the transformed form, the new faith formulation was no faith distortion: its meaning was truly Christian.

Another feature of the transmission of faith and ideas through rhythm is the chant, which, in many societies whose traditions are orally transmitted, was used in pre-Christian times for both educational and liturgical purposes. An indigenous church in such a society would be one which retained the form, transforming it with a new faith formulation. It will be no surprise then, seeing I have been speaking of the dance in Fiji, to find beside it, the educational and liturgical use of chanting. The old Fijian pre-Christian chant has been sanctified and made holy unto the Lord.[25] In the traditional manner, led by the matrons in the village congregations for over a century, the psalms of David, and the lyrical and descriptive passages of Scripture have been chanted both before and as part of the regular church worship service. Here the story of the creation, the building of the temple

---

25 In the same way the original collection of Christian Fijian hymns, created by John Hunt and R. B. Lyth were composed as Fijian lyrics, even with Fijian euphonistic particles. It was a later (and more Victorian) generation which made them rhyme and organized the parts to fit sheet music. The Te Deum was used in Fijian whenever some sinner "bowed the knee" before God, the whole congregation bursting spontaneously into the praise. For an evaluation of Hunt's mastery of Fijian hymnody, see Nettleton (1906, 84).

of Solomon, the glory of the New Jerusalem, the Ten Commandments, the Beatitudes, and David's lament over Absalom (to name but a few of many I have heard) have been features of Fijian worship.

This was a learning experience, but it was far more. It was a communal participation in worship, which was thoroughly Fijian in form and thoroughly scriptural. Originally the form was used over the bodies of the slain, as the triumphant villagers lauded the exploits of their fighting-men before a cannibal feast, and at the time of the presentations at the pagan temple. But, by the gospel, it was transformed and found appropriate for use in transmitting a new and better message from Scripture and catechism.

Events in the life of the village church were also commemorated through chants. This preserved the creativity of the village poets and made the church a centre of village life. In the same way, songs of farewell and dirges in memory of those who had died in the faith were composed and chanted.

For a century now in Fiji, the ongoing operation of the life of each village community has been stimulated by these transformed indigenous forms and patterns, and the strength of the church today is partly due to them. A secular anthropologist working in Fiji described this church as "a Fijian-orientated institution . . . guided by a spirit of tolerance . . ." (Belshaw 1964, 14).

The Risk to Faith

To this point we have been considering the experience of the Christian fellowship group in its encounter with the world and the culture to which it belongs. We understand that the church has to maintain its life and witness in the world, with a message which is transmissible in the cultural forms that are comprehensible in that familiar world. Yet, there is always a danger of becoming so accommodated to that world that it is no longer recognizably Christian. I have spoken of the risk to faith which comes with involvement in the world. Here is our paradox. Here we could well be sucked into the vortex at the "meeting of the waters." Yet our Lord pointed out to His disciples that this was the inevitable risk in the Christian mission, when He prayed for them whom He left in the world, but not of the world (John 17:14b, 18).

Encounters there had to be, but encounters need not necessarily bring about syncretism or faith distortion. Syncretism is not the only kind of faith-reformulation. Cultural forms may be transformed. How this can happen I have tried to demonstrate with examples of forms of art and rhythmic mechanisms. It might have been done in other areas of culture also, but the point is clearly made. The notion of consecrating, dedicating, or sanctifying a cultural artifact or institution unto the Lord is not uncommon in Scripture. Where Scripture is iconoclastic, it is the faith-formulation and not cultural form that is under attack. Elijah's encounter on Mt. Carmel was an attack on the worship of Baal and its pagan associations, not an attack on the idea of sacrifice.[26]

Despite the great social differences between the world of Elijah and that of the New Testament, the basic principle of the divine Word spoken and demonstrated to man through man, is the same. The notion of salvation certainly developed through Scripture history, but the human problem is still the encounter between the religion-man and the apostolic-man. In his work, No Other Name, Visser't Hooft demonstrates numerous New Testament forms of the same conflict. There was the case of Simon Magus, where the issue was the incompatibility of the service of God and the exploitation of divine gifts for self-glorification. There was the disturbance in Ephesus, where folk believed their social stability depended on a harmony between the gods and where the notion of the uniqueness of a revelation in Christ alone had disturbing consequences. There was the letter to Colossae, where folk in the young Christian communion were faced with elemental spirits and cosmological speculations, which Paul dealt with by a dogmatic statement of the exclusiveness of Christ, who was certainly not trying to establish another mystery religion. And then there was Pergamos, the centre of great gods and powerful cults, to whom the Word was decisive—no compromise with other gods (Visser't Hooft 1963, 56–62).

Faith formulation may be developing or distorted. Developing faith has to be related to formal transformation. If the form is not transformed, the faith will be foreign and distorted, and its meaning confused. This builds up problems for the next generation. Any form of religio-social change involves some degree of encounter, and this certainly applies to the Christian mission as it brings the gospel to the non-Christian world. The only tenable and reasonable base for Christian mission, as Kraemer (1938) pointed out is the "apostolic attitude." With him also, while requiring a respectful and humble approach to the non-Christian religions, refraining from too critical a mind against their infusion with Christian values, and recognizing the religious possibilities in the spiritual unity of mankind (the voices of religion-man), I endorse his italicized qualification of these approaches—"provided they are kept in their place." He goes on,

> If they usurp the place of the apostolic motive, which is the alone valid and tenable one, they transform the Christian church into a goodwill agency for

---

26 The scriptural notion of sacrifice is itself a good example of faith-reformulation and formal transformation. The forebears of Israel, who came over the desert, practised human sacrifice until the Lord brought Abraham to Mt. Moriah, in an experience of crisis or encounter, leading eventually to His provision of a lamb as a functional substitute. Thereafter, Israel passed through the phase of animal sacrifice as developed in the Law of Moses. This continued throughout the Old Testament times and is terminated in the beginning of the Christian era, with our Lord's encounter with the forces of human sin on the cross at Calvary. This is spoken of as "a better sacrifice" because, among other things, it is an eternal one. So the faith-formulation grows or is reformulated, passing from Semite, to Hebrew, to Christian faith, and the form of the salvation motif is transformed by a new faith content. Incidentally, converts to Christianity, coming out of a society which practises human sacrifices, need an early translation of the letter to the Hebrews to help them in that journey of faith.

> the diffusion of refined and cultural idealism, which has lost all intrinsic relation with the central apostolic consciousness that we are to be witnesses to God and His revelational dealing with man and the world (ibid., 293).

If the gospel is to be communicated to the non-Christian world, as our Lord instructed, the risk to faith (the risk of the emergence of syncretistic communions) was always a dangerous possibility. But that is no reason why the Christian mission should not continue as he directed unto "the end of the age." My own missionary and research experience suggests that there is a strong relationship between the Christopagan in Christian mission and the religion-man attitude of the missionary, and as a corollary, a rare relationship between Christopaganism and the apostolic-man attitude.

On the other hand, I am not suggesting the apostolic-man has no lessons to learn. Here again, my experience as an anthropologist is that he is rather in danger of the unjustifiable destruction of cultural ingredients, and of planting a foreign church.

The common misunderstanding in both these errors relates to the problem of meaning. In one, the meaning is not Christian. In the other, it is not culturally relevant. And in my opinion, one is as sad a distortion of faith as the other. The greatest methodological issue faced by the Christian mission in our day is how to carry out the Great Commission in a multicultural world, with a gospel that is both truly Christian in content and culturally significant in form. I hope that when we interact with each other in the final presentations of this colloquium that we can come to grips with that problem.

4
THE MEANING OF MEANING

How does one react to a set of presentations such as we have had over the last two days? The subject of this Symposium might well have led us into some strong disagreements in any of three or four areas, but on the whole, there has been more agreement than disagreement. The points of disagreement are present, but they have been latent rather than manifest.

One could argue, for example, on what is really the business of missiology,[27] or how we define culture,[28] or on the point of time when large-scale cultural adoptions should be made,[29] and I am methodologically unhappy about the model of an axis-ladder, with Christians on different steps in their ascent[30] which, in spite of its possible utility, has too many problematical presuppositions. I dislike the statistical use of the notion of a global

---

27 I do not know what Dr. McGavran means by saying that missiology refers only to the adjustments on "new ground," that "adjustments which well-established churches make are no business of missiology," and that "when the church makes the adjustments, the process is no concern to missiology" (Yamamori and Taber 1975, 161). Perhaps I do not read him correctly. I believe the continual adjustments required of the church are part of its mission—for only thus can it hope to bridge a generation gap within its own constituency, and I cover this in Tippett (1973d, 10–16), under the phrase "the inward dimension of mission." This paragraph of McGavran's mystifies me in the light of what he has written under the head of "biological growth."

28 In Dr. McGavran's first presentation (Yamamori and Taber 1975, 35–55), we meet "secular culture," "modern culture," "each culture of the world," "our culture," "Gnostic culture," and "any culture." Sometimes it seems to be a culture pattern, sometimes a philosophy of religion, sometimes part of the patter (without a religion). It is sometimes anthropologically used and sometimes aesthetically.

29 Unless I misunderstand Dr. Beyerhaus, I think he underrates the importance of "making the large scale adaptations" in the first generation (ibid., 140). Functional substitutions made twenty or thirty years later have been notably unsuccessful. We are dealing with conversion from paganism. The very first fellowship of believers should be structurally and operationally recognizable as indigenous from the beginning; otherwise we are building in a cultural void for the indigenes and a "mission to church" problem for the missionary enterprise. I think that whatever indigenous features are to be adopted should be identified and possessed for Christ from the time of the initial people movement and its catechetical consummation.

30 Hoekendijk's first presentation, leaves us with non-Western and Western Christians alive "on different steps on the axis-ladder"—reflecting an admitted necessary humility on my part (ibid., 73). However, the tendency to use some kind of scale like this to measure syncretism in a scientific manner is often used by researchers. It may be useful for measuring behaviour, but when it comes to such things as faith or revelation it fails. Religious experience is so complex that we can never hope to identify the variables for experimental use, let alone eliminate them.

village.[31] I question the exegesis of Mark 5 in Dr. Hoekendijk's second presentation,[32] and I have reservations about how far we can use his schema of Christianization.[33] In any of these, we could get into long (and perhaps profitable) arguments, but they would take us far afield from the subject before us. Therefore, I intend to let these points pass, by merely indicating my reservations, and in this presentation, I shall direct my response to my colleagues in a symbiotic rather than a reactive form.

In the opening presentation, I pointed out that the whole program of cross-cultural communication of the gospel was caught up in the basic problem of meaning, of how a supracultural gospel could be communicated and manifested in meaningful cultural forms. All the papers of my colleagues demonstrate the truth of this fundamentality of the problem of meaning. Therefore, rather than debating a few points of disagreement (profitable as that might be), I shall try to draw together in terms of my own discipline what I believe is a basic ingredient of all our presentations.

Meaning—A Fundamental Problem

Let me recapitulate briefly some of the issues raised by my colleagues which sprang from the problem of meaning, although they did not always articulate it as such. Let me take them one by one.

Dr. McGavran

Dr. McGavran (Yamamori and Taber 1975, 35–55) took up the question of "the pure faith delivered to the saints," and tried to identify its essential ingredients, laying down criteria for validating the message to be communicated to the nations. Taking two phrases of mine, "a pure faith" and "an essential gospel," and presuming that we participants were more or less of one mind in this, he pointed out that for many people there was "enormous confusion" and he devoted half of his first paper to defining the phrase "a pure faith." Thus he identified this basic issue as a problem of meaning.

---

31 The reduction of the world to a global village to make a statistical point (ibid, 151) involves the writer in a false analogy. I do not dispute Hoekendijk's point, but I do challenge the model he uses to make it. It would have been better stated in simple percentages. The analogy assumes an even distribution of the condition (e.g., illiteracy) throughout the statistical universe—which is not so, some places being quite illiterate and others not at all so.

32 The exegesis of Mark 5 (ibid., 145) might well have become a point of debate among us because it implies the authority of a commentator to declare a biblical narrative to be a current heathen folk-tale. This bears on our attitude to the nature of Scripture and its interpretation.

33 Hoekendijk's schema of Christianization (ibid., 146) reflects medieval European history and is useful as a frame of reference for a particular set of circumstances in history; but it is not necessarily a universal pattern, neither does it mean that there is no other quite different frame of reference for analyzing the Christianization of Europe. It may well be that medieval church history will someday have to be written in terms of the dynamics of modern cross-cultural people movements.

Then he went on to deal with secularism, deism, and Arianism. Although I have some difficulty in pinning down just what he means by secularism,[34] and although I cannot accept the notion of "deist culture,"[35] nevertheless, he manifestly is struggling again with the whole problem of meaning—the meaning of the gospel and the false trails which lead into syncretism.

In the case of de Nobili and the Brahmins, and the test of whether this was syncretism or possessio, the answer he received from Rome provided a criterion for meaning. It was not a direct "yes" or "no," but depended on whether the "sacred thread" or "tuft of hair" had Hindu significance, or whether it brought honour to Christ—not Christ as one person of the supposedly all-incorporating Hindu pantheon, but Christ, the only way to the Father. Here again we have the problem of meaning. And this time the focus is on the form (the thread and tuft of hair), rather than the message; but the implication is that the form itself may have a meaning for those who set it in a different frame of reference from the missionary. A similar point arose when McGavran discussed the Christian Christmas festival as a functional substitute for the festival of the winter solstice. The common issue between these two cases is whether the form is given a new and Christian meaning or retains its pagan significance. The meaning makes all the difference in the world—the difference between possessio and syncretism.

Again he speaks of "morphological fundamentalism"—attributing radical new meanings to old words, semantic shifting, to adjust to some cultural or philosophical change, and passing it off as if no change had taken place—we are once again involved in a problem of meaning which, among other things, bears on mission policy and promotion. Likewise, in his discussion of the rejection of "traditional Christianity (creed, cultus, organization, and customs)" for the sake of philosopher-theologians, who want "a radically new form of Christianity," we have a striving for meaning on the part of the armchair missionary theologians.

We have before us a wide range of cases of the problem of meaning—wide enough for me to say that there may be peculiar problems of meaning at every level—the missionary supporter and the policy maker, the observer and critic in the street, the missionary himself as communicator or advocate, and the listening audience—either of practicing Christians or of potential converts. At every one of these levels, we are confronted with some aspect of the problem of meaning.

---

34   Scientific humanistic self-sufficiency and the religio-philosophical incredibility of the idea of God can hardly be part of the same "system" as modern culture which "gives birth to a conviction that life is meaningless." Self-sufficiency and anomie are essentially different attitudes.

35   A worldview which is philosophically deist cannot, in my understanding, be equated with a culture. There is no "deistic culture." Such-and-such a culture may be orientated towards deism—but this is a very different thing. However, I agree with McGavran that when biblical faith is adulterated with the philosophy of deism (as he describes it) we shall have syncretism on our hands (ibid., 35–55).

Dr. Beyerhaus

When Dr. Beyerhaus discussed the separation of mission churches and Afro-messianic movements (ibid., 77–95), he pressed that this was at base a theological problem. His approach to the subject was itself surely an attempt to discover meaning. We placed ourselves in the position of the advocates of the African movements in order to pose the right questions to Western missions. Then we made ourselves critics of the answers we received. It was, I think, an illuminating exercise, and did indeed point up the theological character of the problem—but it was a problem of meaning even so.

Dr. Beyerhaus pinpointed a number of significant things—the failure of converts to realize that the incarnation of Jesus Christ was an historic fact, the failure to appreciate New Testament eschatology, the failure to develop a relevant pneumatology, the failure to achieve a biblical view of the psychosomatic unity of man or to arrive at a true koinonia in the disrupted society. When we confront the penetrating nature of these shortcomings, we begin to ask how missionary communication could possibly be so far off its basic goals—clearly somewhere there was tragic misunderstanding. And we are back again to the problem of meaning, as Beyerhaus cited Freytag—"the gospel heard is different from the gospel preached" (ibid., 89). The Spirit is equated with African life-force, but this never becomes the personal Holy Spirit, and this Beyerhaus rightly points out, is "a hermeneutical task."

In responding to this, I believe that the existence of African concepts like life-force (cf. mana in Melanesia) gave the African a capacity for receiving the gospel. The gospel was potentially credible (Tippett 1972, 133–39). The goal of mission is manifestly to get beyond the notion of life-force to the Person of the Holy Spirit, and I agree this is a hermeneutical task, but it is bigger than hermeneutics. Here the problem of meaning has to get beyond conceptualization to an experience for which we have no words—either in the language of the advocate or the receiver of the message. Perhaps Paul would have called it "the mystery." This, of course, is the work of the Holy Spirit Himself, and it is at this point that conversion to Christ differs from all other kinds of conversion.

When people in a messianic movement "bypass the Crucified Lord" through "seeking a national hero" or confuse the "notion of civilization" with the "coming kingdom of peace," we are dealing with problems of meaning at the acceptor's end of the process of evangelism. This raises the allied question of motivation—why people become Christian. When people, especially large groups of people, become Christian from wrong motives or with wrong expectations, they automatically give a wrong meaning to the message, and eventually are disillusioned. This is one of the causes of nativistic breakaways.

Dr. Beyerhaus has confronted this kind of syncretistic response to the gospel with a better alternative—namely, a striving for possessio. His important discussion on the threefold concept of "Selection," "Rejection," and "Reinterpretation" aims not only at eliminating the heathen elements, but at fulfilling "the adopted elements with genuine Christian meaning"—thus the preservation of cultural forms is not syncretistic, for, "by structured catechetical instruction" they are "filled with the new reality of God's grace." Clearly also Beyerhaus' theological concern is a striving for meaning.

Dr. Hoekendijk

Dr. Hoekendijk confined his first presentation to an historical survey of Indonesian data (Yamamori and Taber 1975, 57–75). But here we saw that at each historical period and in each pattern of Christian mission, the problems discussed could all be reduced to matters of meaning. In a few sentences, let me nominate a few of his ideas which tie up with this dimension of meaning:

> People movements, to be fully meaningful, have to be seen in their sociopolitical contexts.
>
> The missionary is never a speaker only—his whole life is part of the kerygmatic event.
>
> What is said is not always what is heard.
>
> The question is raised of whether syncretism may not indicate the "undetected beginnings of an indigenous theology."
>
> Xavier saw one of his major problems as the task of translating "the mysteries of faith into language one does not understand."
>
> There are cases of pre-Christian mythology being used to bring Christology close to the heart of the people, like the Javanese messianic expectation of "the liberating Lord of Justice."

There is the use of traditional adat for theological developments. Dr. Hoekendijk just mentioned these in passing, but a moment's consideration reveals that they all raise the question of meaning. The same applies in his second presentation (ibid., 143–52) especially his discussion on terminology. However, in my response, I want to go beyond the meaning of our own terms to the meaning of meaning itself. I feel free to do this because strategist, theologian, historian, and anthropologist have all, in a sense, reduced the issue of syncretism to the problem of meaning.

Meaning—A Passive Quality of Cultural Elements

I now propose to analyse this problem of meaning a little more deeply and theoretically in an anthropological manner. The missionary, or evangelist, or communicator—I usually employ Barnett's term "the advocate" (1953) because we are involved in an innovative or decision-making process that seeks a response of acceptance—has the task of advocating the acceptance of the gospel. He is striving to communicate something which is supracultural, but which he only knows in a cultural form, to people whose cultural forms and worldview are different from his own. We have been confronted with the truth that frequently our missionary effort ends up with syncretism or a new form of animism or polytheism; and if the new Christian community is really Christian, its form of Christianity is often unrecognizable by Western Christians who cannot see beyond their own worldview and cultural trimmings. In my first presentation, I tried to distinguish between the two—"syncretism and indigenous Christianity." The data presented by my colleagues also have indicated that we are indeed confronted with these two kinds of community as the result of missionary activity. The humiliating question then is: How does so much sincere Christian missionary activity end up as syncretism rather than indigenous Christianity? [I am not talking about that kind of missionary activity which ends up with a small, enclosed, static, foreign congregation and a Western Christian worldview. That is another problem altogether.]

There are several ways in which we might approach our present problem. Hitherto, our papers, for instance, have analysed it from different angles—theologically, strategically, historically, and culturally—but in each of these areas we come up with the same finding, namely, we have on our hands a problem of meaning. I now wish to probe the theoretical base of that problem a little more deeply and ask another question—For the missionary advocate, what is the meaning of meaning?

The Integration of Passive Qualities

Cultural elements (including say, a Christian hymn or prayer, a rite, a translation of the Bible, or even a cultural institution like a congregational group), according to the anthropologist Linton, have four related qualities, two of them dynamic, namely function and use, and two passive, namely form and meaning (1936, 402–04). In this theoretical unit, I am concerned with the passive qualities of the cultural elements of the cross-cultural Christian mission. What I want to say may be applied to cultural artifacts (like, say, a symbolically carved lectern, or a composed liturgy), or a craftwork design (for an altar cloth), or an institution (like a communion service), or the process of evangelism itself, or an organization (like an operating indigenous church). To ascertain whether or not we are studying a syncretistic or truly Christian cultural element, be it at the level of an artifact, a craft, an institution, or an organization, we have to probe the passive level and consider form and meaning.

Now, on the strength of the variety of data in our present discussions, I wish to go a step beyond Linton's theory. The distinction between form and meaning is not always clear-cut. The form will also have a meaning. It may have a different meaning to advocate and acceptor, especially if they have different worldviews. The same form may have different meanings to the same audience in different situations. Linton's categories are only abstractions. In reality they cannot be segregated. The categorization is merely a mental exercise to help us identify the ingredients of the passive quality of cultural elements.

But I think there is good reason to add a third ingredient, perhaps we may tentatively call it the value. There is some determinative factor interwoven with both the form and meaning. It also influences the dynamic factors of function and use, but it is itself passive and subjective. It conditions the very orientation which strives for meaning, or gives meaning. It covers the principles of an institution, the criteria of an experimental process, and the belief behind an act of worship. It has to be distinguished from meaning because it is largely the cause of the meaning. Change the belief system and you will change the meaning of the form.

Sometimes the value system is articulated in a precise form, as for example, in a code of law, or a policy statement, or a creed. Sometimes it is implied in the cultural idiom of the language, for example, when we say that some action is "not playing the game," or "hitting below the belt." This quality of value in the cross-cultural institution of evangelism surfaces into visibility as the gospel message; which may be considered in terms of "unarticulated belief" or as a concrete form in "the revealed but written word of God." Two of my colleagues have argued, correctly I believe, that one reason why we run into syncretism is by departing from, or manipulating, the message. We can say this when we focus on the value aspect, which conditions the meaning.

Whether we are communicating a gospel for acceptance in the program of outreach into the world (John 17:18) or in the interpretation of Scripture for growth in grace in the program of the inner life of the fellowship group (1 Pet 5:1–11), we need to examine "the passive qualities of value, meaning, and form," as an integrated system, to ascertain whether the program be syncretistic or really Christian, I think this theory, which is itself derived from a data base of concrete missionary and anthropological research, should help us at least to ask the right questions of the syncretist.

The theory may be conceptualized in a diagram which suggests the integrated qualities of evangelistic and educative thrust by means of a rope-like linkage communicating the gospel cross-culturally from advocate to acceptor.

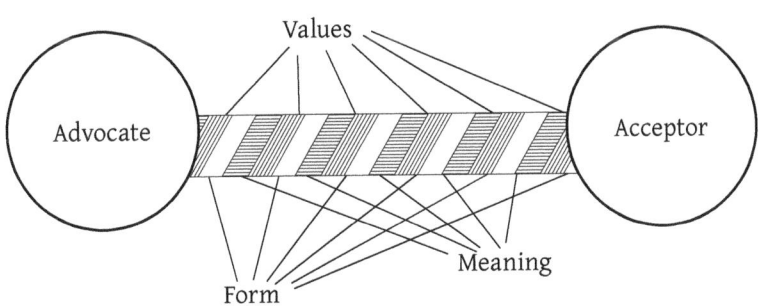

Passive Qualities of a Cultural Element

Let me demonstrate the basics of this theory from the researches of Melville Herskovits, an anthropologist who studied religion at both ends of the slave trade. He worked in Dahomey [Benin] and Nigeria on the one hand, and in Cuba, Haiti, and Brazil on the other. In spite of the Iberian overlay and supposed Christianization in the New World, and in spite of the fact that people called themselves Catholic and Christian, the form, value, and meaning were Yoruban and Dahomean. Herskovits listed about sixty Catholic saints in the New World, which when investigated could be identified as Dahomean and Nigerian deities—some thirty of which he identified by name. Although the worshippers professed to be Catholics and they were led by priests who used normal Catholic procedures—nevertheless, the deities were African and the ceremonialism (forms) and ideology (value) were Dahomean and Yoruban—the meaning was mainly African. One could classify the syncretism of form, value, and meaning. The general religious frame of reference being handed down from one generation to another is African, and enquiry of a Catholic saint will bring descriptions of African deities for a response. These syncretizations have developed independently in each locality—Brazil, Cuba, and Haiti.

If we look at the two ends of the process, we see that although Catholic missionaries advocated their own form of the faith, the acceptors themselves really determine the meaning to ascribe to the forms. Thus enquiries of Christians—devotees of the Christian St. George in Rio, for example—were given the description of the African Ogun; and St. Anthony and St. Peter in Haiti are identified with Legba, the Dahomean trickster. Thus it is the acceptor of the new religion who ascribes the new meaning. This is also seen in the symbolism of Dahomean and Yoruban mythology and worship of the elements. It all holds together as an integrated system, and survives from one generation to another. It may be that the slave lost his freedom in political and social life, but his religion survived as the governor of his society (Wallace 1966, 4) and that religion was African (Herskovits 1937, 635–43)—the religion of the acceptor, not the advocate.

The Advocate and Acceptor Ends of the Process

Let us take a deeper look at that way of studying our problem. We may use the same diagram if we include the "Advocate" and "Acceptor" as the two ends of the process. Both the advocate and acceptor impinge themselves on the process, firstly because they influence the passive qualities, and secondly, because they may have quite different worldviews. We bring out the cross-cultural element by depicting the two ends of the process. Thus either the advocate or the acceptor may be responsible for the ultimate syncretism, the former by transmitting his own worldview with the message, or the latter by misinterpreting the message in terms of his pre-Christian worldview.

I was once present in a gathering when a young Mesoamerican Indian from a syncretistic Catholic background was making his public profession of faith before an evangelical congregation. When he handed over his fetish, as the custom was in that place, I was surprised to find that his fetish was a cross, and I assumed it was a formal expression of conversion from Catholicism to Evangelicalism. I later made some enquiries and discovered that it was not regarded as a Christian cross at all, for there always had been a pre-Christian cross in the symbolism of that tribe. This fetish tied him with the ancient traditions before the Spanish entered the New World. There was no Christian symbolism about it. Certainly it was not a physical reminder of the great event of salvation history—the death of our Lord. For this young man and for his co-religionists in general, it was a magical object with its own inherent power and the shrine of a spirit. After a real confrontation with Christ, the young man felt he had to make a disclaimer of the fetish, as part of his public confession of faith.

The problem here goes back to an earlier generation when the Spanish first 'converted' these New World Indians, and the latter accepted the symbol of the cross as a recognized and approved motif in their supposed Catholic Christian faith. The point I am raising here is that for those early Catholic missionaries, the cross had a precise meaning with a whole set of associated ideas. For the Mesoamerican 'convert' it had a completely different set of mental associations derived from the pagan pre-Christian religion. Each religion used the physical form of the cross, but the matrices of belief constructs within which the cross was used were entirely different. To the observer, these people were manifestly Catholic using a Catholic cross; but in point of fact, the latent belief (which was transmitted to succeeding generations) came from the Indian complex, not the Spanish one. Here is a good example of the point made by Barnett that innovation or newly accepted ideas derive their meaning from the acceptor not the advocate (1953, 338).

In the case I have just described, we had a religious symbol which was common to two different religious systems, but even where there is no common formal element, the form of Christianity adopted may be conditioned or interpreted by entirely secular factors from the pre-Christian cultural system of' the acceptors of the new faith. The gospel advocate should be familiar, not only with the religion of the people to whom he goes, but with their whole worldview. There is no such thing as bringing men to Christ in a cultural vacuum. The missionary who imposes his Western Christianity on his converts (focus on the advocate end) and fails to educate himself on the religion and worldview of the people to whom he goes (focus on the acceptor end) is bound to plant a syncretistic church because his lack of perception of cross-cultural, social, and psychological needs which the gospel has to speak to, will be misunderstood—that is once again the problem of meaning, and one good reason why every missionary should have anthropological training, and understand the worldview of the people to whom he takes the gospel.

Worldview and Cultural Cohesion

Somewhere in this discussion on the problem of meaning, we must bear down on the matter of worldview and cultural cohesion, in particular its significance for the communicator of the gospel, when the advocate and the acceptor do not share the same worldview.

The Worldview: Dynamic Cultural Themes in Equilibrium

The worldview of a people in one respect may seem an extremely complex pattern, but we should remember that its multitudinous features are not of equal value (a trap for researchers who work out scales of variables for measurement). Usually we find a limited number of strong themes which determine a worldview. In anthropology we call these the dynamic themes of culture (Opler 1946, 198–206). They stand out as the marks of normalcy in any given society. They indicate the group feelings of the people. They show how a society meets its felt needs. They reinforce the moral values. They maintain social equilibrium. If greatly disturbed, both individuals and society begin to manifest psychological stress. What is most important to us today is that they condition the nature of acceptable cultural change—including religious change. If we consider evangelization in terms of "directed change" that has to be advocated and accepted, we will understand how important it is for the cross-cultural advocate to appreciate the dynamic themes of the culture pattern and organization of the society to which he takes the gospel.

Normally themes manifest themselves through certain key persons, operating within key institutions, recognizing and using key customs and key artifacts which have symbolic values. Thus it would surely be wise for the evangelist or advocate to recognize these significant persons and things. Malinowski was struggling with this when he said,

> When moving with savages through any natural milieu—sailing on the sea, walking on a beach or through the jungle, or glancing across the starlit sky—I was often impressed by their tendency to isolate a few objects important to them, and to treat the rest as mere background.

and again,

> Out of an undifferentiated background, the practical Weltanschauung of primitive man isolates a category of persons ... (1927, 331–32).

The worldview of the community where the advocate hopes to win men for Christ must be understood—the key institutions and people and values. These are the "givens" of missionary work. These are the frame of reference within which the gospel has to be made credible and acceptable, and the advocate must adapt himself to it. Although the advocate may not be himself of that world, nevertheless, he must minister in that world (John 17:18). He strives to win that world for Christ. To be sure, this will bring changes, but all societies have their regular mechanisms for change, and this should not mean the disintegration of the society or even its leadership patterns.

In my study of Fijian history for over thirty years, I have been constantly reminded how the really great indigenous leaders of the early Fijian church (men like Epenisa Cakobau,[36] Ilaitia Varani,[37] Ra Esekaia[38] and Josua Mateinaniu[39]), all men of tremendous Christian experience and initiative, were previously great leaders in their paganism—chiefs, warriors, heralds, priests, craftsmen, and all of them cannibals. One of the great things about the Fijian mission was that, confronted with the tremendous task of eliminating cannibalism, widow-strangling, patricide, infanticide, and human sacrifice (all tied up conceptually and ceremonially with the value system), the missionaries and their indigenous evangelists (who were the spearhead of the thrust) were able to win these people without dismembering the society. They won the social organization and the leadership, they preserved a great deal of the custom and utilised it in the church, and they captured the natural capacity of the Fijian language for the expansion and the development of a Fijian Christian theology. The society itself continued and experienced a new birth. I do not wonder, then, that compared with some other parts of the Pacific, which I have visited and know well, Fiji has been remarkably spared of nativistic movements. Those which have occurred have been due to local stress situations of a different character, more aimed at colonial government than at the church and based on local factionalism.

The Meaning of Demoralization

On the other hand, as Herskovits pointed out, there is a relationship between the meaning of a body of custom and the integration of the culture, and too much of a disturbance leads to demoralization (1951, 633).

This demoralization may be collective or individual. Collective demoralization leads to a situation propitious for the emergence of a charismatic leader. It is amazing how in the study of cargo cults, one finds that the charismatic figure who captures the stress situation and creates the movement, turns out to be an ex-policeman, ex-schoolmaster, or ex-catechist, who could not get beyond the first rung of the ladder of the foreign structure to which he had attached himself, because the foreign officials under whom he worked

---

36   Ratu Epenisa Cakobau of Bau, known also as Cikinovu (Centipede), was probably the most famous cannibal chief of history and had reportedly devoured over a thousand human victims before his conversion to Wesleyanism in 1854, whereafter his life was completely changed to piety and Christian leadership.
37   Ilaijia Varani (France) earned the name by destroying a French ship and massacring the crew. He was Cakobau's henchman and leader of the forces which upheld Bau. He had a remarkable conversion and lived to be a Christian negotiator and peacemaker of no mean order, eventually losing his life on a peace mission.
38   Ra Esekaia was the firstborn son and heir of the Chief of Bua. He gave up his title when he became Christian as he knew he did not have the loyalty of the warriors and other heathen. However, he protected the small Christian party during the persecution period in Bua. It is hard to see how the Christians could have survived without his leadership.
39   Josua Mateinaniu was a petty chief of Fulaga and a dancing-master of renown, who was taken to Tonga to teach Fijian war dances to the Tongans and was converted there. He returned to Fiji with the first mission party and served as their herald. Thereafter, he was the spearhead of the Christian advance, preceding the missionaries in Rewa, Somosomo, Bua and other places.

did not recognize his capacity for leadership through their use of Western criteria and educational requirements for advance. Here is a beautiful (or tragic) example of the incompatibility of worldviews—again, a problem of meaning. It opens up a whole area of missionary dynamics in which we are abysmally ignorant and which calls for research. The same applies on the level of the individual whose worldview is shattered by acculturation, and who gropes in vain for satisfactions from outside his own world. Here is demoralizing on the personal level, and here again the "solution" is syncretistic.

Dr. Harold Turner has given us an account of a young West African who had truly searched the world for religious satisfaction and had ended up as a corresponding member of religious organizations in England, America, and India. To all of them, he had contributed funds through the post, either to gain merit thereby or to protect himself from possible physical ailments. His bookshelf showed him to be an avid reader of both Protestant and Catholic literature in addition to that of Jehovah's Witnesses, Islam, Theosophy, Yoga, magical arts, and healing manuals. One volume on the Psalms indicated how to use Psalm 119:169–76, for example, as a charm to accompany the dropping of onion juice into the right ear for curing a boil. His sacred paraphernalia lay on a little shrine and included crucifixes, a plaster figure of St. Anthony, a bottle of water, some candles, a Bible, and a box of contraceptives lay nearby. This form of multiple syncretism demonstrates tragically not just how far astray a man can go in his search for peace, but also asks us the question how he had gone so far without being found by an effective advocate of the gospel who could have spoken to his seeking soul (Turner 1960, 189–94).

Individuals of this experimental or searching type quite often end up in leadership roles in nativistic movements. Anthony Wallace has shown that these movements begin with the experience of some individual who first faces stress situations and then becomes innovative (1956, 264–81). Along the same lines the psychologist, Sherif, demonstrated that an individual, confronted with an unstable situation and finding a solution, might well create thereby, consciously or unconsciously, a new norm for a group facing a similar stress situation (1936, Chap. 6). Sherif's research has been brought into anthropology by Barnett (1953, 116–17) and is applicable to people movements to Christ as well as to nativistic movements away from him (Tippett 1971b, 210–20). This is another dimension of the problem of meaning in missiology crying out for deeper research. Until we know more about the dynamics of these movements, we will still fall short in our handling of them.

Subliminal Striving for Meaning

I have argued that the worldview of a people provides a conceptual structure which holds a society together as a cohesive unit. To throw this conceptual structure into disequilibrium is to rob life of meaning. But always there is a "subliminal striving for meaning," as Barnett describes it (1953, 117ff), and this is why people are often innovative in times of stress. However, they will not accept new advocated ideas unless these can be integrated into their universe of experience. They are drawn into what Barnett calls "the matrix of the known."[40] Only thus can the new ideas have significance; and therefore, unless the would-be acceptor can ascribe meaning to an innovation, he will not accept it. It is the would-be acceptor "striving to complete the gestalt" (ibid., 434–35).[41]

The need for fitting a sensation (which for us in mission includes the step of faith) into a framework of known experience, may well distort the data presented by the advocate, and thus the individual to whom the advocate is witnessing may color it by his own interpretation because he is ignorant of the worldview of the advocate. This is a human characteristic. Westerners do it as much as the Maya Indian of my first presentation. Let me for a moment reverse the advocate/acceptor roles. Barnett records a case of an American Indian myth, spoken of as "The War of the Ghosts" which was relayed to a number of white Americans, and passed on among the latter over a period of some months. Each white American rephrased it slightly, mainly at the points of the mythology and the concept of the supernatural in the original Indian story, but even perfectly innocuous elements were changed—for example, canoes became boats—and point by point the story was unconsciously modified to suit the Western civilized frame of reference. In the end, it was absolutely unrecognizable.

In his study of the Shakers, Barnett again demonstrates the process of striving for meaning—the meaningless is given meaning, the unstructured is given structure (Barnett 1953, 120). Barnett says a thing has meaning only when "understood in terms of its mental associates." This meaning may be fantastic by another standard, yet it may be ascribed by the acceptor because it provides a rationale for acceptance (ibid., 335). This explains why a message preached in all sincerity by the Christian advocate with one worldview to an acceptor with another worldview, can be completely distorted by the acceptor, and end

---

40 Dr. Hoekendijk's objection to my use of the word "pagan" is a good example of our failure to communicate because of the "boxing" at the receptor end of the process. He does not (or maybe will not) give my word anything but his meaning and thus distorts the communication. (By the way, I only use this as an example. We all do it.) This is one of the main problems we have in communicating the gospel. All through Dr. Hoekendijk's second paper (Yamamori and Taber 1975, 143–52) his semantic problems are due to his "failure to understand" [his own phrase] and this is clearly because of his "matrix of the known." In his subliminal striving for meaning he gives "pagan" (as also "possessio" etc.) a meaning from his own frame of reference. To people who have trouble over the meaning of the word "pagan," I would recommend their reading Maurier (1968, 22–24).

The same problem arose in Dr. Hoekendijk's response (Yamamori and Taber 1975, 217–23), to which I had no opportunity to reply with respect to his use of the word "hope" as he set *his hope* over against *our certainty*. He says he *does not know* how we "could be so certain." Here, he is in a particular theological "box" which seems to prevent him understanding my particular theology of the Christian hope in terms of assurance—"the full assurance of hope" (ἐνδείκνυσθαι σπουδὴν πρὸς τὴν πληροφορίαν τῆς ἐλπίδος [*endeiknysthai spoudēn pros tēn plērophorian tēs elpidos*]).

41 The Gestaltists have developed the concept of closure to explain the psychological striving or straining towards the completion of an incomplete configuration. The tension is not relaxed until the missing part is realized and the gestalt thus closed.

up as a syncretistic or heretical theology (ibid., 338).[42] Many of the misinterpretations of Juan, the Maya Indian I described in my first presentation, were due to this factor. Many of the contemporary New Guinea cargo cults have emerged because the now disillusioned converts originally misinterpreted and distorted the Christian gospel message, confusing Christianity with Western civilization, and the acquisition of wealth and status with white power. The older missionaries often took conversion at its face value. Today, because of the insights and tools we have through a more developed study of man, and because of the responsibility which increases with the growth of knowledge, it behooves us to pay better attention to post-baptismal instruction.

Now, before I pass from this discussion of the significance of worldview for the problem of meaning, let me pinpoint again three things I have been trying to say: (1) What Dr. Hoekendijk called "the kerygmatic event" must take place within the framework of the worldview of the people to whom we go with the gospel. This is why we have to study a people's cultural world and operate in their language. (2) It is not our task to destroy their worldview, but to bring Christ into it. If we destroy it, they will suffer from cultural voids (Tippett 1963, 60–70), from normlessness (Yinger 1964, 158–73), and from anomie (Durkheim 1951, 258; Giddens 1972, 15, 173–74), which history shows may well lead to depopulation because the zest has gone out of life (Rivers 1922, 84–113). (3) When people accept the gospel they make it fit their worldview and interpret it—as the acceptor and not the advocate is the innovator, and "the gospel" in any society means just what the acceptor (not the advocate) makes it mean. This is why the program of Christian nurture and education must be continuous. Conversion is not a goal, but rather a doorway into the fellowship of believers.

Approximate and Dynamic Equivalence

Once a missionary realizes that to witness cross-culturally he must step outside his own world into a completely different one, to come into encounter with people who have a different worldview and to engage with them within that frame of reference, and in a language of which they are the experts and he is the learner, he realizes the burden of the stewardship the Lord has entrusted to him. The question now comes to him with force: can I communicate the gospel to these people meaningfully? Can I divest the gospel with which I am familiar, of the cultural trimmings I know I have given it, so that the written word may be incarnated in their cultural forms and the Living Word in their hearts? This is the risk of the Christian mission. There is little comfort in knowing that if I fail there may be a syncretistic church there tomorrow.

---

42 Kirk and Talbot (1966) in an article "The Distortion of Information" described three different fundamental types of distortion, which they designated as stretch, fog, and mirage. The analogies offer a useful frame of reference which might have been used for an analysis of the different forms of syncretism.

With some fear and trembling then, I turn to the problem of meaning at the level of actual communication in the field situation.

Getting Beyond Approximate Equivalence

Although Bronislaw Malinowski could not have done his research in the Trobriands without the help of the missionaries, and especially their linguistic work on which he built, nevertheless, he pointed out a shortcoming of their translation and preaching which often led to misunderstanding. He called it the problem of approximate equivalence. He argued that:

> All the words which describe the native social order, all the expressions referring to native beliefs, to specific customs, ceremonies and magical rites are absent from the English (1927, 299–300).

He argued that these words were peculiar to them and acquired their meanings from the life and tradition of the people—that the language was rooted in reality and was meaningful only within what he called its "context of situation."

If Malinowski is correct, and the gospel has to be preached in the language of the hearers, can it ever be preached then without a pagan meaning being ascribed to it?

I must confess that I know nothing so futile as a missionary trying to communicate the gospel to people in a language they do not know. I had a most disillusioning experience of this in a Navaho hogan, and it convinced me that the missionary must use the language of the people. But how does one discuss, say, the Fatherhood of God with a matrilineal people where the father role differs from the biblical one? Where does one find words for such concepts as prayer and worship, and the moral qualities, and the terms for God Himself and the Holy Spirit? One has to find these words within the language and vocabulary of the pagan religious life itself, which is another reason which commits the missionary to a sincere effort to understand that pagan religion, so that he can lead people from pagan prayer to Christian prayer, or from a pagan idea of God to a Christian one.

Yet I am satisfied that it can be done with time and patience. However, it is not merely a matter of finding an accurate word for each concept. Neither is it entirely a matter of translation. These are never more than approximate equivalence. One has to understand the context of the situation and feel something of its nature and atmosphere. Approximate equivalence of vocabulary is not good enough. This is only the way to misunderstanding and to syncretism.

The capacity to place oneself in another religious worldview has to operate in two directions—first backward into Judeo-Graeco-Roman contexts from which the divine message comes, and then forward by looking into the context of the pagan society to which the biblical message is to be transmitted. I have struggled with this two-dimensional cross-cultural adjustment in an attempt to short-circuit my own ethnocentric perception of the gospel, and worked out my own methods on the mission field.

I decided never to translate an English sermon into Fijian. I put myself in the Fijian context and spoke extempore until, after many years, I believe I began to think in Fijian. For three years, I served as the official keeper of the Fijian Synod daily journal and discovered that when it had to be translated back into English, it assumed a vernacular character my normal English never had. I have at home a number of old missionary reports of Fijian testimonies, and I believe I can tell in a moment whether the writers were recording them themselves or translating Fijian documents. When I learned to forget translation and interact in Fijian, I got much better responses.

Sometimes I wanted to communicate a biblical idea, say, a Pauline concept or phrase. In this case, I would try to go direct from the Scripture to Fijian. I might have to take the congregation for a 'guided tour' round Corinth or Ephesus, but not until I felt that cultural situation was clear would I dare use the key phrase. Then, afterwards as we ate our meal together and they talked over the sermon (a humiliating custom they have), I would know if I had got through with the biblical meaning. I know no other way of cross-cultural communication of biblical truths but by narrative reconstruction of the cultural contextual situation in which the key word, or phrase, was first spoken. In any case, the Fijians love to hear how other people live, and have different values from them, and why. Then often, when they had the situation clear, they would tell me how to say it in a single phrase of their own that was not in the dictionary. I have thus accumulated some four or five hundred Fijian situational phrases not in the dictionary because they are idiomatic and not literal.

Let us remember then that the theological terminology of Scripture is already a vocabulary of divine ideas in cultural garments. We should not need to be reminded of this since the day of Adolf Deissmann.[43] Every theological word we have, came originally from a cultural context—redemption, adoption, reconciliation, sanctification, atonement, and so on ad infinitum. And the glory of God is that His purpose for mankind in the "notion of redemption," for example, was capable of enshrinement in a concept from pagan Rome, which happened to have an institution of slavery figuring prominently in its worldview. The essentiality of incarnation is as true for the written word as it was for the Living Word. When God spoke to human beings, He used no universal Esperanto but he spoke in their own language.

---

[43] The older belief that New Testament Greek was peculiar was disposed of by Deissmann, who demonstrated its contemporary use in the secular world of New Testament times: for example, it was thought that Peter invented the term "Chief Shepherd." Deissmann (1927) reported a burial tablet describing the deceased by this term, and indicating the existence of a kind of shepherd guild of which one was chief.

Dynamic Equivalence

The battle for dynamic equivalence is won or lost in the initial program of translation or preaching. The first two missionaries in Fiji quarreled about this subject. One wanted a perfect literal translation of Scripture. He was a skilled linguist; he quickly mastered the grammar and built a good vocabulary, but at best his work was a case of approximate equivalence. He saw words without their contexts even though his translations were literally accurate. His companion studied the Scripture passage he wanted to communicate, and wrote a paraphrase of it, as he would tell the story as if to a Sunday school class. He wrote it out and gave copies of it to the first preachers he trained to read. They studied it, asked questions about it, and went forth into the pagan villages and 'dialogued' the Scripture narrative, as if they were communicating something that had happened on the forest path along which they had come. This second man never gave the Fijians a translated book of the Bible, but the first villages to accept the gospel in Melanesian Fiji were those where his paraphrases were discussed. And these people got the heart of the gospel.

Many years have gone since then. Fiji has a strong indigenous ministry now. Something of this free expression of the gospel remains. I found it thrilling to listen to Fijian preaching, though sometimes the exegesis brought me up with a jolt. I recall a preacher who had done missionary service in North Australia in a totemic Aboriginal community that still practised the cultic rituals in which the religious symbolism, tribal loyalties, and their notion of spiritual unity with the totem were stressed. He had witnessed their elaborate preparations for one of their totemic dances as they marked their bodies with the totemic symbols. After a long and graphic description of this, he led into a discussion of Paul's bearing in his body the marks of the Lord Jesus—a rather daring analogy. His name, strangely enough, was Paul. He carried his hearers along with him in a description of a worldview so different from their own. Then I asked myself—was his interpretation of the stigmata so very far from the original? Where did Paul get that figure of speech anyway—from a pagan brand on the body of a slave, or a Roman soldier pledging his loyalty to his captain, or an offender taking refuge in a pagan temple to escape his just penalty by becoming a slave of the deity of that temple? Whichever meaning Paul had in his mind, the term came from a pagan cultural context, but he used it as a symbolic expression of loyalty and identification with his Lord.

I heard another Fijian preach on treasure in earthen vessels. He did not know Greek, but the Fijian word for vessel has a multitude of meanings in different contexts—a pot, a ship, an envelope, or an object possessed by a spirit. The sermon was a normal one for a Fijian audience though a biblical scholar might have found the exegesis strange. In any case, the congregation was with him and, I believe, strengthened in the faith.

A third Fijian sermon I might mention discussed the atonement. First, the preacher reminded the congregation of the nature of a Fijian ritual of atonement and enumerated the various offences which could be rectified by such an offering. From this he proceeded in the true style of the typology of the Epistle to the Hebrews to demonstrate how the atonement of Christ was a superior, universal, and eternal work of grace, more perfect in every degree than the Fijian type.

Each of these presentations came from a non-Western and non-biblical worldview. Each preacher, in a way, took the risk of syncretism. Yet those sermons were all essentially Christian, not approximate, but dynamic equivalence. They were all preached to the glory of God, and the goal in each case was to bring the congregation to a deeper experience of Christ. They were all well received, and even I, a stranger, felt I was at worship. They all utilised concepts and feelings which would have been difficult to translate back into English. They were indigenous sermons, but they were thoroughly Christian. There wasn't a touch of syncretism in any of them. The problem of meaning had been solved.

In those parts of the world where good indigenous churches have emerged, this is quite normal and has a long-standing history. But mostly the reporting of it to the West has been confined to missionary deputation tale-telling. It has never been seriously studied in the theory of mission as a subject for phenomenological research. One of the new features of postcolonial missiology is the recognition of this dimension of indigeneity and the development of the research area of ethnotheology (Kraft 1973a, 109–26), and under this head a sub-area of dynamic equivalence (Kraft 1973b, 226–49; 1973c, 39–57). We may expect to hear more of this in the next decade or so. It arises from a feeling of our need to solve the problem of meaning in preaching and translation.

Conclusion

To conclude the last of my contributions to this symposium, I ask myself what our encounter here at Milligan College has to say to Christian mission as we enter the last quarter century of this millennium.

Although there are many ways in which we are already speaking of "a new era of mission," we all know that the day of colonial missions is dead, and that postcolonial mission has to operate within an entirely different set of "givens." We seem to have overcome the pessimism of the 1960s and the notion that "the day of missions is dead." It is still an active business, as Stephen Neill has pointed out,[44] and we have no directive from the Lord that the Great Commission is defunct. Already new contours are taking shape, both for missiology as the field of research and theory, and for mission as the applied activity of that theory in the world. The idea of mission (Warneck's phrase), is nothing new, but both the opportunities and the techniques for it have changed out of all recognition. And perhaps

---

44 Neill's opening paragraph in *Call to Missions* (1970) reads, "The missionary work of the Christian church is a fact of the modern world. We may like the fact or we may dislike it. That makes no difference; whether we will or no, it is just there. Not only so; it is a large and ever expanding fact."

it is at this point where I suppose that, as the anthropologist of this symposium, I would be expected to speak.

The problem of syncretism is not a new one. The New Testament church confronted it, as the growing church in every age through history has also done so. However, although it is the same problem, we have certain advantages in our day for dealing with it, and therefore, an even greater responsibility. We recall how William Carey in his day argued that the research of the navigators and explorers, the new charts and techniques of navigation, the knowledge of languages spoken by newly discovered people who knew nothing of the gospel, all gave a new dimension to the meaning of the Great Commission for the church of his day—and thus began a new era of mission (1792).

In our day, many new ways and means of research have opened up to us. We have new disciplines on which we could be drawing for the training of missionaries. We have historical research over a long period of history, which is full of lessons to be learned. And surely to him who has received much, much is expected.

Therefore, at the level of the individual missionaries, we must recognize that there is no longer any excuse for the home church sending out missionaries without adequate training, and in the light of our discussions on syncretism, that availability of knowledge and techniques certainly includes anthropology—social anthropology, applied anthropology, cultural dynamics, cross-cultural communication, and "primitive" religion, as a minimum—and perhaps also a refresher course to update them on each furlough.

At the level of academia, there is a desperate need for more intensive missiological research on both syncretism and indigenous Christianity, in the assembly and classification of data, in theory and in application. The contemporary people movements to Christ, as well as cargo cults away from him, demonstrate the dynamism of our times. For every case of a well-handled people movement, one could counter with a badly-handled one. And how to handle a cargo cult is something in which both the field missionaries and home boards are equally out of their depth. In many ways, the animistic world is 'turning over' today on a scale quite unprecedented in history—and when I speak of the animist world, I am not confining myself to forest tribes, but include the great religions of Asia and the streets of the great American cities. We live in a syncretistic world, and we know next to nothing about its phenomenological character and how to deal with it. A cultural gulf lies between us and the people to whom we have been sent.

The research of the kind I am asking for must come from inside the missionary movement itself. Most of the exciting research has been done by anthropologists, frequently agnostic scholars, who think these things can be studied objectively, or from comparative religionists, mostly armchair scholars who have never confronted the phenomena in the flesh. These human sciences will take us so far, but will not lead us to the "new man in Christ," which requires an apostolic-man not a religion-man, a Christian not a secular anthropologist. In the study of religious phenomenology of this kind, there are two ways of getting into the act—one is by accepting it and readjusting one's theology to fit his new position, and the other is to come into actual encounter with it on the level of faith. Missiology today needs nothing more urgently than an adequate articulated methodology for confronting the dynamistic resurgence of contemporary animism with the Christian alternative.

In this postcolonial era of mission, every cross-cultural missionary therefore, needs a degree in anthropology sufficiently advanced to permit his doing field research; and upon retirement from the field after, say, fifteen or twenty years, the home church should open the door for a select few of these men to be set aside for advanced research—men who, having worked for years outside their own language and culture, can continue their involvement in the dynamics of these cross-cultural phenomenological problems. Every mission field of the world is plagued with some form of syncretism, and every field should have some full-time experienced missionary-anthropologist studying the dynamics of their situation and making it available to the field missionaries. Someday, the Lord of the vineyard will ask our boards and sending churches why they sent men into the vineyard without teaching them how first to care for vines and harvest the grapes; and why they opened fields at all for mission, which they were not prepared to research.

From these experienced missionary researchers, a limited number should serve as coordinators of the total research and the development of a body of missiological theory based on the field data. Our missiological theory is not yet adequate for the missionary task I anticipate our being confronted with in the next twenty-five years. On my recent visit to New Guinea, I was thrilled by certain evidences of indigenous Christianity, and yet appalled by the tragic loss of converts through cargo cults. Our missionary gospel is a glorious one, but our methodology is far short of what the Lord of the vineyard surely expects of his stewards.

5
THE DYNAMICS OF SYNCRETISM IN THE MISSION OF THE CHURCH

I am asked to make a presentation on syncretism, which I understand arises from a direction from your bishop and relates to certain issues which have arisen in your pastoral situations and that you are the committee appointed to examine the theological roots and possible consequences of these issues.

The terms of reference are:

(1) The Commission shall investigate the following areas:

(a) Alleged encroachment of Eastern religious or mystical practises, specifically meditative techniques based on Hinduism or occult incantations.

(b) Participation of Christian people in Yoga, transcendental meditation, Freemasonry, and any other practises that the commission considers relevant.

(c) The use of church premises for such purposes, etc.

Introductory Preamble

Two points should be kept in mind as I make this presentation:

(1) I have no intention of making any dogmatic statement on the specific items listed above, which your committee and indeed every Christian has to decide for himself. What I shall be glad to do is to specify a few theological and anthropological principles that ought to bear on this decision-making and cite a few cases from biblical, historical, missionary, and general religious history, which I hope will bring out some of the dynamics of syncretism for your consideration. Hopefully these will provide some kind of data base for your comparisons and evaluations.

(2) Lest you should think that case studies out of biblical, missionary, and cross-cultural situations in history might hardly be relevant to pastoral situations in modern Australia, let me specify that the common element of all my cases is their cross-cultural rootage, and the more pluralistic the home society becomes, the more relevant are the problems of syncretism in both our faith and theology. As you focus on practises arising from the non-Christian religions, mystical or secret societies, or even demonic systems or astrology and

evaluate their religious status and compatibility with our Christian theology, I venture to suggest that the cases I describe may help you ask such questions as: Is this problem also with us? And moreover, to sort out the causes, the underlying dynamics, and possible consequences of syncretism in the modern world.

With this in mind then, I have agreed to make this presentation and to serve as a kind of resource person if you need one. I want to do this as objectively as I can, although I know full well that is impossible. I am involved in the action itself, and I recognize that I am a witness with strong feelings in the matter.

What Is Syncretism?

The word syncretism actually arose in an historical situation. The etymological derivation is Greek and comes from a political event in the life of Crete, when two political parties coalesced to form an entirely new one, not exactly the same as either of the old parties. In this event there was derived from the verb, συνκρητιζω (synkrētizō), a new word, a noun, συνκρητισμος (synkrētismos), meaning "a union of opposites," an entirely new thing, "coming together the Cretan way."

The word has long been used on the mission field. A tribal animist people, say, becomes Christian. What kind of Christianity do they manifest? Is it really Christian, or still largely quite animist? Is it just a new kind of animism? This has been debated right through the period of colonial missions. Even missionaries in the action have disagreed, largely because as westerners they have not understood the dynamics of the process that is cross-cultural and not Western. Few, if any, appreciated, for example, that religious and magical change do not take place at the same rate of change.

In some regions, notably Latin America, where our liberation theology comes from, the word "Christopaganism" has been more widely used. It places the focus on one specific aspect of syncretism. Yet this is nothing new in Christian missionary history. The large people movement conversions of European history are said to have introduced many pagan practises into the church; although that was really more due to the defective follow-up than the conversions themselves. But in any case, it changed the shape of the church, and ultimately it led to the Reformation. The Reformers were very much concerned with what they saw as the pagan features in the old church. The problem of syncretism is one that has never been far from us.

Syncretism and Us

The problems of syncretism will most surely continue with us in the modern world. It is part of the human predicament, though its form varies with each human situation.

Those two phrases raise several issues that relate to our discussion.

(1) When I speak of the "human situation," I refer to the sociocultural context of the people we are considering, their spiritual and physical state, their cultural practises, their linguistic capacity and its limitations, their felt needs, their value system, their occupational hazards, and their economic pressures, etc. It is in this kind of situation that we must fulfill our ministries. That may be quite different for each one of us. An industrial situation and an academic university are two quite different mission fields, each with its own culture and language.

Over against the diversity of mission fields, I use the term "human predicament" or sometimes "human condition" which implies that all people share the same basic spiritual need. Sin is always with us all, a universal predicament, no matter how varied may be our specific sins in the cultural situations. Therefore we are continually involved in the business of bringing folk to Christ, who is our Eternal Contemporary in all situations at all times. That is, we are in the business of communicating the Eternal Christ to meet the changing human needs in scores of diverse and ever changing human situations.

It is at this point, the servant of God—preacher, missionary, or pastor—has to make his or her own transition in the communication, getting both message and ministry across the gap from his or her own human situation into the other person's human situation. It is in this communication across the gap that we ourselves run into the possibility of syncretism. I shall develop that more later with a case study or two.

(2) So at home or abroad we are cross-cultural communicators. One is a Western Christian missionary reaching out to a forest animist, or to a Hindu absorptionist, or to a Baha'i universalist. Another is an academic theologian reaching out to a community of coal miners, or a lunch-hour assembly of factory workers, or a settlement of transhumant fruit pickers, or a somewhat wild gathering of folk singers, a community of Asian migrants, a gang of motorcyclists, or drug cultists, a teenage boys' club, or a class of high school students with more skill in computer technology than the academic theologian.

For this academic theologian who can draw perhaps from Latin and Greek sources or expound Augustine or Aquinas, every one of these encounters is a truly cross-cultural experience. He has always to jump a barrier to make contact. He has to reach out into the dark. He had to come to terms with a strange value system. He has to master the jargon of another language. He must have answers to a set of felt needs which differ from his own. He knows their human predicament, but he has never worked it out in terms of their human situation, so different from his own. But that unknown cultural human situation in the world into which God has sent one to fulfill one's ministry—that, of course, is what the Christian message and mission are all about. Though we are not of these worlds, we are sent forth into them as He was sent into ours (John 17:14–18, 20:21–22).

In the outreaching ministry of the church into this highly diversified world situation as the cross-cultural advocate of the gospel, trying to introduce folk to Jesus Christ as

Lord and Saviour so that He may be their Companion and Sustainer in those worlds so radically different from our own, we all become involved to some extent in acts that are syncretistic. To communicate at all, it is essential. And the resultant worship patterns will demonstrate it.

To ask a few straightforward questions: The missionary to, say, the Navaho Indians might ask himself, "How do I present the theology of a Father God to a matrilineal people?" Or a missionary to Fiji in the early days might have put it like this, "How do I translate the patriarchal prescription of parallel cousin marriage to a people for whom that is a forbidden relationship?" One could raise scores of such problems, in any one of which, some kind of paradigm shift was demanded of someone, and often led to syncretism. This is formal syncretism. Sometimes it is called "contextualization" or maybe "accommodation." Some really serious situations developed in some mission fields when Christian baptism was related to polygamy for example.

The key question for you is surely: Are we in Australia ever confronted with this kind of problem when people of the Western worlds I have described turn to the Lord?

What kind of theology of Lord and Saviour can be shared by a community of Chinese diaspora in Canberra? I preached to one three weeks ago. They were university students, but it might have been very different. How do you counsel a convert coming out of Buddhism, or out of Hinduism? How do you get him from a cyclical to a linear view of the progress of the human soul? What kind of a worshipping church community do you expect of a "God's Squad" of bikers? How do you get from Confucian to Christian ethics? What kind of a Christian worship pattern can be offered to a group coming out of drug addiction? What kind of hymnology can enthuse a crowd of "rock and roll" enthusiasts? How do you handle a group movement through an occupational community in Canberra? How does one get a group gathering for folk music in a home transformed into a Christian Κοινωνία (Koinonia) when they have no experience of Christian worship?

By this time, it must be clear that these questions are not so much issues inside the traditional church structures, but mostly relate to the church outreach into the world, which indeed the Lord Himself commissioned us to do. In planting new churches in those communities, it is not the traditional kind of congregation we seek. As we sink ourselves in those new worlds and encounter the social issues, values, and cultural forms and try to make Christ relevant there and His gospel meaningful, it is here that we need to be ever aware of the possibilities of syncretism. Or to put it another way: Have we gone too far out into that world, or have we gone far enough? Some degree of contextualization is essential for a new church community to emerge. The right kind is good. The wrong will destroy the venture altogether. How to grasp the potential of the human situation without losing sight of the human predicament! That is the question. And just what is approved and what is challenged sooner or later becomes a matter of debate among us, as is apparent from the Terms of Reference for your committee.

The Inevitability of Some Degree of Syncretism

This is no new problem in the church, although the precise situations exposed to us are more or less new. Whenever we sacerdotalize our Christian theology, faith, and practise so that our religious forms and worship become centripetal (i.e. demanding folk come in to the sanctuary) and not centrifugal (i.e. reaching out into the world) as if they were too holy for the world outside, of course there can be no Christian mission. That is a real danger for the Christian church, and the preaching from the pulpit reflects the dying state. But when the church thrusts outwards into the world, although there is always a danger of its message being secularized and syncretistic, nevertheless that is the risk which must be taken. It is the risk of faith, and it must be taken, even indeed to prove that faith. There can be no Christian mission without contextualization.

The whole history of the translation of Scripture illustrates this truth. From time to time, the church had viewed the biblical languages as holy and other-worldly, and inevitably it was shut off from the Christian rank and file who needed it greatly, and the spiritual ministry of preaching declined. But there were men like Ulfilas whom God used mightily in their day to correct this matter. Ulfilas, you will remember, was evangelist and pastor to the Visigoths. He resolved to give them the gospel as a written word. The leaders of the church said it couldn't be done. The pure and holy gospel could never be translated into the vulgar and uncouth Gothic. But working with prisoners-of-war, Ulfilas mastered the language and took the gospel to a culture of Gothic wagon-dwellers. He broke through his Greek and Latin with great skill in cross-cultural communication; but he did so in spite of the leadership of the church who locked it in as something too holy to be scattered abroad. And Luther did that for the Germans. Wycliffe and Tyndale did it for the English. They broke the shackles of Latin, which the common people did not know. John Hunt did it for Fiji, and in each case, the risk of faith involved daring translation—the use of pagan words (cannibal words in the case of Hunt). Eugene Nida spoke of this as getting "God's word" into "man's language" (1952).

As a degree of syncretism is inevitable in any translation, the same may be said of worship forms, of hymns, prayers, or sacrifices. This inevitability of some formal syncretism is based on the principle of meaning. The advocacy of the gospel must be meaningful in each of its communication, its acceptance, and its ultimate operational system of faith experience.

Having said that, we must also recognize the reality of the danger of this venture of faith. The dangers of syncretism are perhaps greatest at the conceptual level, where error and heresy may enter if we are not watchful. In any area of communication of the gospel to the outside world—be it through translating or preaching the word, planting a church structure, composing hymns or capturing any indigenous lyrics for the gospel—we are ourselves bound by a biblical stewardship and notion of responsibility under God. Our ministry is certainly in the world as salt and light penetrating, seasoning, illuminating, and preserving. As stewards under appointment from above, we are to be responsible and faithful. Any irresponsible thrusts into the world with motives other than glorifying God are not to be allowed. We cannot say "Whatever will be, will be" and leave it all to God. When He appoints a steward to plant and nurture He expects it to be responsibly done. There is a solid body of biblical teaching on that matter. Now, having granted the rightness of the outward thrusts into the world taken in the risk of faith, I want to look at the dangers of syncretism, which are, I suppose, the main reasons for your committee assignment.

The Dangers of Syncretism

I intend now, citing a few cases where things went wrong and maybe in so doing, to bring out a few warnings which speak to that responsibility of stewardship I have just mentioned. First, a few general points:

> (1) Syncretism does not normally come from hostile forces organized against the church. That is open power encounter. Syncretism creeps in through bad decisions, through trying to do the right thing the wrong way, or by compromise to achieve a particular end by too easy a method, and maybe thereby surrendering some spiritual value of the faith.

> (2) Syncretism that is not acceptable is identifiable by its conflict with the biblical and Christian ethic. Being made in the image of God, and having been "called out" to be His people, who are to be "holy as He is holy" (as we are told in both the Torah and the Sermon on the Mount), compromise at a theological or ethical point should warn us to be careful in our contextualization. As His stewards, we are responsible to determine where to draw the line.

> (3) Let us recognize the distinction between contextualization (syncretism that is formal—cultural modes of expression) and Christopaganism in theological, ethical, and philosophical conceptualization which can be heretical and unchristian. It is good, indeed essential, that planted church groups be indigenous, autochthonous, contextualized; but they must be manifestly Christian, whatever the form. It is at that point where the debate always has come down through history. We are considering, then, the point where the faithful steward says, "No!" to the syncretistic innovation.

This is one of the most heavily-documented issues in missiology. It is perhaps right that the first of our case studies should come from Scripture.

Syncretism and the Old Testament

In the Old Testament times, the theological value under threat in cases of syncretism was the monotheism of the Decalogue: the unity, the uniqueness, and single authority of Yahweh. When God calls Israel to be His people they are to be holy unto Him as He is holy and to have no other gods before Him. This is the process of calling out. The world around them was polytheistic, with different gods to deal with every need of people. Every kind of idolatry and fertility cult imaginable was practised by the surrounding races. The celestial bodies were the objects of worship. But Yahweh is a personal God. He calls them. He redeems them. They are His witnesses. It is henotheism only when seen in a "world" perspective. To the Hebrew, it was really monotheism. The Old Testament writers ridiculed any supposed gods with eyes which could not see and ears which could not hear. Isaiah called them "not-gods." Even so, the temptation was for the people to forsake God and worship these not-gods or to mix the two, especially to incorporate the baals and fertility cults, to "make cakes to the Queen of Heaven," and to venerate "the round stones in the valleys" (Jer 44:17). They brought their foreign rituals into the sacred places dedicated to Yahweh, mixing them or substituting them. Down to the captivity in Babylon, this is the main religious encounter of the Old Testament. Lawgiver, Psalmist, and Prophet are all outspoken on the matter, but the people themselves are prone to be like others around them—syncretistic. (At this point, read the description of what young Josiah found to be the state of things after the discovery of the book of law. [Isa 42:1; 43:1–10; 44:6–17, 21–22; 45:5–6; 2 Kgs 22:14–23, 25. Cf. Isa 57.])

Both the historical books and the prophets leave no place for tolerance of any religious exercise which threatened the belief in the oneness of God and His being the only real God. The reforms under Josiah, the episode on Mount Carmel, and the oracles of Isaiah all challenge this syncretism on the theological basis of the first commandment (Ex 20:2–4; 22:18; 22:20 etc.). With this goes the theology of God as Creator and the notion of worshipping the Creator and not His creations or man's creations (Isa 2:6–10; Rom 1:25).

Likewise in the eighth century when the ethical holiness and social justice of the religion of Yahweh are surrendered due to the pagan intrusions, Amos and Micah thundered against the economic shift in values and dishonest trade at the religious shrines, which compromised the holiness of Yahweh and his people—i.e. the covenant relationship. This was just not open for compromise to the prophets.

Syncretism and the New Testament

In the New Testament, especially in the second generation church, excesses of syncretism again troubled the apostles. Ephesus, Antioch, Rome, Corinth, Samaria, Lystra, Athens—they all shared this confrontation. There are many good studies of this for your reading.

Look at Visser't Hooft (1963) for a brief and much to the point study of New Testament syncretism.

There is a passage in 1 Corinthians 10 in which Paul takes some of the Corinthian Christians to task for compromising the theology of the Lord's Supper by their syncretism. "You cannot drink the cup of the Lord and the cup of devils," he argues. The theological threat here is against the belief in the sole Lordship of Christ. This was a day when a Christian could escape all kinds of persecution by simply bowing to Caesar or offering incense at his altar. Emperor worship and Christianity both claimed the phrase "Lord and Saviour," but in one case there could be many "Lords and Saviours," in the other, one and only one. Some Christians escaped being sent to the lions and gladiatorial games by a mere sacrifice or phrase. Others died rather than compromise the theology of "One Lord."

This form of syncretism placed Jesus Christ and the emperor on the same kind of sacred pedestal. Paul deals with this at the Lord's Table, the communion of the κοινωνία (koinōnia) of faith. His challenging question is "Whose κοινωνοί (κοινωνός) [koinōnoi, koinōnos] are you?" "You cannot drink the cup of the Lord and the cup of devils."

There is a principle sometimes stated by anthropologists known as "the continuity of cults" that suggests that cultic movements may recur generation after generation. Interestingly enough, as late as the fifth century, we find the Tanit Cult with Christians also worshipping the Queen of Heaven and going from that ritual to the Christian church for Holy Communion. The Christian apologist, Salvian, took them to task and cited this very passage of Paul to the Corinthians. I have a study (Tippett 1973d) in which I tell of an Indian tribe, supposedly Christian, going from the shrine of Mary to their sun worship. I have met Indian schoolteachers who worshipped as Christians one day and as Hindus the next. I saw them and discussed the matter with them. I know another tribe, whose members (or some of them) worship both as Christians and then turn to Pionyio, the Peyote Spirit. They rationalize that Christ and Pionyio are both "holy people" and are set on the same pedestals. In the presence of these Christians, I was immediately with Paul back in Corinth.

Syncretism and the Christian Apologists

Let us transport ourselves to Lyons in the second century and consider the experiences of Irenaeus, normally remembered as an apologist and writer, but this is to miss the main point. Irenaeus was a pastor of a church in a precise situation. His flock was disturbed by a form of Gnosticism. His great work, Against Heresies (1953), was not so much a theologico-philosophical treatise as an attempt to educate his young converts who were confronting syncretism at several basic points of Christian doctrine. Valentinus and Marcion had invaded his pastorate and threatened the faith at the points of the Person and work of Christ, the incarnation, the sacraments, and other beliefs. True, he established a new tradition by his critical and exegetical method and is remembered for that; but let us not overlook that he writes from a precise situation of syncretistic attack on his flock. It is worthwhile considering the nature of the attack.

He saw that certain persons "by skillful language" were introducing "impious views" which the "hearers could not always distinguish from the truth" because they were "decked out in attractive dress." Those are his phrases. His argument shows the invading teachers to have been restating the Christian creedal statement, or at least, re-using the creedal words, with their own false meanings. Their Father, Son, and Holy Spirit, were far from the biblical meanings of these terms.

Their Holy Spirit was produced by Truth (the offspring of Ineffable and Silence) to inspect and fructify the Aeons. The Logos was one with Zoe, Anthropos, and Ecclesia, and came from the Tetrad of the first and second Dyads. Christ was conceived by the Mother, who was outside the Pleroma with a shadow. Christ cast off the shadow and returned to the Pleroma, leaving the Mother with the shadow outside. By using biblical names, they claimed biblical status and general acceptance. This was all merely another form of pagan philosophy, and threatened to become what I have called in my writing on this subject "faith distortion."

How could the church ever have been disposed to accept such syncretism? Yet this might well have happened, save for men like Irenaeus. As we move on, let us put ourselves back for a moment into their situation. I note:

> (1) The written word was not then in the hands of every believer. Knowledge of the word depended on its exposition by their leaders. Therefore they had no personal criteria for exposing heresy.

> (2) There were formal similarities between Gnosticism and Christianity. They worshipped in congregations, used preaching from a supposedly sacred book, and composed and sang hymns.

> (3) They struggled with similar ideas—redemption from evil and reunion with the supernatural, for example.

> (4) They engaged in missionary programs to win adherents to their form of faith.

> (5) They used identical terminology for expressing their ideas, not only scriptural names but biblical episodes—the baptism of Christ, the request of the mother of the sons of Zebedee, the experiences of Eve and Mary, and so forth. The young Christians recognized these as biblical and did not detect their spurious interpretation.

Do we wonder that Pastor Irenaeus found he had to become an apologist and expositor? After having been away from theological training for many years, it was my confrontation with nativistic movements and the Pacific history of Hauhauism which brought me back to Irenaeus. Te Kooti, John Frum, and Silas Eto were all men who claimed the right to interpret the Scriptures from the angle of their nativistic traditions, history, and mythology. Allegorical preaching can do this with ease. This is one step only removed from the occult and demonic which troubles Christians today when they are not properly nurtured in Scripture. As modern preaching becomes more and more topical and less biblical, the danger is the greater. Valentinus and Marcion may be forgotten, but the expositors of Hare Krishna and Sōka Gakkai are on the march.

Syncretism and the Modern Mission Field

Herskovits, the anthropologist, has left us a fascinating but tragic account of the faith of several groups of American Negroes in Brazil and Haiti (1958). He researched these people not only in those locations but back in Dahomey [Benin], whence they had come as slaves. They claimed to be Catholic Christians in the New World, and the aspect of that form of Christianity which they appeared to have most adopted was the role of the saints as mediators between mankind and God. A more thorough investigation exposed the truth that all their "saint worship" was, in point of fact, a duplicate of their old animism of Africa—its structure, its theological hierarchy, its ritual institutions were all there. They could all be identified. These people had merely changed their old gods' names to those of Christian saints. No doubt there was syncretism there, but more truly, they had really retained the old faith. This is a good example of a struggle with the problem of meaning, which is one of the basics of the dynamics of the syncretism which often follows conversion. If the meaning of the new faith is not properly expounded and understood, the converts will ascribe a meaning congenial to their own perceptions.

Only last week I read the review of a book on the Dravidian gods of India. It was written by a missionary who had showed how even where people had become Hindu, they had still remained Dravidian. The reviewer was an Indian, I presume a Hindu. He did not challenge the researcher's finding but made the interesting comment that the tribals had rather taken over Hinduism. They had been syncretistically absorbed into Hinduism, and with a little accommodation, had survived in a slightly modified animism. That can happen with any kind of conversion if the follow-up instruction is not attended to properly. On the other hand, in the case of conversion to Hinduism, the Hindu does not worry about this. It is covered in his doctrine of the all-inclusiveness of Hinduism. It is seen as the all-encompassing religion which is big enough to incorporate all religions. In this way, a person may be a Hindu and at the same time, a Christian within his Hinduism; and many there are who live in this delusion. At the same time it is the Christian denial of this notion and his insistence on the claim of no other way to the Father but by Christ, that so angers the Hindu. Hinduism is naturally syncretistic. It has been compared with a great lake into which all rivers flow and are absorbed. (However, see John 14:6; Acts 4:12 etc.)

The Dynamics of Syncretism in the Mission of the Church

At this point I want to take up another kind of case study to demonstrate how a process of developing syncretism can really lead to serious faith distortion. I turn to an area of Latin America where we find the Maya Indians. I have been to this location and worked with these people. I have also worked over a great deal of the research of others, and mentored several degree men who have worked with them. I ought to indicate that these people were evangelized centuries ago by Spanish Catholics. They did not claim any perfection for their converts, but argued that in time after several generations maybe, they would become much better Christians. It did not work out that way, and I want to demonstrate how wrong they were in that assumption. I am dealing with a peasant community, and the village leader held both a civil and ecclesiastical office.

As I describe the case of one, Juan, a Maya Indian of the Chamula sub-group, and narrate his experience and testimony, let me first state four things about the nature of the dynamics of syncretism so you may observe them in my narration. You may question me on the points afterwards if you so desire. Remember this man had some three to four hundred years of supposed Christianity behind him. You will want to know how by any kind of conversion, or Christian practise, or Christian education he could get to this position. Meantime I am claiming that:

> (1) Once established, syncretism becomes permanent and becomes a cohesive cultural complex. It retains enough of its pre-Christian animism and structure to be meaningfully operative. It moves in its own direction and never towards a more mature Christianity (except by another conversion event).

> (2) It is established because it lines up with mythical theory and belief which is congenial to the old animist worldview, and the syncretistic conversion is conceptually just a new alignment of old factors.

> (3) Because societies (and individuals-in-society) feel the need of some therapeutic system, if the evangelist eliminates the shaman class, the new worshippers feel the need for some functional substitute. This may well be quite magical and explains why in conversion it takes so much longer to change the magic than the religious allegiance.

> (4) Most societies have some theological notion of the living dead. Nothing will change this but a new and Christian eschatology.

My study of the phenomenology of religion at this level over many years leads me to believe that in the main, these are the four pillars of syncretism. Unless they are dealt with clearly, firmly, and meaningfully in the follow-up immediately after conversion—either group or individual conversion—syncretism will not correct itself with time. My theory of church planting and church growth is based on this assumption. Converts must be: (1) incorporated into the κοινωνια (koinonia); (2) led into active participation in the corporate faith; and (3) nurtured in the meaning of the faith. To fail to follow up conversion in this way is to leave the convert to interpret the new faith in the terms and values of the old pre-Christian beliefs. It can only lead to syncretism and consolidate it. Although I shall illustrate this now from Central America, I think I could argue it on a basis of the exodus of people from my own church in Australia. The situation can only be corrected by a re-conversion, and that, I venture to suggest, may have to be charismatic.

A cultural cohesive complex is a notion embodied in a cultural form with a regular behaviour pattern. The practise continues and the set of ideas survives with it. Juan the Chamula depicted it like this:

> The sky grew bright and the sun came up behind the mountains. My mother put coals into the clay incense burner and went out to greet the first rays of the sun. She dropped some copal into the burner, knelt down to kiss the ground, and begged the sun to protect us and give us health (Pozas 1962, 47).

This is nature worship. It never will become Christian praise of the Creator of the sun. The kissing of the earth for its "personality" will never change. The creations, not the Creator, are worshipped. This is not a Christian corruption. It is an animistic cohesive cluster that has persisted. It was certainly close enough to be transformed, but in three to four hundred years that had never happened. It was still nature worship.

This was supported by Juan's orientation of mythical thinking and belief. Let me quote him again. Note how the Christian elements he has absorbed are controlled and distorted by adaptation into his faith formulation from his original animism.

> The Saviour watches over people on the road. He died on the cross to save the wayfarer from the Jews, who are really all devils, and are all cannibalistic. Originally the sun was cold, like the moon, but it grew warmer when the Holy Child was born. He was the son of a virgin among the Jews. They sent him away because they knew he would bring light. St. Joseph took her to Bethlehem where the Child was born. Then the sun grew warmer and the day brighter, and the demons fled and hid in the mountain ravines. Their activity is now confined to night because the Saviour watches over the day, for the Sun is the eye of God. After three days the Holy Child began to work as a carpenter. He made a door from a log. The log was too short so he stretched it out like a rope to the required length. The people feared him and determined to kill him. The family fled from village to village over the hills. In one village, the Saviour planted a corn field, and the people were bitten by a swarm of flies, but the Saviour said 'Don't eat them, eat me instead.' He visited the afterworld, and then they nailed him to a cross so the people would remember that demons would be punished and they would stop eating people. (ibid., 94–96, abbreviated, but his words retained).

This is a "Christian" account of the life of the Lord covering the journey to Bethlehem, the nativity, the flight into Egypt, the carpenter of Nazareth, the vicarious death on the cross, the descent into hell, and the sacramental partaking of the body of Christ. But there are clear non-Christian elements: the sun and moon, the conflict of light and darkness, the cannibal demons, the biting flies.

Could we ever want a better (or more appalling) example of syncretism, which points up the defective follow-up and nurture in the faith after the original conversions? The rituals of the corn cults and the memory of an epidemic of biting diptera [flies] which had a one-time demonic interpretation are all woven in. The miracle-working three-day-old carpenter is truly a faith distortion. This is certainly pathetic for three to four hundred years of Christian nurture. People do not mature in the Christian faith without planning nurture to that end which achieves the goal in the first generation.

The third pillar of syncretism I specified was a demand for some kind of therapeutic system. For the followers of a Lord whose initial work had such a base of healing miracles, most of them linked somehow with a demonstration of faith, our record has not been that good. True, the church and Christian missions have pioneered hospital work. It has been compassionate and scientific, but on the whole it has not planted many Christian κοινωνια (koinonia). Where it has done so, it has usually demonstrated a strong dimension beyond the medical aspect. In almost every case I know of an independent indigenous church breaking away from an established Western mission, it has manifested a dynamic healing ministry. The same may be said of cargo cults and other nativistic movements. I have researched in areas where the Aboriginal people go to the mission hospital for tablets and medicines for introduced Western sicknesses, but to some shamanic cult or practitioner for custom sickness. Away up on the headwaters of the Nile, three Anuak women argued with me that it was more important for a missionary nurse to go from village to village with her healing than to have the large central hospital which took them a day's journey to reach. If the mission took the healing to their doors, they agreed, the people would become Christian and turn from the medicine-men (Tippett 1970b, 64–66).

Anthropologically this can only mean that the Christian missions have never really offered an adequate solution to the universal felt need for a therapeutic system. Even here at home we often shy off missions and ministries that touch the area of signs and wonders and healing power. The felt need is not only on the distant mission field. But I must come back to Juan and quote him again.

After the death and burial of his father, Juan himself became sick of *komel* (i.e. a sickness due to fear). He called an *ilol* to diagnose it. The *ilol* demanded candles, copal resin, the local native brew, a rooster, and flowers, and returned the next day for a healing ritual. Here I abbreviate Juan's description of his theory of sickness:

> Each person has a chulel (a representative animal in the mountains which shares his fortunes). He reflects the same features—health, sickness, hunger, fatness, etc.) Some hostile chulels prey on those of ordinary people, who sicken as a result. If a demon ties up a chulel, the person whose chulel

> it is sickens. The *ilol* sacrifices a rooster to force the hostile chulel to set the other free. The flowers had to be picked before sunrise and put on a small altar, the rooster hung up by the feet, the candles lit, the resin put in the incense-burner. Prayer was offered to the demon to appease his feelings. The liquor was poured on the ground as a libation, and the following prayer offered: "Holy Earth, Holy Heaven, Lord God, God the Son. . . . Take charge of me and represent me. See my work. See my struggles. See my sufferings. I place the tribute in your hands. In return for my incense and my candles, Spirit of the Moon, Virgin Mother of Heaven, Virgin Mother of Earth, in the name of your first Son, see your child oppressed in his spirit in his chulel."
>
> During this prayer the *ilol* killed the rooster by twisting his neck and Juan records dramatically: "Suddenly I felt free!" (Pozas 1962, 88–90).

The therapy, the psychology, and the belief structure are all thoroughly shamanistic. The only Christian borrowing was the reference to the Virgin and Son, which were probably only self-protective in any case. The Christian mission in three or four centuries had never supplied any Christian functional substitute to meet the felt need and consequently the pre-Christian solution survived in toto and was incorporated whole into the new faith.

What should the missionaries have done in the first place, for manifestly it could never have corrected itself by a few years of maturing Christianity? The theology was wrong. The theory of sickness was wrong. Its totemic-like philosophy was wrong. There had to be specific instruction: a Christian view of faith, a Christian doctrine of the soul, and a Christian ministry of healing. Then it had to be put to the test in a power experience of faith healing.

The last of the points I enumerated was the notion of the living dead. This varies in all cultures with the view of the afterlife. We cannot generalize even for a clear-cut type of ancestor worship, of which I know at least four or five variants. I could give a score of examples, but I stick with Juan, for whom (with his fellow-Christians) focus fell on the Day of the Dead.

> One of my brothers rang the bell to call the souls. I went with my father to the graveyard to weed our family graves and mark a little white path in the direction of our house so the souls wouldn't get lost when they went for their offerings. My grandparents and great-grandparents died in that house. The souls of my mother's parents go over to the house where they lived and died. [The system of kinship and inheritance is tied up with all this, and neglect of the ritual is a cause of sickness.] In every house a table is set with food for the souls of the dead. Pine needles and wild orchids (protective taboos) are set there too. Mother called the souls to come and eat their food. Candles burned all night in the house (ibid., 49).

All that is only part of the story, but it is enough to raise the question, "What does Christianity, the new faith, say with respect to life after death?" Does it offer a credible eschatology? Will this emerge in time if it be not articulated when converts are incorporated into the Christian group?

What have I done in this presentation? Hopefully I've shown that all that is won in a successful conversion can be lost if the incorporating into the group and the Christian theological nurture be inadequate. What I have shown in the case of peasant Christopagans in Central America is not that far removed from things in our great urban centres, which I imagine may well come under the purview of your committee terms of reference.

Syncretism in the Urban West

I have concentrated on the third world because it is the world in which my own ministry has been operating, but I have seen enough to know it does not end there. I know that you have many mission fields at your door. The urban jungle has to be won for Christ, and these things I have described are recurring things if the church is really the church sent into the world. Quite apart from that, syncretism raises its ugly head within our own traditional churches, just as it did in second generation Corinth. It creeps up on us unawares like drug addiction.

In our own world, syncretism is found on two levels. The first of these is with folk redeemed from drug cults, from street gangs, from demonic religion, or from industrial materialism, who come into the church and do not get that instruction which follows conversion and therefore bring their urban animism or value system into the fellowship groups they find—if they find them at all. This set of situations can be exactly the same as the cases I have been describing. It has the same dynamics and the same syncretistic effects. In my youth, the word from the pulpit was prophetic and expository. Today it is largely topical. That throws a heavier load on the ministry of Bible study and Christian nurture, and that is usually accepted mainly by the faithful few rather than those who need it most.

The academic mood of the day that everyone has a right to say his piece and be heard is not geared for Christian nurture and is far more likely to lead to syncretism within the church. I could write a new kind of book today after sitting for a decade in the pew, but it would be an uncomfortable kind of presentation, and I doubt if I could bring myself to write it. It is about twenty years now since Howe's book (1963) appeared. It dealt with the philosophy of sharing viewpoints, both saying your own piece and listening to the other person: two reasonable persons sharing ideas. That point was well taken, but it was something on the human level of two equals. But the book had a bad effect on the Christian mission by humanizing it and denying the evangelist or missionary the right to seek a verdict or decision for Christ, which was described as a "dialogical crisis," which in the 1950s was an academic no-no!

The idea of Christian mission as dialogue did a great deal of harm and stimulated syncretism. It brought the Asian religions into the church. It found the Spirit in all faiths. It played into the hands of the Hindus and Baha'i, the theological polytheists, pantheists, and universalists. It brought the biblical faith under criteria of literary criticism and scientific assumptions which have already, after only twenty years, become exploded theories.

It did all this by making human dialogue the criterion and ignoring the fact that the Scriptures provide for a divine proclamation as well as a personal witness-bearing: in other words, there is a divine message to humankind that we proclaim as heralds of the King, and it is not up for debate at all. Dialogue is approved between human beings as a thing for its own sake; as a rationalization away from the divine proclamation, it is humanistic syncretism of the Christian mission itself. If you want to take me up on that, you'll have to do so on the basis of the linguistic evidence of the New Testament Greek. Moreover you will need to explain to me why the covenant relationship in Scripture is expounded as a διαθήκη (diathēkē), never a συνθήκη (synthēkē). Mission restricted to dialogue with other faiths as a redefinition of the Great Commission is a humanization (and therefore a syncretization) of the missionary mandate. If this be not so, then I have no word at all for your committee, and my own faith is vain, and I am yet in my sins. Possibly the worst form of all our syncretism is the redefinition of the Christian mission itself to escape the implications of the Great Commission.

Now that I have reached urban society and the modern world in this presentation, let me share my own experience in the urban jungle of a great American megalopolis, I went there in the 1960s when the theology of the church was torn by the notion of "God is dead!" and the missionaries of the world were being told "Missionary, go home!" My daughter, in her early teens, brought home from her new school a question which stopped me in my tracks with a jerk: "Dad! What is a ouija board?" Her new supposedly-Christian classmates, rather than searching Scripture and turning to Christian prayer to discover the will of God for their daily lives, were turning to such divination.

I determined to search out the matter and discovered a multi-million dollar business, economically undergirded and advertised to filch money from gullible Christians, and I knew that syncretism was a problem of the modern urban world.

In 1973 the Evangelicals of America determined on a special year of effort at winning the country for Christ. They called it "Key '73," but it turned out very much like every other year. In the initial determination, the journal Christianity Today asked me to give them an article on the spiritual opportunities in the "Secular City" (1973a), a misguided term that came from a book by that name shortly before. I argued that a demonic and syncretistic world was not secular. It was essentially religious. Its greatest felt needs were religious. Its syncretistic and demonic solutions were religious answers. The urban world was responding. The church of Satan had to draw a line when its membership reached ten thousand

and demand the formation of new branches. Sōka Gakkai, a form of modernist Buddhism, was growing at a rate of two thousand a month. The tools of sorcery, magical equipment, love potions, astrological divinatory literature could be obtained in shops wholly devoted to the trade. The best-selling sections in several university bookshops (apart from textbooks) were the satanic and occult—a university market, note. I investigated all this and still have a box of notes and cuttings.

All these are religious, not secular, solutions. They recognized that the felt need of the city was basically religious. Those who exploited the market found it more than responsive. Yet the organized church had no real answer and passed by. Key '73 was a complete failure.

When I hear Australian Christians talking, even in jest, in terms of, say, Scorpio or some other sign of the zodiac; when I see a television audience wrapped in an interview with some supposed astrological expert; when I find folk taken up with systems and practises that are alternatives to the Christian experience, while they are supposedly Christian, even if only in fun as they say, I know that religious syncretism is ever with us, and that any notion of a secular city is a myth.

As I terminate this presentation in which I set out to be objective—quite unsuccessfully I grant—I recall that in that day in America, it was not the organized church but the Jesus Movement which to some extent broke through, and offered a positive solution. They took the demonic seriously. They regarded it as a power encounter. They confronted the power of Satan with the power of Jesus. And they got a hearing. Seekers found the empowering of Christ. I have a similar study statistically documented of the Pentecostal use of the same approach against spiritism in Brazil.

However the tragedy in the case of the victory of the Jesus People was that they had no fellowship structure like the κοινωνια (koinonia) into which to incorporate their converts and nurture them in faith and practise, and their converts were not psychologically or anthropologically one with the established churches. (Maybe a problem your committee should consider.)

I believe there are two basic principles for confronting syncretism: (1) a powerful confrontation with Christ Jesus Himself on a personal level and a challenge to put one's life on the line with Him; and (2) effective incorporation into an appropriate church group for spiritual support and nurture in terms of Scripture study and prayer. Both those may need reinterpretation in terms of our modern cultural mores. The best work I see being done in Canberra along these lines is in terms of house churches and the charismatic communities. Your committee might consider what makes those things "tick" in our modern world.

I think you should explore two questions, then: first, how best to bring focus on Jesus Himself as a person and power; and second, to find structures appropriate to a new type of expected convert for nurture. There is no hope in any of these syncretistic phenomena. The basics are in the Scriptures. The communication and contextualization are up to us.

6
STAR-GAZING

A young couple I know had hoped for a happy marriage, but it went to pieces in a tragically short time. I am convinced that it was all because of the mother-in-law and her astrology.

Back in the 1960s, I was in the United States when a post-war generation was striving to find its religious feet. I was shocked by the teenage addiction to divinatory practises—ouija boards and the astrological columns of the daily newspapers. And I was grieved at how close it came to me personally.

As a practicing anthropologist much concerned with the life of human groups, I determined to do some specific research on these multi-million dollar commercial programs, not so much for their economics (which is bad in itself) as for the demonic nature of their associated phenomenology and their enslavement of the human spirit.

I soon discovered that there were ten thousand practicing astrologers in the country, and every imaginable kind of divination—for fixing marriages, providing information dealing with dreams and omens and propitious days—was peddled freely to any who would buy. I found both European and African forms of witchcraft, from twenty-five to thirty covens in a single city. I had rough statistics of six thousand sacrificial LSD cults. I discovered voodoo dolls for sale by mail, with coloured pins supplied with them for varied evil effects. It was not difficult to get information about wizard consulting services, operating sorcery, crash courses in palmistry, and one regular bookshop had a $25,000 stock of cheap occult literature, which it turned over in a remarkably short period of time. There were little house "'temples" above occult shop fronts. It was easier to strike up a conversation by asking the sign under which a person was born than by mentioning the Lord.

Harvey Cox called it The Secular City (1966) when the post-war world was looking for new values. But one did not need to go beyond Hollywood Boulevard to know otherwise. The felt needs were religious. The search was religious. It was an exploratory world.

Now I am able to stand back and look at it all from a distance, I am certain of one thing: there are several doors wide open for entry into the demonic world, and one of them is astrology. It starts with a mood of carefree experimentation. It is quite as addictive as any drug or alcohol. Nor is it ever apparent just what ramifications may develop from it. That is not just a biased opinion. It is a conclusion on the basis of collected data and anthropological observations.

Let me add to that my Christian conviction, which you may call biased if you like—provided you hear me out on the matter. As a Christian, I submit that we have in the written word of God (the Bible telling of real people over a long period of time and in many cultural situations) as a religious tool in our hands, with Christian groups for studying it together, and facilities for both private and corporate prayer. We have no need for any other form for facing the unknown. Certainly we do not need any pagan divination. Why should I turn to the stars as if the stars in themselves had any answer better than what I already find in Christ?

Anton La Vey of the satanic church, compiler of The Satanic Bible (1969) and The Compleat Witch (1971), points out to his would-be witches that, "Belief in astrology <u>on the part of others</u> is one of the best magical weapons upon which any witch can rely" (underlining his). He goes on to tell his followers not how to use astrology, but why, and to show how it aids them in their bewitching. He gives three pages of reasons why a would-be witch should use astrology as a method based, not on the stars, but on the responsiveness of the witch's intended victims. It is a psychologically insightful passage which shows the point of thrust as, not the influence of the stars, but the influence of astrology which uses the stars to deal with the rank and file of ordinary human beings. La Vey's terms show "the dogma of astrology" not the stars as "the controlling factor."

If the world's most successful satanist, whose automobile in my time moved round San Francisco with the private number plate, reading "VAMPYR," considered astrology such an enslaving institution, I claim the right to consider the holy Scriptures as a correcting institution for freeing victims from enslavement.

Let us turn to the Scriptures then, and see how the men of God—law-giver, prophet, psalmist, and apostle—were inspired to write about it. Of course they did not work out (as we do) a typology of demonic forms. They grouped them all together for one basic reason—namely, they destroyed the covenant relationship between God and His people. Yet there is enough to reconstruct the kinds of idolatry they confronted. The worship of, and serving of the celestial bodies (including the stars) was one. Thus, Moses, the law-giver, makes a long pronouncement on idolatry (Deut 4:14–24) but if we focus on vv. 19–20, we do find a specific reference to serving the stars.

Moses insisted he had these statutes from the Lord "to be taught" (v. 14) for the good reason "lest ye corrupt yourselves and lest thou lift up thine eyes into the heaven, and when thou seest . . . the stars . . . shouldst be driven to worship them and serve them . . ." (v. 19). Moses' point throughout the whole book is that as the Lord's people, the covenant relationship with God must not be jeopardised.

In this early part of the Bible, God is calling out a people unto Himself, to be holy as He is holy (Lev 19:2; 20:6-8). He is God: witness the first commandment (Ex 20:1-5). The law is dogmatic. It is not the opinion of Moses. It is the divine declaration.

The prophets, who also claimed to be speaking the word of the Lord—"Thus saith the Lord!"—were deeply concerned with any departure from the covenant relationship. In the days of the confrontations with the Philistines, the threat comes from the baals and ashtoreth. These are the physical shrines or sacred objects which house or enshrine the presence of the pagan deity—maybe idols, maybe round stones from the river, maybe symbolic paraphernalia—we might say fetishes or symbols today. Samuel called them "vain things which cannot profit or save" (1 Sam 7:3, 4, 20).

By the time of Josiah, the religious state is thoroughly bad, all kinds of idolatrous practise having reduced the religion to a polytheistic syncretism. In the reformation under this young king, the priests and religious practitioners are told to bring forth the sacred objects—baals and ashtora—and there is a great fetish-burning ceremony. These objects marked the worship and ways of serving the foreign gods, and included in the general condemnation is reference to "the hosts of heaven"—the stars and planets (2 Kgs 23).

In a still later period, a prophecy is directed by Jeremiah against his fellow countrymen who had taken up residence in Egypt, and were once more exposed to temptations of the worship of the moon and stars. They are condemned for "making cakes (sacrificial offerings) to the Queen of Heaven" (Jer 44:17, 25).

The prophet Isaiah provides us with a great catalogue of idolatrous practises from fertility cults and religious prostitution to fetishism. Again breaking the covenant relation must bring judgement. Yet the high point of Old Testament prophecy is that in spite of the judgement at the hands of Philistines, Assyrians, and Babylonians, God is always seen as a forgiving God, who will redeem a repentant people. Again the restoration and maintenance of the covenant relation is the essential thing. Manifestation of "a humble and contrite spirit," restores the divine/human relationship. This is the where the biblical religion differs from others.

Isaiah's reasoning through chapters 43 to 47 is based on the doctrine of God as Creator, Saviour, Redeemer, and Holy One. The people of God are "created," "called," and "redeemed" to be His "witnesses" (43:1, 10). This religion is personal—the basis of our having been made in His image (Gen 1:26-27), as distinct from the other creations—sun, moon, stars (Gen 1:16). Isaiah's terms and theology continue in chapter 44. Idols are nothing (v. 9). Idols of wood and stone made by craftsmen and potters are "not-gods" told in a beautiful piece of irony,

> Shall I fall down to a block of wood? . . . Is there
> not a lie in my right hand? (vv. 12-20)

Again the prophet turns to the personal and forgiving God in contrast to it all (vv. 21–22).

The point of the whole passage is again that it is wrong to worship or serve any created object (an idol made by man or any natural phenomena created by God Himself—rock formations, trees, mountains, or celestial bodies). Only the Creator God Himself is to be worshipped and served, otherwise we "strive with Him" (45:9) for He created all things for our use (v. 18). They are themselves creations and cannot save (v. 20). There is only one Saviour (v. 21).

This all-inclusive passage does not exclude astrologers and devotees of the celestial creations:

> Let them stand forth and save you,
> Those who divide the heavens and gaze at the stars.
> Who at the new moons predict what shall befall you,
> Behold they are like the stubble.
> The fire consumes them (47:13–14).

Now, lest it be said that I am only at home in the Old Testament world, let me point out also that Paul regarded those who shifted their religious focus from God, the Creator, to His material creations as being "without excuse." He argued that it was a "bad exchange," using this figure three times in four verses, "They exchange the truth of God for a lie" (Rom 1:25), and this sets in motion a whole series of consequences, ramifying through all kinds of bad exchanges of passion (vv. 26–32), a tragic state which develops from the initial shift from the truth.

What was good for Rome is good for us today. Once we take our focus off the personal and redeeming Lord and put it on any created object or system—including the stars and their astrological dogma—we lose our source of divine guidance, are pressured into situations and ramifications of our "bad exchange," and lose our spiritual self-control in Christ. Maybe unconsciously and unintentionally the astrological mental-set takes over, and we are in deep trouble.

That is what I find in Scripture, and I have no mandate to modify it. What about our "star-gazing" then? Is there anything wrong with it? If we serve the stars and sacerdotalize astrology, follow its divinatory formulae, venerate the signs of the zodiac, and allow this to determine our course of daily life, then please be assured that we have exchanged the truth of God for a lie.

But in themselves the stars are not evil. If we consider them as the wonderful work of His hands, like the psalmist (Ps 8) so that we are led to praise Him who made them and us, that is good.

You will remember that there is still another psalm, which begins with the directive, "Praise the Lord!" that specifies that He who "determines the number of the stars" is also the One who "heals the broken-hearted" (Ps 147:3–4). Therefore the right question for me in my star-gazing is "Do I so live in the right relation with my Lord, that gazing on His handiwork brings me to love Him more and more?"

There is all the difference in the world to see the stars through the crippling and enslaving perspective of the horoscope and being brought to the Creator who is also the Heavenly Father. Either point for viewing the stars will have an effect which will ramify through my whole life experience—one negatively, the other positively.

I am no nature worshipper. I stand with the hymn writer who did not go to nature to find God, but having found God, then saw Him everywhere in His handiwork.

> Heaven above is softer blue,
> Earth around is sweeter green;
> Something lives in every hue,
> Christless eyes have never seen:
> Birds with gladder songs o'erflow,
> Flowers with deeper beauties shine
> Since I know, as now I know,
> I am His, and He is mine.

7
THE ETHNOTHEOLOGY OF THE PEOPLE OF GOD AND THEIR COVENANT RELATIONSHIP
(A Biblical Reconstruction as a Paradigm for the Contemporary Church's Self-Analysis.)

Introductory Preamble

The ethnotheology of the people of God and the covenant relationship[45] may be considered on any of three wavelengths: (1) the nature and the purpose of the divine election; (2) the nature and spiritual quality of the human response; or (3) the character of the requirement of "holiness unto the Lord" from His people in the world where the effect of the whole harmony is to be felt.

The relationship is so finely tuned that error in any dimension will create discord and threaten the whole rhythm and harmony. Yet this theological construct comprises a basic set of movements and motifs which run through the Scriptures and hold its diverse books together theologically, as an orchestral composition is held by its interweaving harmony and chords. It is meaningful only, however, when it is "in tune."

Error respecting the nature and purpose of God's election of Israel as His people (or the "calling-out" of the New Israel to inherit the promises) has no discord to the ear of rational or secular mankind, whose ear is not sensitive enough to pick up the motif of the purpose of God for mankind as a whole, to be achieved through His chosen people and their mission to the nations. On this wavelength, the mission of God and His salvific purposes come under review. To be "not in tune" with this leads the secular audience to reject the idea of God's mission to the world, to people, through people, which is the whole principle of the incarnational theology either for Christ or for his people.

On the second wavelength, the human side of the covenant relationship between God and His people, error frequently lies in the assumption that a "Covenant of Grace," διαθήκη (diathēkē), is like a commercial covenant between two equal partners, συνθήκη (synthēkē),

---

45 For a development of the biblical theology of "people of God," "covenant relationship," "fellowship of believers," "Christians as salt and light," etc., see Tippett (1988) in which each has a full chapter to itself.

For the original use of the "people of God" for the biblical base of church growth missiology, see Tippett (1970a) where ideas like the biblical awareness of social structure and cohesion are discussed.

a secular but not a New Testament term. This presupposition introduces a further error—the supposed human right to vary or reinterpret the covenant to our own fancy. Ideas of "human will," "human reason," and "human rights" obscure the idea of a free offer of grace from above. Both ethnohistory and ethnotheology show how this leads to discord, fractures the covenant, and introduces syncretism.

On the third wavelength, the failure to hear the message of the purpose of God and the readiness to reason with Him as equals about the nature of the covenant relationship itself lead to further error respecting the nature of "holiness unto the Lord" in the world. A wrong view of divine election leads to arrogant exclusivism and self-worship instead of the Servant ministry; mission is distorted, justice is flouted, legalism destroys love. Where there should be music, there is discord; instead of holiness unto the Lord, there is self-satisfaction. To change the figure, the people of God should "penetrate the world as salt and light" (Matt 5:13–16).

Ultimately then, the ethnotheology of the people of God and the covenant relationship leads to three areas which call for better understanding: (1) the salvific mission of God to the people of the world through His "called-out" people; (2) the danger of syncretism as redefinition of the covenant relation; and (3) the nature of the application of the ministry and mission out in the secular world. Each of these is a subject for study in its own rights. In this paper we shall take up the second, but the point is made in passing that to be out of tune on any of these wavelengths can destroy the harmony of the whole.

Using the ethnohistorical methodology of the cultural continuum,[46] we shall arrange a diachronic sequence of studies of the fracture of the covenant relationship through the biblical narrative, making a synchronic resume at various crisis points in the history of the people of God. The writer submits that this will be ethnotheological in that each synchronic level will manifest cultural features to be expected at that point in time; and yet a continuity of theological principle will be manifested through the diachrony.

We may then project the analysis to our own point in time and examine our own covenant relationship in the light of those continuing principles and threatening fractures by our present-day forms of syncretism.

In reality the probing at three wavelengths cannot be truly separated. They do interrelate. We segregate them merely for the purpose of analysis, that we may detect the process going on and do something about it. For instance, the notion of the mission of God to the world concerns our confrontation with other religious beliefs and involves us in such questions as how to evangelize and how to communicate cross-culturally. That is an external thrust. The examination of syncretism that damages the covenant rela-

---

46 The term "cultural continuum" was used by Linton (1936) and by Barnett (1942) and refers to a continuum in equilibrium within itself, yet "moving like a gyroscope through time and a subject for ethnohistorical investigation at points along the way" (Tippett 1973b).

tion is an internal matter within the company of persons "called out" of the world and incorporated into the fellowship of believers. This is not evangelism of non-Christians; it is our own self-examination. They are quite different things—and yet they will concern the same theological systems and belief structures which we confront. Our expectations and procedures will differ but in each case we need to understand the same phenomenology of encounter with non-Christian systems.

Our data base is biblical. Our focus is on the historical periods of religious crisis. Our evaluation is more anthropological than critical. Our ultimate goal is to bring the biblical criteria to bear on our own present-day experiences of syncretism within our fellowship of believers and to test our own covenant relationship as the people of God in the present-day world. This paper will lead up to that point, but the analysis will be left for a later study.

Frame of Reference for Analysis

I take my stand on the biblical specification that the Christian church as the "people called-out" ἐκκλησία, (ekklēsia) to be the "people of God" who "inherit the promises" made to Israel (Heb 6:12; 9:15; 10:36) are such because of a covenant relationship, which specifies the need for being "holy unto the Lord, as God Himself is holy" (Lev 11:44; 1 Pet 1:15) and observing the first commandment of serving no other gods (Ex 20:2-4). I see the church as commissioned to be the fellowship of believers, κοινωνοί in κοινωνία, (koinōnoi in koinōnia) to support and strengthen each other in prayer, worship, study of the word, and growing in grace, and as sent forth into the world to perform the ministries of Christ there—serving those in need, reconciling those at enmity, nursing the sick, that is, ministering to the body, mind, and soul of needy humanity. I find the voice of the written word unified in this specification, and this might be called the holism of the church's program as the people of God as the body of Christ in the world. I recognize that such a program is possible and even credible only insofar as the covenant relationship is a reality. We live by the Sermon on the Mount only inasmuch as we relate personally to Him who gave it to us.

There can be no question of the consistency and faithfulness of the divine side of the covenant. The only threat lies in the possible disloyalty from the human side. Nor can we escape the many references in Scripture to this human inconsistency and its effect on the continuity or fracture of the covenant. The prophets and historians of Israel were continually pointing it out. Moreover it was because of this fracture that God sent forth His Son in whom the New Israel inherits the promises and purposes of the Father. If this be not so, then the Scriptures do not hold together—their vision is unreliable; Christ is false to Himself; and my faith is vain.

The fracture of the covenant relation comes at a point of disloyalty to God as the One Lord. We may follow through a select series of crises in the history of Israel when the covenant relationship is actually "on the line." As we look at a few of these, let us remember that the people of God were surrounded by people with religions that were highly syncretistic. They were polytheistic, and one more deity was no problem to them. Indeed it was desirable to them, to increase the resources on which they could draw. But when Israel is called out of this to be the Lord's in a covenant relationship, God must be received as One Lord. It must be so if this "called-out people" is to be His mouthpiece to the nations.

Israel's eventual exile into Babylon is not so much God's punishment on them as the result of their own departure from the covenant contract. Even in the severest prophecies of doom, there is always the hope that a remnant will be saved and the covenant relationship re-established. The fracture is not from anything on the divine side of the covenant but from the human. The Lord still wants to save mankind and to do so incarnationally. Although the temper of the context changes after the exile, as soon as the Christian church moves out again into the syncretistic and multicultural world of Graeco-Roman times, the same preexilic atmosphere returns, and it speaks to us again in our own times.

The problem which was a stumbling block to the Jews and foolishness to the Greeks is still a cry of the critics of modern missions and the other faiths. When Jesus assured the apostles they were "not of this world," but were "sent into the world," He was putting them into this so-called "scandal of particularity."[47] Satan came at him at the same point, and got a dogmatic response "No syncretism! Not even coexistence!" (Matt 4:8–10). Then Satan left him, as Luke qualified, "for a season" (Luke 4:13).

From the giving of the 1aw on Sinai, when the principle was specifically articulated to this present day, the problem of "One Lord" has been with us. On the mission field, rural and urban, syncretism is met in "101" forms and options. Our basic paradigm for evaluating it comes from Scripture, so to Scripture we shall go now.

The Psycho-Dynamics of the Mount Sinai Crisis

It was in the power encounter events between the Lord's chosen servant, Moses, and the magicians of Pharaoh that we first meet the terminology of the "people of God." It is really a cry of religious demand, not merely a cry for justice. It is more than a command: "Let my people go!" It is "Let my people go that they may serve me." We often cite or sing a song of liberation and forget the accompanying purpose which implied a religious relationship. However, note that the establishment of the authority and power of the Lord does also have the concomitant notion of "His people." He calls a people unto Himself—eventually to serve as His mouthpiece to the nations, although as yet it is only rudimentary.[48]

---

47 For writing on the particularity of the Christian way to the Father, see Tippett (1973d, 17–24).
48 At this point the concept is linked with the communal liberation of a people from slavery in Egypt, but in the Psalms and Prophets, the people of God are definitely to win the nations to the Lord. For an overall development of this concept, see Tippett (1979).

After the deliverance from Egypt and again at the Red Sea, which Israel never forgot thereafter, and prophets and historians designate Him by this achievement—"I am the Lord thy God, who delivered thee from the land of Egypt and the house of bondage . . ." becomes the opening formula of subsequent legal enactments for Israel.

The focal point in the Book of Exodus is the giving of a formal legal structure, especially in chapter 20. The foundation principle of the whole theology and institutionalized system for Israel's worship is the first of the Ten Commandments, which, after the above identification formula, says "You shall have no other gods . . . you shall not make yourself a graven image . . . you shall not bow down to them or serve them . . ." Thereafter everything proceeds from that statement.

The divine articulation of the law is followed immediately by a demand that their religious relationships differ from those of Egypt, and that they never again enshrine any gods in "gold or silver" (v. 23). Yet in point of fact, that is the very thing they did. Moses climbed the mountain to receive the tablets of the law and to learn the structures and the personnel of the religious system utilizing "forty days and nights" to master them, only to find on his return to the camp that they were all corporately engaged in religious dancing and worship of the golden calf (32:19ff.). Here indeed is an anti-climax. The sacred writer designates it as "sinning a great sin" (v. 30) for "they have made themselves gods of gold," and an atonement for sin had to be made. The symbolic tablets were shattered and had to be renewed. Eventually a covenant was made, and there is to be no mixing of religions taken from the peoples whom they will meet on their journey and worship of no other god but the Lord (34:14). To make a covenant with gods of the land, or sacrifice to them is described as "playing the harlot" (v. 15) and there are to be no idols (v. 17).

To a social anthropologist, the psychodynamic of this biblical description is pretty well exactly what might have been expected at this point in the history of religion (even if a scholar feels that some of the detail of the legal structures are projected back to the time editorially, the basic phenomenology and dynamics are right for this point in history). Moreover the narrative shows a basic early theological awareness that syncretism shatters a covenant relationship, and the analogy of harlotry is a powerful one to make the point meaningfully, for the marriage and lineage ideas go back a long way in human history, and prostitution was their most ancient threat.

The Psychodynamics of the Crisis on Mount Carmel

Passing far beyond the cultural context of the wilderness period when the tribe was only being transformed into a "nation," we find ourselves in the period of the divided kingdom and looking at the northern kingdom under Ahab and his disturbing foreign queen, set over as they were against the prophet Elijah. It is the period of the non-writing prophets, and their record comes from the Hebrew historians.

Under royal patronage, Israel has fallen sadly under the strong influences of baalism with some focus on fire ceremonials and child sacrifices. The reign of Ahab is summed up by the Jewish historian with the well-known formula—"Ahab . . . did evil in the sight of the Lord above all that were before him" (1 Kgs 16:30). Several chapters of dynamic confrontations follow, the most significant of them both theologically and anthropologically being 1 Kings 18. Here is an account to follow step-by-step because it shows the normal structure of an encounter, where physical, social, political, and religious authority are "on the line," where the acceptance/rejection dynamics are determined by contest/ordeal encounter and where multi-individual decision-making is affected. This pattern is anthropologically absolutely true to type in this kind of society. Every step is culturally meaningful to observers and participants. Both Elijah and the priests of Baal take the encounter to the power centre of their respective deities. By agreement, "The God who answers by fire, let Him be God!" This is arrogant confidence on the part of Elijah, fire being the domain of his antagonists. It is furthered with the saturation of the Lord's sacrifice with water. The people participation, the meaningful sacrificial and symbolic elements, and the demand for ocular demonstration are all true to pattern. The drawing out of the performance to the sacrificial psychological moment, with Elijah's prayer at the hour of the evening sacrifice, is the theological focal point—"Let it be known that Thou art God in Israel!" and the fire fell; and then comes the popular multi-individual verdict of the whole group, who have corporately agreed to accept this ordeal/trial contest.

Once again the dramatic sequence is perfectly structured and culturally contextualized for that stage of ethnohistory and ethnotheological dynamics. It is not our worldview. It is not our way of doing things, but it is absolutely as it would have been in that day and age and synchronic analysis; but viewed diachronically, it re-established the basic theology of the first commandment, the basic truth running through time. The social and religious stability depends on the Lord being One Lord and there being no syncretism.

The Psychodynamics of the Encounter with the Great Religions of Other Nations and Their Exposure under Josiah the King

The political structure of the oriental monarchy had now taken more concrete shape, with many cultural borrowings from surrounding nations. In 2 Kings 22, we find the king with his advisors—secretaries, heads of government departments, and so on. Josiah, who had become king as a boy of eight, "did that which was right in the eyes of the Lord," but was very much under the guidance of others, at least down to his eighteenth year.

Hilkiah, the priest, brought to light the book of the law from the temple and had Shaphan, the secretary, read it to the king, who in culturally symbolic pattern immediately "tore his clothes" in despair when he realized how far his people had departed from the law of the Lord. Neither the prescriptions nor proscriptions had been observed, and the religious decay of Israel was manifest. He saw Israel under judgement because they had "forsaken the Lord, and had burned incense to other gods!" It was only because of the distress, repentance, and tears of the king that the judgement was lifted (vv. 17–20).

In this type of cultural structure, the king, as the cultural focus of the people, was the competent and responsible authority for public action. Josiah set out immediately to restore the relationship between God and His people. He called the whole population of Jerusalem together for a multi-individual assembly, and had the Law read to them, standing himself by the central pillar. He is the competent authority and responsible figure to them, but he will have them know he is about to act on the law of the Lord, and the whole company is then asked to support him in a multi-individual acceptance of the covenant (23:1–3).[49]

Here we have an anthropological window into a transitional stage in the history of Judah (it is worth a study in itself) which shows a real-life situation of greater acculturation than we had in the Elijah/Ahab episode. The people of God have been subjected to encroachments from both neighbouring peoples and superpowers living as they did in the no man's land between Egypt and Assyria and eventually, Babylon. The pressures are international and politico-military. Their very survival seems to be in jeopardy. Over the years of uncertainty, all kinds of religious experiment have been tried and even invaded the temple worship. Not only were there revivals of Baalism, but astrological worship had been set up at the Hebrew holy places; sacrifices were made to the sun and moon and other heavenly bodies; forms of necromancy were practised at burial places; prostitution fertility cults abounded; military horse and chariot offerings were made to war gods; altars were set up to the divinities of the Sidonians, Moabites, and Ammonites; bones of human sacrifices were heaped in sanctified piles at the sacred sites. There was not a great deal of evidence that they were the people of God at all. Second Kings 23 is a terrible catalogue of religious decay.

Josiah's righteous anger made a clean sweep of all this. He destroyed the pagan altars around the countryside, defiled their religious paraphernalia, smashed or burned all religious symbols, scattered the deposits of sacrificial bones, set to work on their unfaithful priesthoods (that indicated the extent of their institutionalization), and then returned to Jerusalem in a spirit of hot catharsis.

This kind of religious action can never allow it to remain a "cultural or religious void." The iconoclasm was consummated at Jerusalem where the people were called together again and the Passover was celebrated as an ocular demonstration of their return to the Lord (23:21–23). Nor did it end there. He continued to wage a holy war on all mediums and

---

49 This type of dynamic leadership is much illuminated in missionary experiences of the culture contact period of Christian missions. For the role of this key person, see "The Structure and Validity of People Movements" (Tippett 1971b, 198–220), and Tippett (1976a, 231–42).

wizards and anything which could be regarded as a teraphim or idol. The Hebrew historian sums it up: "He turned to the Lord with all his heart, soul, and might according to the Law of Moses" (v. 25).

Once again the cultural trimmings of this narrative reflect a specific context, which is not our Western way of thinking, and many westerners have difficulty projecting themselves into that kind of action; however field missionaries, who have confronted fetish-burnings over which they themselves have had no control, will understand, as will a good social anthropologist who has trained himself to cross this kind of cultural barrier and look at a worldview not his own. To this anthropologist and ethnotheologian, the whole thing is credible and according to expectation.

The important ethnotheological point here is that the young king, when he discovered their error, knew that he had to take his stand on the Mosaic tradition and act in meaningful terms. If his people were indeed the people of God in terms of a covenant, he himself as their competent and responsible authority had to act within the terms of that relationship and he did so on the basis of the first commandment. The context is dramatically cultural. The theology is dramatically continuing Mosaic tradition.

In passing, I point out how this biblical historian used a powerful judgemental word to refer to the earlier king who had set up that heathen altar at Bethel which Josiah had pulled to pieces and desacralized. He described Jeroboam as the king "who had caused Israel to sin" (23:15). If there is anything in Scripture about the terrible responsibility of a communal competent authority, it is surely this word. He—the king—"caused Israel to sin" by introducing syncretism into the sacred place and worship of God.

The Ethnotheology of the Writing Prophets (8th to 6th Centuries B.C.)

The Reformation under Josiah is an interesting synchronic study more or less a complete thing in itself. After that, history moved on and the Reformation which had taken place under the power of the king's own personality fizzled out after his death. The international unrest and pressures from outside became more and more complex. Assyrian dominance gave way to Babylonian. Yet the very pressures of acculturation and syncretism over the two hundred years or more, led to the emergence of the great writing prophets. A huge library of expository literature has been written about them, but we can only mention a couple of points here—points which bear specifically on our theme. Their importance of course extends far beyond this.

Two great themes are in creative tension and both have their roots in tradition. Once again the covenant relation of the people of God is threatened by disobedience and the sin of syncretism. Over against this is the urgency of the role of the people of God as communicators of the purpose of God for the nations.

The prophetic oracles are vivid in their descriptions of the spiritual apostasy of the people of God. These dirges and laments are just as informative. Indeed one could prepare a long glossary[50] of the precise forms of their religious excesses, from their "setting up round stones from the valley," craftsmen working on "idols of silver and gold," of "making cakes to the Queen of Heaven," and "adding sin to sin." Some of these are associated with systems of economic and moral injustice, and there are false prophets, not a few, who manipulate their oracles for economic gain or political power.

In Amos we have a social window on the dishonest trade and oppressive injustice at Bethel, supposed to be a holy place. The moral life is lost because the covenant relation is ruined by insincerity of what sacrifices are made. In Hosea the figure of Israel playing the harlot is met again and most highly developed in a sustained metaphor.

The great disclosure of the prophets which marks a spiritual advance on the contextualized reformation under Josiah is a better approach to the mission of the people of God to the nations. A reading of selections through the prophecy of Isaiah brings out this theme. If the reader reads through the following passages—42:1-2; 43:1-3, 5-10; 44:6-17, 22-32; 45:5-6—he or she will see the prophet's argument.

In spite of this high level of prophetic preaching, they still have to warn the people of unfaithfulness and syncretism. They still prophesy the fall of Jerusalem and the captivity, and it is in captivity that we have their finest preaching and their confidence in the restoration.

The mission of God through Israel as His suffering servant eventually leads on into the ministry of Jesus Himself, for when His time comes, He stands squarely on the prophets (i.e. Isa 53 and 61). His own designation of the world as the field for apostolic mission (John 17) is in line with this prophetic vision.

The period of the writing prophets immediately before and during the captivity is again a sociological context quite its own, with its own political science, literary and conceptual distinctives, but it is still the scriptural universal of the covenant relationship of God and His people. The new feature is the sanctified suffering experience of Israel and the hope of restoration. As Jeremiah put it "I will make a new covenant.... I will write it upon their hearts" (31:31-34).

---

50   Typical prophetic catalogue of idolatrous practises, Isaiah 57.

"Sons of the sorceress, offspring of adulterers and harlots;
Offspring of deceit, who burn with lust among the oaks under every green tree,
Who slay your children in the valleys under rock clefts,
Among the smooth stones of the valley is your portion,
To them you have poured out your drink and cereal offerings,
Upon the high mountain you have set your bed, and made it wide,
You have set your symbol behind the doorpost,
You have looked on nakedness with perfumes to Molech.
When you cry out, let your collection of idols save you!"

Theological Distortions Confronted by Jesus

The Israelites were bewildered by the Fall of Jerusalem and the destruction of the city and the captivity; but the prophets showed it to be the result of their own sin and folly (e.g. Jer 44:20ff).

The experience was one of sifting out, and the remnant who returned represented a strong degree of moral reform. References to idolatry disappear so that the period has been described as "the exorcism of the spirit of apostasy."[51] The return was possible with Persian support but the political character of the rule under which it was effected determined rather that Israel became a kind of theocracy rather than a monarchy. Greater significance was thus ascribed to the scribal and priestly leadership, and the system of control confronted by Jesus was open to different kinds of spiritual distortion.

Power was concentrated now in the temple and the law, both of which were distorted. The covenant requirement of "holiness unto the Lord" was distorted towards a pedantic legalism and the covenant perspective of God's elected people was distorted towards a self-satisfied national exclusivism that had no time for, or mission to, the nations. This self-righteous view of the covenant relationship was the subject of much outspoken condemnation by Jesus who saw the scribes and Pharisees as "a generation of vipers" (Matt 3:7; 13:34; 23:33).

Jesus Himself, as we have seen, stood squarely on the prophetic tradition, especially the second part of Isaiah. It supplied him with both the popular and theological statements concerning his mission in the world. (Luke 22:37; 4:18-19; etc.)

Moreover he called his disciples "from the world" and sent them back in mission "to the world" (John 17:13-16). This is all in line with the theme of the covenant relationship. The context of Jesus' ministry was in Judea and Galilee; but He sent them forth as "lambs among wolves" (Luke 10:3) into the Graeco-Roman world where they immediately confronted, not the distortions of scribal and Pharisaic self-righteousness (and self-deification if you feel that way about it), but back into the world of religious pluralism and syncretism as severe as any hitherto confronted by the people of God.

Thus, even though the synchrony of Jesus' day in the Palestinian context is so different from all the other scriptural synchronic and ethnohistorical levels, we still find the basic abiding values in the covenant relationship as Jesus creates the disciple band and sends them forth in mission (Matt 28:18-20; Acts 1:8; etc).

Confrontation of the New Testament People of God with Syncretism

Because of the expansion of the Christian movement beyond the Palestine of scribalism and Pharisaism, we need to digress a little here to see what was going on in the Empire at

---

51 The notion of the "evil spirit of apostasy" being cast out comes from Fairweather's reconstruction of Pre-Maccabaean Judaism (1908, 59).

large. Outside Judea, in spite of the cohesion of Empire, the world was multicultural, melting pot of religions and religious phenomena, and utterly syncretistic. The higher gods of Hellenism coalesced with every imaginable form of cultus and magical system and local religion. Even old Semitic deities received Greek names.

In the Empire, Jewish and Christian particularity were regarded as scandalous—but only the former was legalized. Male and female deities coalesced. Religious blending accompanied every transportation of subject or conquered population with cultic interchanges. Certain old Greek ideas which had been deified persisted. Power, wealth, and state were deified and institutionalized. Astrology, magic, and emperor worship were interwoven wherever some advantage could be derived thereby. Religion was generally directed towards power, control, or wealth.

Even where abstract virtues were deified and honoured with temples and sacrifices (Libertas, Victoria, Pax, Concordia, etc.), the personification usually derived a degree of wealth or power there from. The cult of Tyche (Luck) was the most widespread popular expression of human greed like our gambling systems today. The major gods gathered hosts of demons and lower spirits in their train.

It was in this phenomenological atmosphere that the first Christian churches were planted outside Palestine in both the rural and urban world. Astrology was linked with fate and given divinity status. It captured astronomy and mathematics. Magic through figurines, statuettes, amulets, healing charms, and private divination were everywhere on the increase in late antiquity. Gods of the household, the family, the hearth, the doorway were worshipped through 'fetish' shrines (e.g. the shrine of Zeus Ktesios, god of the pantry, was a snake kept in the pantry for worship).[52] Protective household spirits were worshipped as Agathos Daimon. The roadsides were marked with wayside shrines, heaps of stones (herma from which we have Hermes). Some like Hermes and Artemis (leader of the nymphs) became major deities.

From the Roman side of the syncretism, each house had its shrine (lararium) for worship of protective spirits (lares) and the lar of dancing and drinking for whom libations were poured out. Meal offerings were made for gods of the pantry (penates), the goddess of the hearth (vesta) and doorway (Janus). Lares were placated at wayside stopping places by travellers. It was on this religion that Augustus superimposed his own worship as Lares Compitales. He divided Rome into districts, set up shrines for superimposing himself on the whole system, extended the household and district structure over the provinces, set up Lares Augustales at the crossroads, and established priesthoods to keep them operating.

Beyond this were civic cults, city patron deities, and others calling for sacrifices and supported by public funds derived from local taxes. Greek and Roman systems were inter-

---

52   The spirit involved in divinatory possession was often conceived as being enshrined in a snake, as designated by the Greek of Acts 16:16.

woven. Shrines to Athena, Delos, Olympia, all had their Augustus shrines side by side. The cult of emperor worship incorporated oracles, healing systems, sorcery, with divination, sacrifices, and rituals. The systematic overlay of occultism with charms, spells, and magical papyri trade is more than one researcher can handle in a lifetime. These all illustrate how religious performance drew from every possible source of wealth or power. It is covered in hundreds of papyri back into the second century. This is the phenomenological background of the Acts of the Apostles, the Pauline and Johannine writings. It was from this kind of community that the apostles won the early converts.

This has two significant bearings on the Christian missionary expansion: first it was the setting of the missionary confrontation with the world (Acts 13:4–12; 14:8–18; 16:16–24; 19:13–20, 23–41); and second, those who converted to Christianity sometimes brought some of these ideas with them. It is this second group with which we are concerned in this paper. It may not be that these converts bring the pagan syncretistic systems into the churches, but it may well be that first generation converts see the gospel through those syncretistic eyes and ascribe wrong meaning to the gospel. This is why the follow-up after evangelism is so important: the incorporating of converts in the fellowship of believers and their spiritual nurture, as Paul's letters demonstrate.

The New Testament descriptions of evangelism show the requirement for the convert "cutting himself off" from his old religious allegiance. When Paul and Barnabas started their evangelism in Lystra and the hearers interpreted it in terms of Greek anthropomorphism, Paul stopped it immediately. He would have no misinterpretation at this point (Acts 14:11–18). Simon of Samaria would certainly have contaminated the fellowship there after Philip's evangelism, but Peter would have none of it. So easy would it have been for Simon Magus to have been accepted by the church in Samaria. There is some evidence that he was associated with the cult of Helena there relating to the Phoenician Astarte and, as a priest of that cult, could have claimed his own divine status (8:9–12). In any case his intention of exploiting the new religion was quite in step with the local contemporary syncretism. Peter observed that (1) the syncretistic assumption was wrong and (2) the gift of the Holy Spirit was incompatible with economic or power exploitation. Luke in Acts has several episodes exposing economic exploitation or power control of religious syncretism—sons of Sceva, Demetrius the silversmith for example. There is no doubt that the Christian leaders were sensitive at the point of religious syncretism, and the non-Christian world outside was aware of it. There are supporting records also in secular history (e.g. Pliny's discussion about the butchers who lost their sacrificial trade).[53]

A long volume could be written on the references in the Pauline letters to cases of syncretism in the Christian churches. He did not always deal with them in the same way,

---

53 The Pliny reference to the disturbance of the butchers is found in his official correspondence with Trajan.

but he never let them pass without some kind of correction. In the case of Corinth, where the syncretism touches the inner performance of the Lord's Supper, he is sharp and to the point: "Ye cannot drink the cup of the Lord and the cup of devils." Here are Christians who profess to be faithful but who also engage in external non-Christian cults. The passage starts "Flee from idolatry!" (1 Cor 10:14–21). Strange, is it not, to find that kind of crisp demand in a letter to a Christian congregation. I recall being pulled up with a jerk the first time I came to the sudden end of John's first letter with its parting comment "Keep yourselves from idols!" (1 John 5:21).

Much of the syncretism which entered the churches was subtle, not always apparent until the Christian was unwittingly "hooked." Both Paul and Peter warn about it. Paul has much to say to the young Timothy by way of pastoral advice for the young pastor. He talks of "seducing spirits" and "doctrines of devils" (1 Tim 4:1). It is always possible for a Christian to turn aside after Satan (I Tim 5:15; 2 Tim 1:15). Timothy is urged to keep his trust and avoid "profane babbling and false knowledge" (1 Tim 6:20; 2 Tim 2:15). The Greek suggests Gnostic invasion. Chapter 3 in the second letter is full of such warnings, and Timothy is told to rely on the study of the Scriptures in dealing with it. Paul rebukes the Galatians for taking their eyes off Christ and considering these false ideas. "O foolish Galatians: who has bewitched you that you should not obey the truth of Christ crucified, it having been so placarded before you?" (Gal 3:1). There is "no fellowship with the unfruitful works of darkness" he tells the Ephesians (3:11), and again that "no fornicator, unclean or covetous person, no idolater, has an inheritance in the Kingdom of Christ," (3:5) these being the marks of invading religious groups. Paul commends the Thessalonians for rejecting idolatry (1 Thess 1:9).

We have seen how the Graeco-Roman religions were prone to syncretism, even to the extent of capturing philosophical, mathematical, and astrological elements. New Testament history is not without examples of this kind of invasion of the Christian congregations, although most of the allusions are generalizations rather than specific. They call for investigation of the localities concerned for interpretation. It can be done with painstaking research, and one often comes up with information on healing religions at locations of medicinal springs, syncretistic distortions due to the influence of local vested interests or schools of philosophy. This is why the contextual study is important in interpreting a New Testament letter, say.

Even though the converts of a particular congregation may have a clear notion of their salvation from sin by the gospel of Christ, they did not always separate this from erroneous ideas about the universe and cosmic forces, which might indeed link up with some local school of philosophy or even a mystery religion of some kind. It was always quite possible they would end up, as it were, with two quite incompatible gospels. This was the kind of situation Paul confronted at Colossae.

Paul warns the Christian converts there, "See that no-one makes prey on you" or "lest any man should beguile you with philosophy and empty deceit" or "with enticing words ... according to human tradition, according to elemental spirits of the universe and not according to Christ." This introduces us to the "elemental spirits" (stoicheion) and the realm of intermediate powers between God and humankind. Here we have the spirit beings associated with religious festivals, local belief, legalism, and ascetic formalities established with worship bases. Some of these had linkage with Jewish syncretism, some had Persian cosmological speculations, and others were oriental. This was Colossae. Paul was having trouble with them at the point in missiology we call "the problem of meaning." They were ready to accept Christ but were having trouble discarding their old pre-Christian syncretism.

Paul's approach was positive and sympathetic. He pleads their emptiness in the face of the Cosmic Christ, in whom all things are summed up, and he asks what more is required than this. "Solid reality" (NEB) says Paul to the Colossians "belongs to Christ" (2:17). Any elemental spirits which might exist are, at the most, only part of the world, and this world Christ has overcome. Christians belong to Christ not to the world. They have passed beyond the reach of the spirits. Christ disarmed the principalities and powers and made a public example of them, triumphing over them). So Paul, rather than denouncing them, draws them out and demonstrates the sufficiency of Christ and the ultimate irrelevancy of the elemental spirits.

This is the rational way in which Paul dealt with converts whose faith in Christ was clear but were having difficulty in escaping theological chains from their past. This is very different from cases wherein converts had cut themselves off from the old way clearly, and subsequently compromised their faith either for some advantage or to avoid pressure. In any case, Paul never let syncretism pass unchallenged, but he tempered his challenge to the mind-set of his audience and the type of counsel he felt was called for. This is why it is important to know the context out of which the biblical writer is making his pronouncement. There is a passage in Paul's second letter to Corinth where we have the apostle throwing a series of oratorical questions at the congregation, having told them not to be unequally yoked with unbelievers:

> What fellowship has righteousness with unrighteousness?
> What communion has light with darkness?
> What concord has Christ with Belial?
> What part hath he that believeth with an infidel?
> What agreement hath the temple of God with idols?

Then he sums up, "You (Corinthians) are the temple of the living God, for God hath said, I will dwell in them and walk among them and I will be their God and they will be my people. Wherefore, touch not the unclean thing" (2 Cor 6:16–17). This is a powerful piece of rhetoric in terms of the people of God and the covenant relationship.

Paul does not stand alone. The Petrine letters show similarities. We have several warnings of false teachers in their midst (2 Pet 2:1) and strong words to those who, having been enlightened by Christ, return to the old syncretism (2 Pet 2:20–22). None of these things are spoken in a vacuum. Peter is writing to Christians who have cut themselves off from the past—from the lusts of men to the will of God, from sensual cults and idolatries to a new way, so that their old pre-Christian companions are mystified by their transformation (1 Pet 4:2–4). In the meantime, they are subjected to persecution and temptation to accommodate. Peter writes to strengthen them to stand firm and not to compromise. He writes to them in the covenant terminology as being a "chosen generation, a royal priesthood, aholy people . . . in time past, not a people, but now the people of God . . ." (1 Pet 2:9ff).

This is the New Testament picture I get of Christian communities in the multi-religious society pressured to compromise, certainly at the point of accommodation to emperor worship. They confront martyrdom by their refusal in each succeeding wave of persecution down to the Fall of Rome: witness the case of Antipas, martyred at Pergamos, the first city of Asia to set up the Augustus shrine beside that of Zeus and their Egyptian healing cults (Rev 2:13). There are also terms like "following the way of Balaam" (2 Pet 2:15; Rev 2:14 etc.), and "the works of the Nicolaitans" (Rev 2:6, 15) which indicate the continuing exposure of the Christian congregations of syncretistic distortions, the heresy of Balaam being a general compromise with idols or other faiths as distinct from the direct encounter with the Augustus emperor worship.

As we leave this synchronic analysis of New Testament times, having observed how the young Christian church from the start was thrown into open encounter with religious pluralism in both the rural and urban world and also an encounter with syncretism within her inner congregational life, we see these confrontations as part of that Graeco-Roman context of their mission in the world. We also see how the Christian leaders like Paul, Peter, and John presented the Christian cause in terms of the covenant relationship of the people of God and demanded loyalty to Christ and holiness unto the Lord.

Conclusion

The finding of this paper is that the problem of syncretism and its danger to the stability and genuineness of the church—either at the level of the ἐκκλησία, (ekklēsia) at large or in the local κοινωνία (koinōnia) is one which needs continual watching, being not confined to one time or place. A diachronic study through various synchronic levels at crisis periods in biblical history shows its continuity.

Much the same kind of analysis may be done through levels of church history since New Testament times leading up to a study of the phenomenon in our own day and generation.

This would seem to be an appropriate field for serious contemporary research, and this writer believes it should be based on the paradigm of our role as the people of God in the covenant relationship. The precise nature of the syncretism will reflect our own cultural mores but the phenomenology will be similar with that in this paper and must be assessed ethnotheologically.

But that is not all! A new dimension is added to the Old Testament diachrony with the incarnation of the Son of God and His entry into the earthly context. Any study of syncretism in Christianity needs to recognize that both the secular and religious academic worlds might view Christianity as just one religion among many, even if it be the greatest of them. This is certainly not the Christian view, as I pointed out at the Milligan Discussions [Chapters 2–4 in this volume], citing Visser't Hooft's No Other Name and Daniélou's study of the religions. Visser't Hooft spoke of Christianity as not "one of the general expressions of the phenomenon of religion." He challenged Christians to rediscover that Christ did not come to add something to the storehouse of mankind's knowledge of religion, but that the world might be reconciled to God through Him. Both Daniélou and Visser't Hooft throw this truth against any syncretism in the churches and the failure of Christians to think from this perspective, and the writer of this paper concurs.

8

TOWARD A TYPOLOGY OF CONTEMPORARY IDOLATRIES INVADING THE KOINONIA AND CAUSING SYNCRETISM, IN BIBLICAL PERSPECTIVE

The scholar W. A. Visser't Hooft viewed the temple life in Jerusalem just before the exile, the days of the Roman Empire when Christianity spread through the Empire, eighteenth century Europe in the days of Rousseau, and the present day as periods of religious rationalization and syncretism. He argued the great danger of the rational character of syncretism and its threat to the life of the Christian church.[54]

In this article I shall look at the present-day aspect of this subject, not with the intention of arguing against it (I have done that elsewhere) so much as working out a typology of some kind that the general phenomena may be critically examined and also its potential for rationalization, as suggested by Visser't Hooft. However I shall do this with the biblical models before me, and I frankly admit that any biases which should show through will be biases of prophet and apostle.

As a preliminary preamble, I wish to deal with the point of view from which the article is written—first the biblical character of the terminology and values used and the theology on which it is based, then the field to be considered as the typology is worked out. It is hoped in this way to provide a framework for the honest study of our contemporary syncretism.

Terminology

The choice of the word idolatry is deliberate, because it is biblical. It is not conditioned by the early debates of the first anthropologists about "What is an idol?" although this is not excluded for anyone who feels it needs to be assessed.[55] Nor am I troubled by those biblical

---

54 *No Other Name* (1973), a successor to an earlier *None Other Gods* (1937). As a World Council of Churches official, Visser't Hooft was in a good position to know the wide range of cultural material on this subject.

55 Early debates about the nature of idols were around the point of whether they involved human creation (carving, decorating, painting, etc.) or whether natural objects (round stones from the river, or strangely shaped rocks or mountains, say) became idols as objects for worship. Many of these were "shrines" (i.e. objects entered by the spirits for the occasion of worship). In this paper we do not obtain our definition from the shape or category of its creation, but the fact of the worship offered and an offence against the first commandment.

scholars who say it is an Old Testament idea and disappeared after the exile.⁵⁶ I am using the term in the New Testament sense, as the best one I can find to express idolatry itself and all these phenomenological associations with which we have to be concerned to study syncretism.

The English word *idol* is indeed a Greek word. Paul used it in the Old Testament sense (or one of them) in his description of the worship of the golden calf (Acts 7:41). The word was εἴδωλον (*eidōlon*) and its derivatives form a cluster of words—εἰδωλολάτρης (*eidōlolatrēs*) [image-worshipper, or image-servant, i.e. idolater], εἰδωλόθυτον (*eidōlothyton*) [image-sacrifice]) and εἰδωλεῖον (*eidōleion*) [an idol's temple] and so on. We have over thirty references to this concept in the New Testament. We may take it as a New Testament word.

The terms are invariably associated with other terms suggesting a variety of complexes, which is exactly what we know to have been the characteristic of the Graeco-Roman world, which was itself highly syncretistic as far as its religious practise was concerned.

In the writings of the Apostle Paul, we have idolatry associated with sacrifices (1 Cor 8:1, 4, 10; 10:10, etc.); with fornication (fertility cults) (1 Cor 5:1; 6:9; Eph 5:5 etc.); with covetousness and extortion (Col 3:5; Eph 5:5; 1 Cor 5:10 etc.); with witchcraft or sorcery (Gal 5:20 etc.); and with drunkenness and revelry (Gal 5:19-21). Peter has a highly descriptive passage (1 Pet 4:3) with an interesting lot of qualifiers. It is linked with divination, lying, and murder; there are warnings against it from Paul (1 Cor 10:14) and John (1 John 5:21); and there are several passages to indicate the exclusion of such people from the church of the consummation (Rev 2:8, 27; 22:15). The term repeatedly found in these descriptive passages is idolatry.

The term divination is more an Old Testament than a New Testament word, but there is a reference in Acts 16:16 where the power encounter involved the exorcism of a spirit of divination and soothsaying under spirit inspiration, μαντευομαί, (*manteuomai*).⁵⁷ In Old Testament prophecy, the idea is used of false prophets, especially those who divine for money or political purposes. It is most common in Ezekiel, but see also Micah 3:11 and 2 Kings 17:17 for its association with enchantments. It is the opposite of the oracle from the prophet of God.

Astrology belongs mostly to the Babylonian period. It is linked with magic and power control of enchantings, sorcery, and in the interpretation of the unknown. It features mainly in the book of Daniel where the magicians and interpreters are always set over

---

56 It is true that oracles against idolatry more or less terminated with the exile. The remnant which returned was cured from this particular problem. As a theocracy, emphasis fell on the law and the temple. There was national self-expression again under the Maccabaean period. However the outside world remained intensely polytheistic and syncretistic. Israel withdrew into its own self. Her pride, self-righteousness, and distortion of the mission to the nations may be considered her own type of idolatry (Type III).

57 Divination by possession was common in Greece at all levels of the hierarchy of practitioners from the Delphic Oracle downwards. The identical performance is still found in much of the tribal world. See Tippett (1976b).

against the Lord (Dan 1:20; 2:2, 27-28; 4:7; 5:7, 11ff.). The nature of interpretation of the mind of God as over against that of man is important in this book.

There is a word to the culture of Babylon in the prophecy of Isaiah, and in the oracle against Babylon (chapters 45 to 47) the prophet goes further. Not the stars, but the God who made them (v. 12) is alone God and Saviour. Their idols count for nothing, they cannot save (vv. 16, 20). Their idolatry includes their sorceries and enactments and astrology (47:13).

All this related phenomena is included in the general term idolatry, and that is the way I shall use it. If the reader does not like it, he or she is free to substitute the term of his or her choice, but what I am describing is a concrete phenomena, a network of related forces which the Scriptures say, in both the Old and New Testament, fracture the covenant relationship of the people of God. My typology will cover the modern counterparts of these forces.

The scriptural linkage of these forces in complexes demonstrates their capacity for syncretism.

The Theological Underpinning

Following the biblical theology of the people of God and the covenant relationship, I do not intend to concede the point, which underlies most rationalization about syncretism, that the Christian revelation can be treated as one religion among the religions. The religions are religious systems not revelations. When we perceive "Christianity" as an institutionalized system, we may make it into a religion, and that is where our trouble begins. This system can be attacked by syncretism like the religions. But the covenant relationship of the people of God, "called out" to be His, is not syncretized, it is "fractured" by such a phenomenological invasion. As the prophets put it, "playing the harlot."[58]

Granted that the earthly expression of the people of God—the κοίνωνία (koinonia), or fellowship of believers—which is our physical incarnation, and should be a cultural dynamic equivalent, is the locus where our loyalty or disloyalty to the covenant relationship is apparent, the real spiritual state is indicated by the relationship with Christ more than the manifest form. This is more than just a differentiation of real and ideal, although in one sense it is that. The question at stake is our personal relationship(s) with Christ Himself—believers as "individual-in-group." There has to be a κοίνωνία (koinonia) for our witness to be possible in the world. If our mission is to be practicable, and "in the world" as His was "in the world" (John 17:18), there has to be a structure of some kind. The people of God are thus incarnated in the world of human life and exposed to the forces and temptations of human life.

---

58 For a developed study of the people of God, their covenant relationship, and related theology, see Tippett (1988).

Our relationship with Christ is all important; but we can only maintain the sanctified life in the strength of Him who demands it. His demand for our Christian maturity in the Sermon on the Mount (Matt 5:48) is only possible again through Him who demands it. It is here, of course, that the Christian code differs from those of the so-called great religions—the Person of Christ stands beside His code as the power in which it is possible. We are not confronting an impossible law, but a personal relationship that uplifts and gives maturity to those who live in relationship with Him.

It is the relationship with Christ which is so vital, so precious. It demands our complete loyalty and sincerity. If, in this secular world where our mission and witness lie, we are to be responsible stewards of our physical gifts (household managers is the biblical term—οἰκονόμος (oikonomos)—the personal relationship with the Lord must be sincere and not fractured. To this end, we have His assurance of His presence to the end of the age (Matt 28:20). Moreover we have the promise of the Spirit to interpret and guide and strengthen. This is not ultimate or complete here on earth, but is a foretaste, a pledge and promise of the ultimate to come, a strong feature of New Testament assurance to the people of God, a qualitative connection between the fellowship here on earth and that in the life to come (Luke 22:18; Eph1:13, etc.).

This fellowship is not a matter of law or merit, but of relationship and thus the apostle's deep concern for the churches is the tragic possibility of the fracture of this relationship, which he perceives in terms of any invasion of polytheistic or polydaemonistic forces, the "powers" (Eph 6:12). It is from this biblical position that I shall probe the forces of the "powers" confronting the churches today.

It is interesting that Paul could conceive these powers in terms of relationships or fellowships of "partakers together." He had to confront the Corinthians specifically: "Ye cannot drink the cup of the Lord and the cup of devils; ye cannot be partakers of the Lord's table, and the table of devils." He talks about idolatry and sacrificing in the same passage, and of our "provoking the Lord" (1 Cor 10:20–21).

And in passing, we are not dealing with the mission of God to the secular world, which has not received the gospel; but to those within the churches who have heard and accepted and are in danger of losing touch. The word for other faiths is the subject for another paper. We are concerned with what is going on among believers.

So much for the biblical orientation to the study of syncretism, but before turning to the typology we shall prepare, perhaps one more point needs to be stated, in passing. We do not consider animism as one of the religions as many comparative religionists have done.[59] We do not set it in any evolutionary system or history of religion as a primitive form. It is a phenomenon which invades any religion or religious thinking, thus creating

---

59 This was done in most textbooks for the comparative study of religion round the turn of the century; a misguided effect of using a biological model (Darwin) for imagined social and religious evolution.

something syncretistic. Some religions receive it naturally. There is a sense in which it is really the basic distinction of a phenomenological perception of what is religious—the spiritual as distinct from the materialistic. In this sense, we ourselves are animistic because we recognize the encounter of the powers.[60] It represents the spiritual as distinct from the rationalistic approach. Because of it, the Christian evangelist and tribal religionist can relate. It is not a precisely defined entity, but is a basic awareness on which discussions of powers in encounter or sympathy can interact. It is not actually a scriptural perception, but is implied in Scripture.

Wanted: A Typology

A recent writer has given us a book entitled *Religion in Chinese Garment* (Reichelt 1951). Elijah of Mt. Carmel gives us a picture of religion in power encounter of Baal and Yahweh. Paul depicts the threat to Christian fellowships in Graeco-Roman power struggle. In each case, it would be possible to prepare a structured typology of the forms and powers involved. If Visser't Hooft is correct in suggesting that we are in such a time of crisis (and I think he is right), a typology would help us greatly to identify just what is going on.

The temptation might be to classify this religious/magical/occult/psychic phenomena regionally. This writer wants to avoid that in favour of a phenomenological typology. As I believe the threat is coming mainly in urban settings, I desire to use an urban data base, which calls for a clarification or two.

The category urban is used in a fairly wide manner, meaning more than just city (although it does mean this). I shall look at urbanizing communities (because we may observe emerging processes in them) and also fringe-urban areas where urban expansion is enclosing rural units and making them suburban or urban perhaps against their will, and where rural values may survive or be forced to adapt to rapid change.[61] I want to include new types of community development due to migration movements, industrial development, or resettlement programs, factory, plantation, or mill towns, especially in their early stages when we can identify anthropologically the stresses and adjustments called for and their ethnopsychology and power dynamics. A study of social change after this manner bears on the shape of urbanizing in the creation of new social problems and felt needs, which turn out to be in point of fact, the issues new syncretism seeks to solve or satisfy.

---

60   The term animism, revived by E. B. Tylor for developing a science of phenomenological research, in its simplest form meant "a belief in spiritual beings" to set off his research world over against that of the materialist outlook on life. This, of course, included Christian believers. The agnostic scientist might find this convenient for his own belief structure; but in point of fact he did us all a great service by providing a perspective that showed how Christianity could relate to all kinds of religious phenomenology including the idea of power encounters, which many scientific persons are quite unable to deal with.

61   To cite two quite different case studies, both worthy of study, see Anderson and Anderson (1965) and Marris (1961), and for my use of the latter, Tippett (1973d, 118–21).

The writer's data base is worldwide but limited to locations he has researched or observed for himself, or from informants he has personally interviewed, or from his own research from official records and documents. The urban/urbanizing complexes covered include large towns and cities in Latin America, North America, Africa, and Oceania.[62] The obvious gaps in the list are Europe and South Africa, and there must be many magical ways of dealing with crises in the latter. Nevertheless the list probably does include cases of most types of urban/urbanizing situations, and hopefully most types of phenomena that should be included in our analysis. In any case, the typology which would seem to be derived from the biblical study does fall into line with the urban experiences of this researcher.

Therefore I indicate the three broad categories under which I will discuss the idolatries observed. I believe they are universals, even if the precise sub-types do vary a little. I certainly believe that they bring biblical and anthropological researches into line with each other and permit a comparative evaluation in which the biblical criteria may be utilised for examining the current social scenes. For the want of better terms, I shall call them:

(1) Rival Gods and Religions

(2) The Spirits and Related Powers

(3) The Deifications

Rival Gods and Religions

There is a word which Luke used in Acts, putting it actually in the mouth of Gamaliel. θεομάχος (theomachos)—"an opponent of God," derived from θεός (theos) plus μάχομαι (machomai) [quarrel, fight, dispute or fight against]. Under this head we look at the religions, in the sense that they may usurp the place of God in the loyalties of the Christian. Any allegiance to them that fractures the covenant relation of the people of God comes

---

62 One person can research only a limited number of urban situations in a lifetime. It is better perhaps to study one or two locations in depth through time. What this researcher lacks in depth he makes up for in his range of coverage, which has exposed a greater number of situational types. The following have been researched at varying depths—churches, social structures, communities, and individuals. They have covered the use of questionnaires, schedules, graphics, interviewing, and library checking, and so forth. Urban/urbanizing data has been collected in Latin America (Mexico City, Monterrey, Navoja, Toluca, Aguascalienteo, Guadalajara, and many emerging towns by visitation; and Sao Paulo, Recife, and other places by interviewing persons and documentary research); in Africa (personally in Addis Ababa, Dembi Dollo, Nairobi and through documents of maybe seven or eight places); North America (Hollywood, Greater Los Angeles, San Diego, San Francisco, Yuma, Farmington, Gallup, Flagstaff, Washington D.C., on and off reservation towns; and documentary work in a dozen or more libraries including Chicago, New York, and other university centres; and some New Orleans-based research); in Asia (personal research has been done in Den Pasar, Kuta, Seoul; and interviewing of good informants from Bombay, Madras, Hong Kong and other places) and in Oceania (in Honolulu, Suva, Guadalcanal, Port Moresby, Papeete; and in Australia, Melbourne, Sydney, Canberra, and other places). Two bad gaps need filling before this writer may regard himself as a citizen of the world; one is Europe and the other South Africa, and there must be many magical ways on dealing with the present crises in the latter that would bear on this paper.

under purview here. We are not dealing with their entities in themselves but the results of their entry into our Christian faith.

The Spirits and Related Powers

Luke again speaks of "unclean spirits," "evil spirits," "possessing spirits," "spirit of divination (possessing)." These passages bring us into conflicts and power encounters of many kinds—healing, exorcism, and the whole area of polydaemonism. Paul speaks of "seducing (misleading) spirits" and "doctrines of devils" in writing to Timothy. We also meet "tormentation by spirits." Type II differs from the first, being less structured and theological, direct power encounter rather than sophisticated rationalization. "How, after ye have known God," Paul asks the Galatians, "how turn ye again to weak and beggarly elements, whereby ye desire again to be in bondage . . ." (4:8). Luke has cited the words of Jesus that "all the powers (δύναμις) [*dynamis*] of the enemy" are nothing in face of the Lord's "power-with-authority" (ἐξουσία) [*exousia*] (Luke 10:19).

The Deifications

These are various forms of mankind's self-worship. The Graeco-Roman world deified social values, built temples, exacted heavy levies, and generally made profit by parading its own virtue and political entity. Wine, sex, war, and wealth were deified. And of course the idea of empire was enforced by emperor worship, rejected by Christians often to their own martyrdom. This kind of idolatry is often linked with greed and extortion. The body of Pauline references to this dimension surely means that somewhere along the line we need to take a look at our contemporary self-deification, for although often hidden, it is just as pernicious and destructive to the covenant relation, and even if hidden their mechanisms are just as structured.

From these three broad angles, then, we shall turn to the precise forms of modern idolatry which tend to invade our Christian κοίνωνία (koinonia) with syncretism.

Anthropological Terminology and a Theoretical Point

To move now from the theological or biblical terminology to the ethnological that this may be a proper ethnotheological analysis, one recalls that the pioneer ethnopsychologist, Ralph Linton, defined the terms "items," "traits," "trait complexes," and "activities." The "trait" for Linton constituted an overt expression of a given culture in individual acts and/or objects. Any one of these could be analysed into smaller units, "items." A number of traits in association might be regarded as a "trait complex" if they operated together as a functional whole. A larger complex of a number of these, Linton termed a total "activity."

Many subsequent writers in anthropology used this construct to discuss social structures and the model proved very useful.[63]

This permitted the identification of, say, economics or politics or religion as activities within which culture trait complexes were quite discrete components. This was not the only anthropological construct which could have been used, but at least it was one, and a good one.[64]

In other areas—one of them missiology—the terms might have been used with profit. Thus, for example, at the Milligan discussions on syncretism, this present writer utilised the same idea, using his own term "Cohesive Cultural Cluster" in the same way as Linton used "Trait Complex" to identify those complexes within animism which retained their cohesion in the general process of a change from animism to Christianity. This writer had drawn from the linguistics of Edward Sapir at the point, but we are indeed talking of very much the same kind of cultural phenomena. It seems appropriate that the point should be made again in our present context, because it helps us identify the precise nature of much of the syncretism before us, and explains the cohesion of certain aspects when other aspects are changing.

As an example of a cohesive cultural cluster or culture trait complex, this writer identified three components of surviving animism in many forms of syncretistic "Christianity." These were: (1) the orientation to mythical thinking and belief; (2) the demand for a therapeutic system; and (3) the notion of the living dead. It does not follow that these components need always be the same, although they frequently are; but the point of importance here is that syncretism is due to the existence of such a complex and its cohesion, a subordinate unit of a greater whole. Thus a person may say he is not a Taoist or a Hindu, but yet may very well cherish a complex that comes from Hinduism or Taoism.

Linton's terminology regarded these trait complexes as overt. More intensive research would have shown that they could be broken down into subordinate traits and items. It is surprising that no missiologist has taken up this matter for deeper research, as it offers a model for a penetrating and useful disclosure of our current syncretism and could pinpoint areas for much needed teaching and nurture within the fellowship of believers; and to this extent, speaks to the equilibrium of the whole "activity." Ethnology, theology, psychology, and pastoral counselling all meet at this point; both respecting the exposure of what we confront and how it should be dealt with. The current dislocation surely calls for inter-disciplinary cooperation.

At this point, I am merely declaring that to study syncretism, we look at culture trait complexes and that they are cohesive constructs but not whole activities; although that is

---

63 See Linton (1936 [1964], 397ff.).
64 Malinowski (1945), through his instrumental imperatives and integral systems, provided useful models for missiology when it was developing its theoretical base for the postcolonial changes.

not to say they may not open a door for the takeover of a whole activity at some time in the future. It is not difficult to find such cases in ethnohistory. From the angle of theology, a different question is raised, namely, what the pagan or animistic trait complex does to the cohesion of the fellowship relation between God and His people. This is a theological question, but its investigation requires an anthropological insight: hence it is ethnotheological.

A quite different yet related question needs to be mentioned. I refer to the missionary character of the Asian religions in Australia at the present time. One can only mention it in passing, but this must be done because it complexifies the situation. Moreover the nature of Asian migration makes the confrontation inevitable, and there are issues we need to be realistic about.[65]

First we must recognize its existence in our midst. A certain sociologist recently implied inaccuracy in statistics stating that the Muslim faith claimed a greater adherency than the migration numbers. So what? Muslim growth is not confined to migration. They are increasing their numbers from other parts of the population. Certainly every uncommitted Asian group is a target for them. Their land acquisitions and building programs do not go unnoticed, and their roving missionaries travel our bus routes with tracts and indications of their sponsorship from Muslim centres in the West.[66] We know also of Buddhist and Baha'i activities, Taoist and Hindu. Inasmuch as these are often whole missionary thrusts, they do not fall within the scope of this paper, although they are our concern in themselves. It draws on a different body of data. The encounter of the religions is the stuff of another paper.[67]

However, when they make inroads into Christian communities through their modern cultic forms, philosophies, rituals, or medicines that hold together as cohesive trait complexes, they are very much our concern here. Either at the point of overt traits in the complex or of covert items in the traits, they may very much concern us, for there are "101" ways in which circumstances can draw out latent forces and make them quite manifest. Any habit-forming drug only needs an apparently harmless entrance, and an addiction is

---

65 It is not merely that we must learn to witness in a multicultural society, but the inevitability of increasing population shifting means we will be shortly operating from a minority position in it.

66 I see a Muslim working a bus route in Northern Canberra, armed with a shoulder-bag of literature which emanates from a Muslim missionary organization in New York. Some of the distribution of religious promotional material, especially that in the mailboxes, is manifestly organized.

67 I researched this in Suva when the old colonial town was taking the shape of a city in its own right, and wrote it up at the time purely for my own record. It is available for researchers at the Tippett Collection, St. Mark's National Theological Centre, Canberra. The item is entitled "Non-Christian Asian Influences in the Fiji Islands" (1959). A file of field notes and a questionnaire are also housed there. Among other things it showed how the Asian religions tried to establish their credibility by claiming their rituals and theologies as "the same kind of thing" as the Christian items accepted there. Often they equated them. For example, they claimed to have the doctrine of the incarnation, even though in a myth or dance or song, rather than in historical event. They equated Diwali with Christmas. Their stamp issues since Independence have perpetuated the equation, and given them equal legitimization.

always a possibility. One does not need to be either a theologian or anthropologist to know that this is so. The journey down the trail always starts with an "act of rationalization."

It matters little if an anthropologist, theologian, or moralist points out afterwards that the error was in starting on the journey, or opening the door in the first place. I know I use analogy to make a point, and that is no proof. But don't miss the point I make. Not that syncretism is like drug addiction (it may be so, but that is not my point) but that we should take a critical look at this whole idea of rationalization. After all, that is where we began with Visser't Hooft.

Both the open missionary thrusts of the religions and their more subtle argument and advocacy of their internal cohesive trait-complexes are often aimed at the academic world (where Christianity first attempted to evangelize Asia), and many operate in urban centres and even on church properties. They utilise the public media, the mails, letter-box distribution of tracts, storefronts, and so on, on a basis of the freedom of opinion and religion enjoyed in this country, although in some cases this would be denied to a Christian in their own country.[68]

Rival Gods and Religions

At the beginning of the 1960s, I came home to Australia after twenty years on the mission field. I came back to a place I did not recognize. Its general atmosphere was to me a spiritual depression. The theology was pessimistic. The idea of mission was virtually dead, and where it was not dead, it was "old colonial." There was no awareness of the spiritual opportunities for the people of God round the third world. I found its form of Christianity coloured by the church driven underground and quite unaware of the signs of new life which had excited me. I found my home church really did not want to listen to me. They saw me as "out of touch," yet in spite of my twenty years on the mission field, I was more aware of the wider world than those at home.[69]

I found the more spiritual part of the ministry at home in a state of semi-despair. The catch phrases were "God is dead," "Missionary go home," "The day of missions is dead." and the Scriptures had to be "demythologized" (by which they really meant "remytholo-

---

68 A discussion of just where and under what terms of freedom Christian missionaries may go in postcolonial times is discussed in Tippett (1973c). It was a subject assigned to me for the conference on Frontier Missions held in Chicago, 1972, when the right of entry to Muslim, Hindu, and Coptic countries was coming under strict control. In some places a Christian could enter to teach or do medical work—but no more.

69 Two of my articles survive along this vein from those days. One was entitled "The Church's Cutting Edge" which was an answer to the idea of "churchless ministries," which saw the church driven underground in a secular world and came from the European theology of Hitler's world. In 1961 I was asked to deliver the Layman's Missionary Lecture, an annual event using some missionary on furlough and hitherto published by the Layman's Missionary Movement. I took the theme "Current Interacting Forces in Pacific Missions." The home church was still lost in the old colonial paternalism, and (except from one missionary from India) I had no evidence that they knew what I was talking about. They sidestepped the idea of publishing it. I should have liked a few copies to circulate today among those who were present then. These articles may be researched at the Tippett Collection, St Mark's.

gized"). I had returned from the mission field determined to speak to a younger generation about getting from colonial to postcolonial mission in a program of optimism. But I was "beating the air" with futility. Like Walter de la Mare's horseman, I knocked. No one answered.[70]

It was about this time that Visser 't Hooft was pointing out that our day and generation was torn apart by "rationalism and syncretism."

I spent the 1960s struggling to express the theological positives as they related to Christian mission. I explored another mission field which had been far more colonial and dependent than my own and became even more convinced that I was in the stream of God's will for me. As a result I turned to America, where I really found myself in the thick of the battle. But at least the battle was on, and I knew what I was fighting for and who stood beside me in the battle. In that setting, I did some years of research in the sociology of the religious changes that were distressing me—and Visser 't Hooft.

Michener's terrible distortion of history cost the American church a whole generation of missionaries.[71] Harvey Cox's idea of The Secular City was also a half-truth, half-distortion. Both these were having a major effect on thinking within the church, and it was wrong thinking.[72]

Having come from a more biblical world of power encounters, I was far from convinced that the world was secular. Even the secularity was a form of deification of man himself (our Type III). What stood out in the research was rather that the world was intensely hungry for some spiritual relief. It was ready to listen to any offer of salvation, any way of meeting its unsatisfied felt needs, any religion that offered hope, any crazy religious advocacy. It was ready to try anything.[73]

---

70 Walter de la Mare's poem "The Listeners," (Clark and Gillespie 1937).

71 Respecting Michener's Hawaii, see (Tippett 1971a) at St. Mark's on the research done in Hawaii while Michener's informants were about and those who knew his research could be interviewed. See also the works of Albertine Loomis (1966 and 1967), based on her grandfather's records. The original missionary letters as published at the time are also at St. Mark's. See also "Skeletons in the Literary Closet" in Tippett (1973b).

72 Cox (1966) utilises an unscientific progression of social development in his introductory essay, his categories being not a comparable sequence. Even if one allows the importance of a probe into secularity, that the phenomena is "secular" is not proved. To be secular one might assume it to be materialistic. I looked at the same world at the same time and saw it as satanic, and that is religious, not secular. Unless, of course, we speak of departure from the dominant religion as secularization, as the Romans defined the early Christians as atheists. But the biblical writers, it would seem, did not see it this way. Neither did Jesus when he told the evil spirit to come out of the man. Theoretically, and for purpose of discussion, we recognize these two views of the "secular," but when we confront a power encounter situation like "drugs in cultic form," or "possession that calls for exorcisms," we can hardly ascribe the materialist meaning. Maybe the whole problem is not a matter of semantics, but of perception.

73 It is crazy, of course, only to a person who sees it as superstitious, as a return to the "primitive," as unscientific in a scientific age. Indeed such a person can never understand it at all. He sees himself as a sophisticated person looking at something crude, simple, primitive, unworthy of consideration, pathetic, and calling for the help of modern psychology and counsel. But neither Moses, nor Elijah, nor Isaiah, nor Paul, nor Luke, nor Jesus took this kind of confrontation lightly, or underrated it. "It was wrestling against principalities and powers." It called for "power-with-authority, ἐξουσία (exousia)," to confront "power, δύναμις (dynamis)," and that was a confrontation to the ultimate, and on the religious level. This battle is not fought on the level of rationalization. When I met the

A rationalizing Christianity saw itself as rejected—as of course it was—but it did not see the doors open, the searching souls, the hungry multitudes. In point of fact, the so-called secular city was intensely religious. We entered an era of drug cults, magical panaceas, and experimenting with the religions. In view of this mental set, one had to ask what was wrong with the advocacy of Christianity. Both the world of the cults and the Asian religions got more and more hearing. The hearing was experimental at first, and for some became addictive, but it denied the simplistic idea of a purely secular city. If God was dead, the gods were not. Some of the religions and their modernist expressions had phenomenal statistics. Research showed, for example, that thirty-five thousand Americans turned to the Japanese Buddhist cult known as Sōka Gakkai in the 1960s; and another Japanese cult was winning two thousand converts a month (only 5 percent of them Japanese). A new syncretistic Korean religion was winning similar support, so much so that these movements became the subject of sociological studies in the universities.[74]

Many of these were actually using the Christian missionary techniques both in their structures and communication. They held monster rallies, no doubt with Christian mass crusade models. They held conferences in specific locations, bringing delegates from various countries, and developed programs for world mission. They developed literature programs, circulating materials in the mails, through letter box delivery and house-to-house visitation.[75]

In Los Angeles, where I was resident, I found cults, ritual performances, shrines, covens, small group operations, and shop-front book sales all over the city. Some book shops did their major trade in religious and occult books and papers. (I shall return to this when we come to Type II). To designate this as the age of "the secular city" seemed to me a strange misnomer. It was religious "through and through"—the religions were on the move and getting a hearing.

One reason was that they were rationalizing about it all, and the hungry world was ready to listen. The basic point about rationalization is that it explores, develops, and

---

powers—the spiritual powers—of animism and satanic religion, I knew the inadequacy of our biblical training. I tried to put it down in black and white as best I could. I sent it to a premier journal in the area of religion because I knew they needed it, because they were bogged down (or stuck up) in the super-structures of the so-called great religions in philosophical rationalization, but their readers rejected it. One of them, K. S. Latourette, sent it on to the *International Review of Missions* where it duly appeared. No comments came from the West, but I got letters from Africa, India, and the Islands, where readers knew what I was talking about. See Tippett (1960, 415–417) and note the case of missionaries A and B.

74 Books produced on the Japanese religious movements at the time included McFarland (1967), Brannen (1968), Thomsen (1963), and Elwood (1974). The Moon Movement out of Korea into the West was evaluated sociologically in Lofland (1966). Sōka Gakkai publicity broke into print with a professed goal of world mission.

75 I had the opportunity of many interviews with missionaries from Japan in those days and have a whole box of their papers. They demonstrate how Sōka Gakkai and other movements actually used the methods of the Christian missions and developed similar structures and programs. They were often bewildered by the fact that with the same techniques of advocacy folk had converted to other movements; but that is another subject.

experiments on the basis of what is going on in one's own mind. There is no external criteria for testing. The authority of Scripture may be disposed of; or if preferred, it can be manipulated to suit what one wants in his own mind. Visser't Hooft had identified this characteristic of the era in which he was writing, and I found it so. He had also identified accompanying syncretism, and this also I found true.[76]

One must not miss the fact that probably from the 1950s, but certainly during the 1960s, the religions in general became intensely missionary, as they still are, even if sometimes the more missionary thrusts come from their modernist prongs.[77]

Syncretism is no problem to many of the religions because of their polytheism, and some are ready to incorporate Christ among their deities. Hindu all-inclusivism, for example, is always ready to make additions to its reservoir of truth. The doctrine of the spirit in Hinduism, for Christian thinkers about the Holy Spirit, may be seen from either of two quite incompatible theological positions, one open to syncretism, the other not so. One leads to universalism, the other to the biblical doctrine of prevenient grace. And it all depends on whether the Scripture be used to support one's own thinking, or as the authority base from which one's thinking is derived.[78]

If anyone knew about the nature of the revival in Buddhism, it would have been D. T. Niles. He depicted it at the time in terms of four strongly emotional factors: (1) "the emotion of mass devotion" which as a religion of festivals and pilgrimages became intensive

---

76 Visser't Hoofts appraisal was "Syncretism has no centre, no point of reference" (1963, 89). See Tippett 1973d, 113). It is interesting to note that out of the context of the Social Gospel years, which have some theological similarities to our own P. T. Forsyth (whose theological skill was not valued in his day) who said, "The recent decay of missionary faith has gone with a genial creed of much sensibility, but no grandeur, and little power" (1908, 32–33).

77 To take just one case as an example—the Buddhists of Ceylon (as it was then called). It was Colonel Olcott, who went there in 1873, who gave them their Buddhist flag, as used in the festivities and pilgrimages. But it was the conversion of the Hindu, Dr. Ambedkar, to Buddhism which marked the transforming event. He had come very close to becoming a Christian and his turning away shattered the hopes of men like J. W. Pickett and D. A. McGavran. They were people-movement missionaries, and Ambedkar took with him hundreds of thousands of Harijans—a whole caste. He had missionary enthusiasm and pleaded with the Buddhist World Fellowship to develop missionary strategy. Waves of Tamils came over to Buddhism from time to time. A Centre for the Propagation of Buddhism was set up in the heartland of Hinduism at Jaffna. Buddhist missionaries returned on furlough reporting conversions of Westerners to their faith. D. T. Niles depicted this as "a new emphasis on man's sufficiency but no radical repentance or turning to God." Their converts, he says, were disillusioned liberal humanists. It was a rationalizing kind of conversion. Niles said that a missionary Buddhism with an emotional kind of expectancy is a fact of life now. The newspaper The Buddhist World began to appear. Then it began to change the shape of the political structure. That is a picture of the development of an idea of world mission at a point in time. I do not give it as a report of today but as an example of a movement Christianity nearly won, but lost. There is a good deal of material from other sources in my repositories respecting this movement. Every modernist movement also has its story of this kind but in various ways, with different techniques and stressing different aspects of their theology, they are all expectant, aggressive, and missionary.

78 The "Spirit in Hinduism" to some people means that God is already there in its theology as in other theologies of other religions. The Spirit is the universal in which all religions are ways to God. Many Christians respond to this kind of Universalism. The other and quite different meaning lies in what is known as the theology of prevenient grace, the Spirit of God going before the evangelist or witness and preparing the way for Him. This is a strong biblical idea, as the Lord said to Cyrus "I have girded thee though thou hast not known me" (Isa 45:5). "Providence and the Spirit of God go before and open up the way." (Wesley, sermon on "The Means of Grace").

especially when sacred relics were on display and were the object of homage; (2) an aggressive and flag-waving expectancy of people-movement conversions; (3) a new message of man's sufficiency; and (4) a movement among Buddhists of a sense of grievance (and let it be noted that D. T. Niles made that point, and he was speaking of what he saw and knew of his homeland, and he saw it as a move "to forge an instrument with which the Christian movement could be countered").[79]

Shortly after that, I met Buddhist activity in a large American university, but in the form I encountered, it was a thoroughly syncretistic movement. The advocate had identified the Christian community that had survived in Japan through the years of foreign closure, as having been absorbed into Buddhism. They had appropriated the crucifix as a symbol of their own, removed the crucified Lord, and substituted a praying Buddha. This was preserved as a relic and was offered to Christians as an example of a Christian idea within the totality of Buddhism.[80] They obtained a hearing in the university and considerable press publicity. Since then I have met a number of ex-Christians who have entered Zen and other forms of Buddhism. Many of their literary figures are such, and mostly they have rationalized their positions philosophically. It seems to me that this kind of missionary activity is directed towards the more academic West, especially towards thinkers who see the human being as self-sufficient, and/or those who place little authority in the word of Scripture or have become otherwise disillusioned with Christianity. That is as it has seemed to me at least. Philosophical dialogue or the circulation of literature seem to me to have been most widely used. I myself have been the recipient of much unsolicited material through the mail. I have a record of 120 Buddhist titles offered to me in one month in the mid-1960s from a single Buddhist bookshop. I was known as a missiology teacher at the time and was selected as an appropriate target.[81]

At the same time, but on a more animistic level, I was offered Buddhist jewelry including Dharma pendants of various kinds, Amida pendants and other Dharmacakra lapel buttons, pins with safety catches, gold and silver chains and tie tacks; also meditation gongs and In Kin hand-bells. In addition to these were art objects, records of translations

---

79   D. T. Niles was witnessing his country becoming enmeshed in laws and enactments that were closing doors to the Christian faith and matters that had been possible under British control. Buddhists were taking over because of their sheer majority and Christian values were being undermined. The term Buddhist "sense of grievance" was Niles' term at that point in time. He was writing with hurt. He wrote for World Dominion and his article was widely copied overseas.

80   I was researching at that university at the time and made my notes there and then, and obtained a picture of the Buddha Cross.

81   This is not the only thrust of Asian interests I have felt through the mails and bookstores. They regarded theological students, and particularly their teachers, as being so softened by rationalization, that they were a good target. Four or five university bookstores I visited regularly had large sections on Eastern religions, much larger than that on Christian theology (if they had one). Within a five to ten mile radius from my residence, there must have been seven or eight bookstores devoted entirely to Eastern thought and philosophy. I am talking of a book choice range into four figures, as in a catalogue I still have on file.

from old Chinese Buddhist texts, esoteric iconography of Japanese Mandalas, illustrated ritual texts, woodblocks, and textiles all identified as this type of Buddhism or that, and all of them offered at that time, unsolicited by me. I guess I was a kind of target. However I don't need a gong or bell to say my prayers, and my God knows my sincerity or otherwise without having to be so called.[82]

The practise of Yoga, according to a celebrated Buddhist teacher, whose article came to me by mail, although a good method to cope with life, is really only for those who have the competent teacher; otherwise it becomes just a substitute for gymnastics. To which I would add, which is just exactly how Christians using it rationalize.[83]

One is disposed to deal with the Hare Krishna and the Baha'i and so on, but I have used my space for this Type.[84] Roberta Winter's story of the encounter of the former with the

---

82 The urgency and impetuosity of prayer with the aid of a gong, drum, or bell, is a rather sad commentary on the nature of prayer, surely for any religion. Many of the Christian missionaries in the East never did come to terms with it. One recalls the experience of David Hill narrated by Rattenbury (1949).

83 Many Christians practise Yoga. Invariably when questioned about it they defend themselves with a question "What is wrong with it?" a quite wrong question of course. Where do we get that criterion for testing—what is wrong with it? By what kind of measuring tool is the thing "not wrong" necessarily right, or even advisable? The second line of defense is, "I only use it for the sake of the mental relaxation or exercise, or whatever. It certainly isn't religious." Well, here we have it from the Buddhist scholar, Karwath, Chairman of the Buddhist Cultural and Medical Centre at Scheibbs (Lower Austria)—it certainly is not "just gymnastics. It only becomes that when you have not a competent teacher." It is not for playing about with. You need to know it through and through. I cannot profess to be able to interpret that properly, except to say that to him the answer "I only use it for exercise" is just not the idea at all. Indeed he regards that as undesirable. So one is not disposed to listen to any rationalization about it. My question is "What does it give me or do to me that I cannot get from Christ?" And an honest answer to that question I can deal with!

84 Hari Krishna is well known for street performing and the distribution of literature, some of it quite "impressive." See Prabhupādav (1970), an elaborate production with a multi-coloured jacket produced by the International Society for Krishna Consciousness. Baha'i stresses that the foundation of all religion is one, the Holy Spirit. God is not divided. Divisions are caused by man-made religion. Even the antagonism of science and religion disappears when the Holy Spirit is present. God alone (through the Spirit) is to be realized as the one power which animates and dominates all things. To cite Abdu'l-Baha from City Temple, London in 1911: "The call of the Kingdom is heard in all lands. The Holy Spirit is felt in all hearts that are faithful. This is a new cycle of human power ... the hour of unity of drawing together all races and classes. ... There is one God; mankind is one; the foundations of religions are one." As a faith this must have theological problems for Christians at the point of incorporation of all religions—a kind of pantheism as it were—and how it relates to Moses, Buddha, Muhammed, and Christ, who though they seem to be different, and found different religions, are really one in essence. (This information from Baha'i sources.) Arya Samaj, a Hindu reform movement supposed to reform from within, I met a good deal in Fiji. It did reform service projects, but it also set out to win back lost Hindus, and that meant operate against Christianity, which it certainly did, often in an underhand manner which I shall not narrate here.

The Divine Life Society from Andkutir in the Himalayas, established a branch in Suva in 1952 as a part of their world mission. This is a movement seeking God-realization, or realization of Self. It is more than meditation. One studies the Hindu scriptures and one develops the Atman within, observes certain rituals and visualizes the Lord who resides in his children, and so on. This comes from the material they sent to me unsolicited. It is a letter to me as one of Nectar's Children; and is signed—Prem and Om, Thy Own Self, Sivananda. And the whole letter is surrounded with "Om! Om! Om!" and promises me "rapid progress in the spiritual path." A second similar letter tells me what Hindu literature to explore for my journey to bliss and immortality, purity and salvation, and the particular form of yoga I should employ. It does not suggest doing anything just for the exercise. I really do not know anything much about this, except that I am to make "prostrations to the Supreme Brahman, Lord Krishna." It doesn't say anything about what it may do to my fellowship with the Lord Jesus. I shall have to leave the discussion of the missions of the Jain traveller and the more established Ram Krishna Mission, but I have my notes in a file.

Center for World in Pasadena speaks to our case, because it deals with the actual dynamics of the encounter.[85] Taoism, as a religion, is distinguished by its search for blessing and long life, a balance in life, certain physical exercises, a multiplicity of gods, temples, images, and ceremonies. It has numerous sects and societies based on different elements in its philosophy of unity, harmony, and self-power. Usually it does not stand alone, but links with Buddhism or Confucianism, showing a syncretistic tendency. It deifies celestial bodies, immortalizes ancestral figures, and sometimes utilises alchemy, geomancy, and charms, and some of its forms emphasize physical exercises or piety.[86] One form of Taoism is known as Tai Chi, which claims to be physiotherapy from Chinese medicine but traces itself back to the Taoist origins. Its breathing techniques are supposed to link the person with the One—the Tao. The name means "Extreme Ultimate" or "Absolute," and supposedly generated "yin and yang," the "symbols of polarity in balance" in the universe. It is difficult to relate Taoist ideas of the cosmic forces and the many deities with a biblical theology. They are just incompatible theologies. Indeed Taoism is self-centred rather than theocentric. It is propagated from eight centres in Canberra.[87]

Another Eastern movement which seeks a market in Canberra is Mahikari. Promotional material claims it is not a religion in the usual sense and offers as proof that Catholic priests, Lutheran ministers, Shinto and Buddhist priests, and Muslims all practise Marikari. That, of course, requires a degree of rationalization, it being claimed also that "Mahikari (True Light)" obtained by the practitioners is "the Light of the Creator God." It also utilises a locket, a holy object (Omitama), as a channel of that light for transmission to people, things, and spirits with amazing results. That is a religious practise well-known in the tribal religions and in sorcery. It solves marriage, financial, and other problems, including sickness. Said to be followed by scientists, medical men, political and other leaders, teachers, and housewives, it is therefore "not religious." So! Yet it tells us of one Kotama Okada, or Sukuinushisama ("Great Saviour") the long-awaited master from the East, who brought Mahikari to the world. Yet this "non-religion" supports its claims by the following quote: "I have yet many things to say to you, but you cannot bear them now. When the Spirit of truth comes, he will guide you into all truth etc." (John 16:12–13),[88] which is precisely what Valentinus and Marcion did with Scripture among the Celtic Christians at Lyons; and Irenaeus would not have a bit of it. It was this type of syncretism which led to the recognition of the canon of Scripture to test this kind of heresy. It is this kind of ra-

---

85 The struggle for possession of a small university campus was a power encounter between the Centre for World Mission and a Hindu movement's determination to obtain it for their own missionary purpose. Roberta Winter, who lived through it, tells the story under the symbolism and title of Once More Around Jericho (1978). She discusses the mysterious forces employed and pinpoints the power encounters.
86 See the brief but comprehensive article in Encyclopedia Brittanica (1984).
87 Their promotional literature specifies the claim for developing self-centred concentration—a quite anthropocentric rather that theocentric value system.
88 All these claims are quoted from their own promotional literature as currently available in Canberra.

tionalization which always shows up in these cases of syncretism, and Scripture is either bypassed or misinterpreted. May I cite Visser 't Hooft again on the point: "The strength of syncretism has always been its inherent plausibility." It fits our culture and our mood. It calls for a mutual understanding of Buddhist, Hindu, Taoist, and Christian ideas as "reflections of the same ultimate reality." "The weakness of this position," says Visser 't Hooft, is that it leaves it "within man's power to change the content and shape of truth. . . . It is not within man's power to change the truth that has come to him from God."[89]

Ultimately then, Christians may be confronted with the religions in their "original form," an "adulterated" or "modernist form." There are only four possibilities before them: (1) confront them, recognizing the authority of the first commandment and the word of the Lord; (2) recognize them as valid options and coexist with them; (3) become absorbed in them, which means reject the gospel, or (4) absorb them which means make our religious life syncretistic. The people of God have to decide, and their covenant relation is "on the line."[90]

The Spirits and Related Powers

Technically a performance is magical or religious depending on whether the act is manipulative or worship/prayer—respectively, whether the participant is himself or herself in control or drawing power from without. I accept that distinction and at many points find it useful for description and understanding. However for the purposes of this present study, the point at issue is whether or not some deity or spirit other than the scriptural God—Father, Son, and Holy Spirit—is involved. On this level of belief, a manipulative act of

---

89 Visser 't Hooft (1963, 85).

90 Christ has to be "the sole Redeemer, and sole Agonizer of Salvation, the one bearer of the world's sorrow and sin so as to take them away . . . The more we know of the Father the more do we confess we owe it to Christ, the more do we see that it was possible by Him only, the more do we see that no man really, practically, permanently cometh to the Father but by Him. Those who have lived nearest the Father have been most forced to confess that it was only by having in Christ what Christ has in none—a Mediator" (Forsyth 1908, 215). Do we agree with Forsyth? In the light of that dogmatic claim of John 14:6, the text Forsyth was expounding turn for a moment and consider this dogmatism in reverse: "A guided tour took me to a Moslem Centre in the heart of America—Washington D.C. in 1956, and there I read the following statement in a book, Our Foreign Missions (interesting title!)":

> The task of shattering the cross to pieces demanded that, just as Christian missionaries had been penetrating to the nooks and corners of the earth, Admani missionaries should roll the tide back, and carry the fight into the homelands of the Christians themselves. The wind is now beginning to flow from East to West. (Ahmad 1965).

Quite apart from the mixed metaphors, here is a reverse mission, a drive for world Islam, using the Christian model; and pinpointing the event on the cross as the crucial point for destruction. What is it about the cross that is so vital? The fact that He died, and also my belief about it! It is in the light of that statement of only thirty years ago that we ought to look at the Muslim growth figures for Africa south of the Sahara, Indonesia, America, and Australia at the present time, with Islam this is not an offer of syncretism, as with Hindu, Buddhist, and Taoist attractions and alternatives. With Islam we have a different set of problems, which do not concern our subject for discussion, except that our covenant relation is "on the line" in each case, and the more we rationalize about our own beliefs the more impotently we present the gospel.

sorcery, say, or an act seeking possession of a spirit for divinatory purposes, is a willing involvement with some spiritual being other than the Lord.

What Tennyson said of Christian faith and practise, that "our wills are ours to make them Thine,"[91] is true for any god or spirit worshipper. Both magical and religious performance offends against the first commandment and fractures the covenant relationship of the people of God, whether it controls the powers or is controlled by them. Thus both sorcery and possession come under purview as we study the Type II.

Before analysing a selection of these types of spirit phenomena, there are a few general observations to make from the point of view of an anthropologist, the scene being as complicated as it is, and the performances and their group acceptance being by no means mono-causal. Historical, cultural, theological, and psychological factors must all be recognized.

(1) The tendency of some reports of enquiries to place all these movements in "the radical or unstable fringe of society," and a failure to challenge the church to take the matter seriously is tragic and short-sighted. These are highly significant issues.[92]

(2) Wherever in history we have had heavy migration movements, free or forced, programmed or otherwise, movements from one culture to another and especially from rural to urban life, there has been an increase of magical and religious forms, and more often than not, new syncretistic developments. Any period of history which has the data preserved will demonstrate this, and numerous reasons for it have been identified anthropologically.[93]

(3) With all kinds of economic reorganization and the establishment of new lines of communication and market centres, ports of entry, transport exchange locations, etc., there has been an increased trade in magical paraphernalia, religious prostitution, etc; once again with new syncretisms.[94] Paul's letter to Corinth is not fully meaningful without an awareness of this.

---

91 Both in Christianity and animism the surrender of the will is all important in any power-encounter with evil. See Tippett (1976b, 146–47). Remember the old Haitian words to the padre in Cave's tale, "You're too questioning. Even if you wanted to be possessed and tried to be, you'd be searching your own feelings too much. To be possessed a man has to let himself go . . ." (1959, 250).

92 We call in experts, pay them a large research fee, receive their professional report but seldom act on it unless it suits us to do so. We decide what we always intended doing—report or not. Few of us really read the report in full. The report was only to save our faces in any case—it saves us from criticism. If we don't want to act, or have not the courage, we rationalize about it or sweep it under the carpet. Most reports on syncretism in the church are treated thus. Don't push me: I might start citing cases pretty close to home!

93 See Tippett (1967b, 341–45, 350–51) where I am describing "Plantation Christianity" in an area created from migrants recruited for labour in plantations from various parts of the group, speaking different languages, with different religious persuasions (even the Christians were diverse) and different standards of English (where they had it). I show how and why magic and sorcery come with the migration, new forms develop, and then counter-magic to meet the new situation. The complex of injury and attempted cure arises out of the crises and dynamics of the context and formulates its own patterning.

94 The reader is referred to my article on Ethiopian markets in Tippett (1970b, 110–15) in which I show how they are centres of diffusion and meeting places for people over widely scattered localities, speaking different languages, exchanging their craft produce and animals, many of which are for sacrifice. These markets are microcosms of

(4) The aftermath of every homecoming after war has introduced borrowed religious and magical ideas, especially forms of sorcery. Often these tools and concepts have spawned in the new location like plant and insect pests, especially when some cultural factor in the new climate has been stimulated.[95]

(5) A diachronic analysis shows basic phenomenology that recurs in waves of emphasis stimulated by various factors as suggested above. In anthropology we speak of the "continuity of the cults." In church history we speak of periods of religious revival. The causes and contexts may differ greatly, but there are dynamic features which run through them like themes. There may be new items, new shapes, new syncretisms, but there are basic phenomenological continuities. The church should be alert to their reappearance and learn a few lessons from her long and checkered history. I say this as an ethnohistorian and a missiologist.[96]

(6) These forms of religious performance that spring up like mushrooms in these times of heavy activity are invariably not only featured by cultural borrowing, but they are also contextualized in some way or other. Their syncretism takes on a meaningful (to the participants) form relevant to their peculiar felt needs and cultural expression.[97] If the church desires to handle the problem pastorally, it must at least enter into that area of understanding. It is quite unsatisfactory to end a report with, "The movement has now died

---

the countryside and some of the trade reflects the witchdoctor paraphernalia. I met a Tishena witchdoctor at the Chebera market. He was apparently doing well in business and was better dressed than anybody else, but all out of character with his people—brown rubber boots, a sun-helmet, and a blue canvas coat, a mark of his emulation of Amharic colonialism. His extortions had built up one of the biggest herds of cattle in the region.

95   For example, a Fijian Battalion had gone to the Solomons to support the Americans in World War II. Soon after their return when I was ministering in Suva, and there was considerable suburban settlement, I became aware of the growth of a form of sorcery which I did not know, and I had thought myself well informed in this area. I checked it out and made notes. Subsequently, when I was researching in the Solomons, I came across the same form of sorcery and some of its associations. Some of the Fijian troops had taken them back home: a straight case of cultural borrowing. In Suva it took root in the urban situation. It never penetrated deeply into the countryside, at least not in my time. Likewise much of the sorcery introduced into Australia after World War II came from southeast Asia and has continued to the present-day. I ran into evidence of a regular flow from Bali, through Kuta and Denpasar, when I was researching there for the indigenous church.

96   The idea of "the Continuity of the Cults" was applied by Worsley with a sequence at Buka (1968, 114–22) which sequence I have extended in Tippett (1967b, 216, 371). There is more information on the Hahalis Welfare Society and its Baby Garden on file in the Tippett Collection, St. Mark's. Some day this continuity of nativistic cults will need further ethnohistorical examination. It speaks very much to continuing spirit phenomena in our own country.

97   In the study of innovation, and especially religious innovation (which includes cross-cultural conversion, messianic and millenarian cults, and magical formulae), the acceptor is really the innovator (not the advocate or agent of change) because he ascribes the meaning. In anthropology this is spoken of as "the problem of meaning." An evangelist supposes he preaches the gospel correctly. A Hindu or cargo cultist may ascribe a completely different meaning. See Tippett (1973d, 124–25) and (1970b, 262, 272). Basic definition: Barnett (1953, 334–38). For the theory in missiology, see Tippett (1987b, 307–09). For a brief analysis of the importance of the social context in the study of a movement involving spirit phenomena, see Tippett (1976b, 158–62) where attention is paid to cases from Haiti, Ethiopia, and sub-Saharan Africa and also an Eskimo case. The researcher must master the worldview because the value system may be the direct opposite of our own, a point brought out well by Benedict, who showed how normal behaviour in one culture could be abnormal in another and how an abnormal person could perform a 'normal' role in a society where his abnormality was accepted socially as normal.

down." It may have found its own solution, or the "people movement" may have completed its structural entity and established a new supposed integrity of its selfhood. Or it may have turned to another experiment.

I think these points will be demonstrated in the case studies to follow if the reader looks out for them. There is probably no better example of a cult growing out of its ethno-historical context than the case of spiritism, which will serve us as a useful springboard. Please note I said spiritism.[98] I did not say spiritualism.

Spiritism

Spiritism, which many people call voodoo (but voodoo is only part of it), is probably not found in Australia. This permits us to start by looking more objectively at the phenomena and relate it to its own unique context. We can examine from a distance how a context shapes a movement and how it settles down to a permanent form or practise and becomes a new religion in itself.

Its region extends through Brazil, the Caribbean, and into the southern states of the USA, and especially its large cities. Historically it is a vestige of the West African slave trade, Portuguese, French, and British. It emerged in the colonial plantations as an ethnic self-defense against plantation controls—especially Portuguese and French and the Catholic religion they imposed. In time the slaves became Christian and accepted the form of their masters. Internally they reshaped it to suit themselves and gave it their own meaning (that aspect of the study of meanings ascribed to accepted innovations is well understood in anthropology).[99] The components of that context were thus unique to that situation, and spiritism is a good subject for analysis. I can study sorcery or divination or

---

[98] Spiritualism is a performance, a séance, in which people seek to communicate with the dead through a medium. Spiritism is an experience of possession within a form of ritual performance (like worship). It is an act of worship with a specific theological base. It is probably the most extreme form of syncretism invading Christianity. It has a superficial Catholic shell but is really African religion. It is centred in Brazil, the Caribbean, and the United States. In 1960 there were over six thousand spiritism assemblies in the USA. They were dominantly black but attracted quite a few intellectual and affluent whites from "across the tracks." See Tippett (1976b, 55ff) for a brief survey. But there is a huge body of descriptive literature. The main authorities are Herskovits, Bastide, Metraux, Deren, Bourguignon, Courlander, Johnson, and others, some of the sources being in French. The French influence of Kardecism is strong in Brazil, but there are many forms of spiritism. Spirit possession is the universal feature, and there is absolutely no scientific doubt about the genuineness of the possession. One of the features of this possession is its equestrian descriptive terminology. The possessed participant is the "horse." The spirit "mounts" him and "rides" him. It concerns our subject because of its attachment to Catholic Christianity. Catholic theology is taken over, reinterpreted in terms of African religion, of which there are diverse forms. A good survey of the varied components of the different types of spiritism (Johnson 1968) is found at the St. Mark's National Theological Centre Library.

[99] The reshaping and developing of the theology is creative. The first dominant syncretism and reinterpretation came from Dahomean religion. The manner in which the Haitians drew this together and then added Yoruban elements (which had a different theological thrust) and produced a new theology has been researched by Courlander. "Vodoum" originally Dahomean "spirit" or "deity" became more and more applied to temple ritual with spirit songs and dances. The "Loa" for the possessing spirit came from Congo. The integrations in the system indicate the common inherited African religious feature forming a true religion, the purpose of which is to transform the chaos of the slave life—a creative performance. See Courlander (1960).

possession from anywhere in the world; but when I study them in Brazil or Cuba or Haiti or New Orleans, they have their own contextual and historical peculiarities, and they have bound themselves together in specific structures to fit the context.[100]

And to study the effect of this syncretism on the church, it will have to be the church of those countries, and more particularly the Catholic pre-Vatican II form of it. We ask what happened to the liturgical forms, the theology, the hierarchical ecclesiastical system, the hymns and prayers, and the adoration of the Catholic saints of Portuguese and French Catholicism when the churches were flooded with West African slaves, who came to the New World with a well developed theological and formal religion of their own. What we find, in point of fact, is not that they became Christian, but that Christianity in some ways became African; yet not wholly African for there was a wave of French intellectualism among the colonial elite, and this provided a further element for syncretistic development.[101] Thus indeed has Harmon Johnson analysed ten different forms of spiritism tabulating their componential differences—a very nice piece of research. Because he understands this, he can speak very clearly to the churches, Catholic and Protestant. So there are levels of spiritism to suit the levels of society, under the title of the church. But what has it done to the nature and function of the church?[102]

I read up my notes on one situation. A ceremony of initiation is being described, initiation into spiritism in terms of the Christian church into which it is incorporated: French in this case. The initiation is a rite of passage. Its format is a process of rites—a dying to the old life, a purification (washing ceremony), and a resurrection, both spiritual and physical. It has similarities to the theology of baptism, but is essentially a spiritist ceremony. It did have a Christian confession before the start. An act of Christian worship preceded every voodoo rite (Paul had something to say on this). A bush priest is present at the voodoo ceremony to invoke a Christian blessing. Really he has no Christian status, but is a kind of link-person between the two powers—a cultural innovation on the lines of social role-creation to maintain the unity. The worship directed to God as Creator is new and Christian. Hitherto they had not seen a primal creator god as related to the events of daily life; but the idea was acceptable and they adopted it, as also they accepted the pictures of the Catholic saints as images of lesser gods and spirits. These under African influence

---

100 A situation which is socially or religiously dynamic and contains cohesive structural elements can modify its accepted new ideas to suit its own context. The new syncretistic entity we call spiritism might have been an indigenous church with better guidance or advocacy. Even so it would be the local adherents who did the reshaping. An example of this would be the case of the Bataks in Sumatra. See Tippett (1987a, 285–301). For another treatment of the same dynamics (i.e. a common ethnic cluster of components) see the pattern of conversion to Christianity in Tippett 1967a).

101 Most of the resource material for the background in the French sources, but see Johnson (1968), typescript material at St. Mark's.

102 Melville Herskovits' descriptive account is (1937b), but his most illuminating critical analysis of the relation of the supposed "Catholic Church" to the African hierarchy of gods, now served under the names of the Christian saints is found in an article (1937a).

joined the gods of the wayside, the house-building, the gardens, etc., and moreover there was an act of name-exchange and many African gods survived and merely assumed the names of Christian saints.[103]

The dances, rituals, symbolic vestments, and drum beats of the performance identified both the saint and the African god whom he actually was. The sacrifices offered, the possession by the spirits, and a dash of necromancy could hardly be twisted in any manner to be considered Christian.

Fortunately we have anthropological research done by scholars familiar with both ends of this story and competent of comparing what happens in Dahomey with what happens in Haiti where the slaves were taken.[104]

Research on the mainland of USA shows a slightly different pattern of development. Let me give a few quick vignettes. The voodoo ceremony develops into a precise format, quite African. Any Christian element surviving is Africanized. Practitioners are set up in the business of performance and trade like American medical men and psychologists. Shop-fronts market magical potions and powders. Practitioners compete for areas of power control like gangland territoriality. These cases all came from urban America.[105]

(1) A shop store front advertised some of the concoctions available inside. It read:

Dragon's Blood	50¢	Easy Life Powder	$2.50
Love Powder	25¢	Boss-Fix Powder	25¢
Sacred Sand	$1.00	Get Together Drops	$1.00
Black Cat Oil	$1.00	Devil's Shoe Strings.	25¢[106]

(I imagine there has been a price rise since those prices).

(2) Julia, a voodoo practitioner for thirty years, had extensive rural and urban connections. She had made a good deal of money and had acquired an automobile for business. Her testimony makes a good point: voodoo requires faith. I quote her: "I makes me own stuff and saves money. They say I walk with the devil in the graveyard at night; but wait till they get into trouble. Then they come for help. They bring me money and pay what I ask

---

103   Maya Deren, (1953 and 1973). See also Meträux (1959 and 1969) and McGregor (1966).
104   Herskovits researched in Dahomey and Haiti and has made good anthropological comparisons at some theological depth. See also Courlander and Bastien (1966). The relation of "rider and horse," processes for protection against possession ("mooring the loa") and descriptions of the intensity and duration of possession, of which the possessed "horse" knows nothing thereafter are numerous. See Meträux and Pedro McGregor references in my survey (Tippett 1976b, 156–58).
105   Satanism and possession in America have been researched by sociologists and journalists, the former constructively, the latter descriptively with a good level of observed data. Reconstructed cases are illuminating. See Tallant (1946). An anthropological survey of glossolalia and allied phenomena associated with possession was prepared by May (1956), enough to demonstrate the worldwide range of possession.
106   This is an abbreviated list. The catalogue of such magical cures available in American cities runs into hundreds. Indeed it would make a fine data base for a study on Firth's model of cultural florescence (1963), or that of ethnoscience.

for chicken feathers, earthworms, oils, and powders. When they know they're dying, I cure them; partly by what I know and partly by faith. Don't forget the faith, even in Voodoo."[107]

(3) Here is an item printed in Creole in a city newspaper. Everyone knew the local voodoo queen was on the warpath over a threat to her professional territoriality. "They think they frighten me, the crazy rogues! They don't see their misfortune, or are they drunk? I put on my lovely head kerchief. I do not fear the tomcats' shrieks! I drink serpent venom! I walk on pins and needles and on golden splinters! What can they do with their 'Big Malice'? I'll paint their doorsteps with gris-gris and make them shake till they splutter!"[108]

(4) It was supposedly a Christian act of worship. The names of the saints were Christian, the first components of worship, the Apostles' Creed, the prayers to the Virgin Mary. A statue of the Virgin was near the altar, but that was about all. The chanting and dancing came out of the heart of Africa. Bodies swayed. Brandy libations accompanied the swing and rhythm of the dance. The tempo increased. A participant thrust an ignited candle into the brandy, and a burst of liquid fire lit up the faces of the dancers, and exposed their ever-increasing ecstasy, until the rhythm and chant became a wild chanson africaine. Believers came forward and knelt for healing treatment from the witchdoctor. At the height of the frenzy, a white woman, who clearly did not belong, a respected married woman from the affluent side of the city, joined in, was whirled about with the others, sprayed with sacred brandy in her trance.[109]

I grant that all comes from a very special kind of context; but hopefully it shows how context can shape innovation and religious change. Hopefully also it will show how innovations can become permanent; how the precise meaning is given by the acceptors and performance is twisted to suit their purposes and felt needs. Any study of religious syncretism demands this kind of research, whatever the context. It is not good enough to say "a movement died down" or "the situation eased" which is a "cop out." Was the problem solved? Did the innovation or movement become permanent? Did it shift to another location? Was there a compromise? Was the syncretism legitimatized? Or was the matter just swept under the carpet to emerge again some time in the future?

There are two occasions when this kind of inbuilt problem can torment and divide the church: (1) when researchers try to be so objective and non-committal that the situation

---

[107] The economic contextualization and desire for power and prestige here reflects the cultural context, especially in the American South. However note the place of faith. I remember a sermon in Fijian by a bush Fijian, in which he discussed the power of faith either for evil or good. His preaching point was "Faith in what—or whom?"

[108] Desire for power and prestige again reflects the dynamics of the local context. This is an open challenge of one spiritist force to an entrenched system. The Mt. Carmel challenge would have been quite meaningful here. See Footnote 58.

[109] Here is the religious level of the contextualization. Christian Catholic components are forced into a meaningful structure. The felt needs are clearly religious. Linton's "psychic needs," Maslow's "self-actualization needs," even for the affluent, respectable, white woman. We have a considerable number of cases of this out-of-class type of person becoming involved and experiencing a complete personality change. For the reality of this see Herskovits (1937b and 1958) and Mbiti (1969) for an interesting case.

can be rationalized away; and (2) when the church leaders have not the courage to face the facts and sweep it all under the proverbial carpet, again by rationalizing the situation.[110] In spite of the peculiar situational components of that description of spiritism, which scarcely touched the surface, there are several aspects of it which are found the wide world over—its universals. They include sorcery, possession, and divination, with which I shall have to deal because they are at our door.

There are also other factors about which there is a great deal of confusion because we have never sorted them out and the terms are used in so many different ways—satanism, black magic and witchcraft—even by the practitioners themselves. Nor have we appreciated the antagonism and power encounters between them. That will have to be discussed.[111]

Then there is the whole question of the healing ministry, which the Lord wrote into our own Christian mandate, but which we have neglected enough for there to be movements out of the church because of this neglect. That calls for an evaluation of shamanism and the Christian commission.[112]

The wide range of cultural diversity round the world does not help but rather complicates our consideration.

Sorcery

Sorcery is quite specific, even though it is often spoken of as black magic or as witchcraft or satanism, in which it may or may not be involved. In all my cross-cultural research I have found it clear-cut. People know what I mean, which they do not know with the other terms.

Sorcery is magical in that it is manipulative. It is personally conceived by a sorcerer, and intended to work evil against some individual, group, or institution. It may cause sickness, depression, or death. It may injure programs, destroy property or animals, or gardens or building projects. It is evil, and it is premeditated; and it is usually individually initiated even when done for a communal purpose. Power politics or personal jealousy or rivalry may be behind it. It cannot be used for healing, except when the sorcerer is induced to withdraw a spell, and that has normally a formula of its own. Counter-sorcery is sometimes used to break a spell.

---

110 This tendency has been behind much Christian inaction, and the forces of organization have not failed to observe it. At the same time satanism warns its adherents not to get lost themselves in "the quagmire of grey forces."

111 The power encounter mentioned in footnotes 98 and 99 even breaks in on the occasional case of possession, where two loa strive with each other for the right to mount the horse. If one is vulgar and the other elite, the struggle may result in a glossalaliac battle of the spirits and the poor possessed creature becomes exhausted switching from the high speech to the vulgar. This can happen where the spiritism is diversified as by Kadecism in Brazil.

112 The term "shaman" has been variously used by different writers dealing with different cultural regions, but normally we reserve the term for the role of curers or healers, who in a sense fight the sorcerers. To understand this in a locality one must master first the theory of sickness. See "Theory of Sickness and Religious Belief" in Tippett (1970b, 199–225). Christian missions have often failed to differentiate between shamans and sorcerers with unhappy results. The breakaway independent prophetic movements have usually emphasized this unmet felt-need for healing.

To counter the sorcery of another person requires a stronger power (mana, for example), and has a technique of its own.[113]

The sorcerer must understand the ritual of his art perfectly, and apply it correctly. Wrong application at the simplest level will make the sorcery impotent. At the worse level, it may rebound on the practitioner himself (cf. Sons of Sceva in Acts 18:13–17). At the worst, it may kill the sorcerer himself, and this is a terrible thing.[114]

The antidote for a sorcerer's sickening potion operates in its own power and is a risky business. The only certain cure I know—and I have lived in this kind of situation—is the power of the Lord (Luke 10:19).

Black magic refers to this kind of injuring operation. Sometimes the term white magic is used for the healing program which cures custom sickness. Normally, but not always, a diviner is needed between them. In this type of situation, the diviner diagnoses the cause of the sickness and may specify the cure required. One must learn the system and the correct path through it. The important factors are that there is always a cause of sickness, and there is usually a cure. Sometimes in our world, a person claiming all these skills is called (wrongly) a witch. Sorcery, as I have met it, has usually been used by a person of ill-will, an individualist, not well-received by his community and generally feared. He operates in his own interests, or is open for hire (like a Western "hit man"). He is normally used to fight a rival, to intimidate or pressure somebody, or humiliate him, or to retaliate or repay an injury (e.g. "payback"). He plays the same role as a vandal, a fire-bug, or a terrorist in the contemporary West. He is an unsocial person, and normally his motivation (or that of the person who hires him) is either a desire for wealth or prestige or power, either personal or political. It can be used against corporate bodies like a school or church. These I have known.[115]

---

113 A form of evil or any kind of pressure enforced on the Fijians by the use of a sacred whale's tooth (in pre-Christian times said to be charged with powerful mana) could only be stopped by the presentation of another whale's tooth, a larger tooth, or a collective offering of ten, thus with still greater power to "press down" (bikai) the other and wipe out its dominance. This is what the gospel writer, Luke, would call "power over all power" using ἐξουσία (exousia) over δύναμις (dynamis).

114 When I was living in Kadavu I remember a sorcerer dying from his own venom. He had an evil record and had caused many deaths. When his power rebounded on him through an error of bewitching, his whole body broke out suddenly in blisters which were quite unknown in the medical understanding at the regional hospital. It was diagnosed as not a complaint for hospital treatment. (The idiom was "pricked with his own bone.") Nobody would drink the counter-magical potion on his account (bese me gunuva) because of the general hate of the man. He died a tragic death and a couple of bones he used as his "locus of power" literally performed a remarkable agitation as his spirit master claimed him. This I know. I lived nearby at the time.

115 The circumstances relating to my appointment to Kadavu concerned a case of a mission school complex being bewitched by a sorcerer. Time after time the school gardens were uprooted by pigs. There was one accident after another among the school children. Each of these was quite out of proportion as I verified. No normal cause was ever found and not until the sorcery was exposed and dealt with did things return to normal.

Witchcraft

Witchcraft, the ambiguous term, I mention only to deal with the data. I am not concerned with a good definition because I use the term only in the African sense. The satanists and white witches cannot agree themselves on the meaning so I'll deal with the phenomena rather than the term. The old medieval witchcraft, to all intents and purposes, has been shut up in the archives for the use of historians.

In African witchcraft again, it belongs to a specific social structure. The witch is not one who victimizes people. She is herself the victim. She does not know she is a witch. A crisis situation, a social breakdown of some kind, a series of unexplained deaths creates a mental set of expectant discovery on the part of the community. Somebody is destroying us with witchcraft. Witchcraft requires such a communal mental set, because it is an imaginary evil. With this kind of situation, there must also be a functional role in the society—viz., the witch-finder. Witches and witch-finders go together as a dyad. The witch-finder selects (by divination maybe) the victim, who is declared to be a witch. Usually it is a useless person, a person with a social problem or an idiosyncratic person who can be disposed of without much concern. The witch has no idea she is a witch; witchcraft being performed in sleep at night, etc. She is duly dealt with by the prescribed social mechanisms. The community returns to a state of equilibrium and the witch-finder is the "good guy." This is all culturally and contextually reinforced.[116]

That "in my book" is witchcraft; and that is still found today in many rural areas and in cities where it has been brought in by migration as suggested above. Its "justification" is as an adjustment mechanism in situations of social crisis. That can happen in urban areas over-crowded with rural migrants having this kind of communal expectation. Western judges have seldom come to terms with it.[117]

That is a very different thing from the common usages of the term in our Western urban world today; when I indicate, for example, that in San Diego as I knew it in the 1960s,

---

116 See Parrinder (1958).
117 One of the demands behind many nativistic movements is for native offences to be tried by native magistrates, partly because they know what lies behind them, and partly because they know how to deal with them to the satisfaction of the tribe. Cf. Marching Rule in the Solomons (Tippett 1967b, 204–09). Or to outline a good example of misunderstanding in legal matters from Africa, the trial of Elard, the magic-man, by Sir Edgar Unsworth was reported in Time Magazine (5/4/63) Elard was solicited to dispose of a troublesome girl by her grandfather for an agreed sum. Elard waited by the riverside, dressed in his appropriate attire for the event. The girl came to get water and was attacked by Elard, the crocodile. He broke her arm with his tail and dragged her into the water. When Elard wanted to collect his fee for turning himself into a crocodile for this purpose, the grandfather went back on his deal, and Elard took him to the native court for his money. Sure enough the native court made the grandfather pay. However, a government policeman who chanced to be there reported the matter higher up and the two men were brought up on trial for murder. Elard pleaded not guilty as he was a crocodile at the time and not a man. Sir Edgar called in the government psychiatrist (escape route #1) to test Elard's sanity. He was found to be quite sane. Sir Edgar turned to the Court Assessors, three tribal elders (escape route #2). They were unanimous: "He was a magic crocodile when he killed the child." Since African belief and western law found no common base for discussion Sir Edgar ignored tribal opinion and sentenced both Elard and the grandfather to be hanged.

some thirty witch covens could be located, with an average of twenty-five to thirty participants each. There was also the Witchcraft Convention in Los Angeles, which attracted quite a number of trained school teachers. I watched a television program at the time in which a person calling herself a witch described how she made voodoo dolls for sale and dispatched them by mail. These were made to order, personalized to meet the requirements of those who hired her. She gathered dried leaves from a graveyard, for use with chicken feet. She drew the faces of the victims from photos sent by those who employed her, and supplied black- and white-headed pins for sticking in the voodoo dolls. That, of course, is straight sorcery.[118] Had she called it sorcery she would have been arrested. Witchcraft had been legally cleared.

This redefinition of witchcraft, now the term is legally clear, has led to this open espousal of the witch's witness. Now we may read an open confession of a witch's activities in her autobiography. I read much about her adventures along the way and her growth in the craft from childhood through her grandmother's tuition, as she made her pies and tarts and ornamented them with astrological symbols. She describes how every child born had his horoscope worked out at birth. The angry grandmother, after trying to obstruct her being sent away to school, cautioned, "Remember I have had her from the beginning and she will come back." There is no doubt that her childhood experiences of her witchcraft shaped her later life.[119]

Perhaps one incident may be narrated here. At one time she fell ill, indeed apparently was sick unto death and very weak. Her grandmother brought in her pet owl, for which she had a really loving attachment. Grandmother asked, "If you had to choose between your owl and yourself to live, which would it be?" Eventually the old woman disclosed that the owl would have to die for her to live and took the owl out. The very next day she began to feel better, but she never saw her pet owl again; although it was some years before she understood what a sacrifice was.[120]

She composed her first poem at the age of eight. Her skill in folklore and with rhythm attracted her to psychic interests. She had learned the importance of rhythm and vibration and subsequently linked it up with mantras, psychic forces, and trances. The personalities she tells about in her story were all the same kind of character.

---

118   This was on the Los Angeles Channel 9. Moreover it had good press coverage and a photograph of the "witch" (sorceress).
119   Sybil Leek (1968) has written her autobiography and done so under her own designation "witch."
120   'Religion appeals to a power outside the person, for any of a number of reasons. Often it is for the cure of sickness. The vicarious principle is clear. This was a costly sacrifice for the girl. The grandmother's training was certainly religious. I remember a case in the Solomons when an old man, very sick, was offering a pig sacrifice for his life. The fire and the pig sizzling on it were so close that he could have touched them. He was enveloped in the smoke and heat. The sweat was pouring down his body. He was quite confident his god would heal him as the procedure was ceremonially correct under the eye of the medicine-man who watched nearby.

Her description of the full initiation ceremony into the witch profession discloses her emotional feeling "when she became fully aware of the great cone of power which can be raised by a group of people all endowed with psychic qualities."[121] Then reflecting on it afterwards there came to her "a great surge of peacefulness" and a "feeling of thankfulness that I belonged for all times to a group of people whose roots went back into eternity."

She showed some hostility to organized Christianity on account of her witchcraft, and opposed the established church, but allowed people their freedom of religious choice provided they lived consistently within their religious frame of reference; but as to her own religious position, she spoke of the "Old Religion," by which she meant the original religion before any of the religions emerged, before Moses and any of the religious founders.[122] She believes in a Supreme Being, but not a God who can walk the earth. To her, an image of a God who can be incarnated is an impossibility because humans are good and evil. She speaks of Christians following Christianity but has no idea of following Christ anywhere in her writing as I recall. Nor do I remember any biblical reference except that she had studied the Bible as a child.

This is a missionary volume, but her mission is an attempt to whitewash imaginary ideals and Old Religion, the original pre-religion. She sees witchcraft as a saving force for humanity.

Anton La Vey, of the satanic church and author of The Satanic Bible (1969), will have none of this "white witch" working for the benefit of mankind with sanctimonious definitions, herbs, charms, and healing; it is writing new rules for the game. It only came after the repeal of the witchcraft laws in England in 1951.[123]

Satanism

This is poles apart from La Vey's own writing on witchcraft, and he wrote a textbook of the methods of success in the art, a shocking and frightening work oozing with subtle trickery and sexual traps. He still holds to the all-evil image. He criticised other new ideas about witchcraft, as used by the "self-convincers," like the dependence on herbs and drugs, which cause discontinuity with reality. He requires that magic be concentrated on one compelling desire in the performance of the ritual and that this quality is lost by drug-

---

121 This is a fairly developed theological construct "a cone of power" generated by the corporate group. I am reminded of a corporate healing service of peyote cultists. The peyote service is for healing. The whole extended family has to be present, concentrating and straining for healing power. The performance is not likely to be effective if some are absent.

122 This is an idle speculation. Her view of the Old Religion before ever there was a Moses or a Buddha is a ploy to escape the living religions, and it is too transparent. She knows nothing more of that precursor of the religions than I do (probably less if I tested her knowledge of prehistory and early archaeology). Moreover the whole idea misses the key issues of God's disclosure of Himself to mankind as in Scripture. The more one thinks about her Old Religion the more one meets theological and historical problems. She has cheated again. It just refuses to hold together. You cannot project a Western morality into an Old Religion and still make and market voodoo dolls. How naïve can one be?

123 Anton La Vey (1971), a terrible and carnal work.

effect. Spells are generated only in intense emotional concentration. Bewitching must be deliberate and active. The magician must know himself, must know the one he intends to bewitch. One studies personality types and fetish-finding in them. He is concerned here with how witches bewitch a man and take him from his bewildered wife.

Likewise he had little time for the multitude of unskilled practitioners of witchcraft around California at that time, using palmistry, tarot cards, crystal balls, and ouija boards, all of which involved credibility factors. They are known in satanic magic as "convincers." The witch learns what they are supposed to achieve, and thereby knows how to manipulate those who believe in them. The credibility factor is no problem to the witch, but it is to the person to be bewitched, who wants to believe in them.

This is as it was in the 1960s. Intermediate between the polarity of satanism and the white witches lay a whole army of magical practitioners, fortune tellers, psychics, diviners and sorcerers, herbalists, and vendors of magical books and paraphernalia. For a period the LSD drug cults were active and experimental, and the story of The Exorcist, which was founded on fact, was frequently enacted in California.[124] Animal sacrificing was widespread, and all these had their regions of concentration. On the whole, those at the poles thought little of the intermediate rank and file of magicians, but in the period of greatest drug cult activity, things with them were very serious. Without going out of my way to seek these things out, I was astonished at the frequency of their crossing our paths.

In the attic of an inconspicuous house near the place where I lived was the Temple of Esoteric Wisdom operating under a priestess. The adherents used to worship the Great Feminine Principle, the Great Masculine Principle, the Primordial Principle, and the Dark Womb. The sponsors of this fertility cult supported themselves by means of an occult bookshop. Public prayers had been abolished in tax-supported public schools; but a university student could do courses in magic. He could, and some did, do enough units to obtain a master's degree in religion and magic and set himself up in business. One such called himself a druid, set up the Wizard Consulting Service, and was available for sorcery for a fee.[125]

---

124 The text of a letter has been preserved in which the author confesses that the book (Blatty 1971) is founded on fact, real experiences.
125 This claim is all well documented. The first accredited MA degree with a major in Magic was awarded by the University of California at Berkeley to Philip Emmonds Isaac Bonewits, 16th June, 1970. The matter received a full page write-up in a San Diego publication Uplook. The same number had another item on the teaching of "Witchcraft" in the schools under deceptive titles like "Literature of the Supernatural" in spite of the Supreme Court ban on the teaching of religion in schools. Courses in all aspects of religion are taught at the universities as intellectual study and can hardly be eliminated. The inconsistency was in the fact that the negative of "teaching religion" in the Supreme Court ruling did not apply to the teaching of magic for the specific purpose of practicing it. One could hardly study, say, philosophy without touching religion. I myself did courses in Magic in my degree work and learned much from it. But once a course in magic qualified a person to go out and practise sorcery—that should have lined up with the Supreme Court ruling, because a fuzzy notion of religion or failure to define it properly can make a law anti-Christian and pro-magical by its semantics.

The mood set was such that public enterprise and what we call the private sector soon became aware of its financial possibility. The "world's most experienced airline" offered tourists a "Psychic Tour of Great Britain" at $629 (1972 price), each participant to receive his own personalized astro-numerology chart and the experience of a séance.[126] Occult literature was so big that one bookshop with an occult stock of $25,000 turned 65 percent of it over each month, and offered crash courses in palmistry at $25. So it went on.

Featured also in this wave of the occult were the huge sales of astrological material and literature, divinatory equipment, and ouija boards. Ten thousand professional astrologers earned their living on astrology which had a market of forty million Americans, 25 percent of them said to be addicted. One author on the subject sold twenty million copies of his book around the world. Two thirds of the newspapers in the land ran astrology pages or columns. Educationalists prepared special books to help parents teach their children in the art. A quick trip round the stores that Christmas showed the toys being offered included vampire sets, crystal balls, fortune-telling sets, zodiac medallions, and a variety of astrology games. A series of Christmas cards celebrated the Saviour's birth with a set of horoscopes.[127]

Anton la Vey, master of satanism, though he had no faith in astrology argued its value as an index to the understanding of human affairs. Man may be studied and reveal himself so that the witch may reach out to bewitch him. Of course we never learn to understand mankind by working from the other end of the universe. A witch believes astrology only for one reason, namely "because everyone else believes it." To know this then is to know how to manipulate him. To this end, astrology is a great magical weapon. The stars affect no one, but astrology does. It is a shot in the arm for the witch's ego; it is a point of contact, and a door to conversation and rapport, and eventually for manipulation—because it appears valid or is believed to be valid.[128] That is the cold, practical view of a satanist. For a Christian view, see "Star Gazing."[129]

As to the ouija board, a Christian youth counsellor wrote in 1975 that one of the most common questions he had from parents of young Christians concerned this instrument. Yet many parents and teachers had no concern at all about it. Their common reaction was—"Why, what is wrong with it: it is just a game?" Following up the matter, the counsel-

---

126 This was regular tourist publicity advertised in the press, available in the publicity rack, for commercial reasons, to sell tickets for world travel in competition with other airways. This was a Pan-Am [Pan American Airlines] offer.
127 Eugene Nida's book appeared about this time. Here is a quotation from his writing: "Horoscopes and crystal balls are thought to foretell the future, while ouija boards, tea leaves, and lines on the palm of the hand are supposed to be sure guides to impending events. The extent to which communication from the impersonal supernatural world are believed in is almost incredible. For example, it is estimated that over 30% of the people of France believe in and consult horoscopes and clairvoyants. Probably a roughly similar percentage of Americans do so. Certainly it is difficult for a society as a whole to claim an advanced 'scientific outlook' when most hotels have no 13th floor and many airplanes have no 13th row" (1968, 25).
128 Lyons (1970).
129 Chapter 6 in this volume.

lor was surprised to discover (1) how widely used, and (2) how little understood was this occult device. He came across numerous cases where the device lightly played with had led to serious personality change and broken friendship. He found it one of the normal instruments for opening doors to demon-possession. On the story of The Exorcist, Blatty admitted in a letter (13/11/72) that, "The book is based on a true story, and the involvement with demon-possession was through a ouija board." Whether there is anything essentially evil in the board is not the point. It is certainly used for evil. Moreover there is a whole area of research still to be done on the manner in which spirit force operates through a material locus of power, and whether any mana adheres to it when it is temporarily not the shrine of the spirit. In any case, the question "What is wrong with it: it is only a game?" is far too simplistic. This is an area of ethnopsychology and ethnotheology in which the research has scarcely begun.[130]

Divination

Divination may be defined as "the ways and means of discovering the unknown." It covers everything from propitious days for marriage, for journeying or trading, events to be expected, the wisdom or folly of specific courses of action, the mind of a deity on some matter, the best place to build a house, and so on.[131] Basically it is to "tune" the person to his god(s) and to maintain harmony between his own behaviour and decision-making and the forces of blessing on which he draws help from outside himself. When a person becomes a Christian, does he cast aside all divination? Is there a Christian functional substitute? Does one still need to know the will of God in his/her life? Are there artifacts and procedures for this in the Christian life? Surely the tool is henceforth the written word of God which discloses to us the mind of the Lord. The procedure is the method of prayer—not only asking, but also listening to Him. It follows, then, that instead of tarot cards, ouija board, and the like we should be developing our prayer and Bible study. I have always taught that when animists have come to Christ, and I have always found it meaningful to them.[132]

The chairman of a Californian graduate school made a critical study of the ouija board using questionnaires and sociological tools and had access to the data of a large New York toy store, a good cross-section for study. Many customers had been drawn to the board as a toy or game for innocent fun. The board was a good seller, attractive to young people, the majority of them from Christian homes where divination would have been rejected. The questionnaires showed up that the "toy" did somehow lead to (or was associated with) psy-

---

130 For the idea of a spiritual force or power in a physical "locus of power," in an idol, a fetish, or a sacred object, which is thus its "shrine" (i.e. enshrines it) for the moment of offering, or worship, or prayer, or "whatever" see Tippett (1971b, 211ff. and 1976b, 164–67).
131 See typology of divination performances in Ethiopia in Tippett (1970b, 167–77) for the diversity over one territorial region.
132 See Tippett (1967b, 12–13, 280–81).

chic development and increased dependence on the board for decision-making. There were also clear signs of exposure of the young players to "the danger of occult entrapment."

At the time of my investigation, two million ouija boards were sold in America over a period of three years. This was at the same time as the cultic developments I have described. While our researches should not be strained to say more than they actually do, I am convinced that the tool has an inbuilt capacity for undermining the covenant faith, for making the operator dependent on it, and for picking up any bad vibrations in the surrounding world. I think I should rather explore the Bible and talk to God in prayer about what He wants me to do.

But material artifacts (ouija boards, cards, crystal balls, and tables of propitious days) are not the only forms of divination. There is another which is ceremonial, and in which a person becomes a shrine of a spirit or deity. He may pass off into a trance, or he may retain contact with reality. The latter is normally shamanic. The former, by far the more common, is the subject for a whole book. The reader is referred to a "Spirit Possession as it Relates to Culture and Religion" in the report of the Christian Medical Society's investigation at the University of Notre Dame in 1975, which surveyed the anthropological literature on the subject.[133] The subject has a long history. I have two Fijian reconstructions of possession prophesies from missionary reporting of the contact period, and I am astonished at their similarity with Dryden's translation of a possession prophecy of the Greek Delphic Oracle (1932). This is a dominant element of the spiritism described above, and I have met it myself in the present-day third world.[134]

In that paper I questioned whether or not the Christian church had provided its members with the kind of faith needed to deal with the ever-increasing confrontation with spirit forces of our times.

I also asked whether we had really adequately assessed our own social context to understand our increasing number of sodalities of persons so disillusioned with society and the church that they felt they had to turn to these cultic forms, and what they supposed they really got from them.[135]

What are the features which brought these disillusioned individuals together into corporate groups for cultic exercises shared in "fellowship"—a fellowship after a Christian model but serving a demonic power? There was a body known as "The Fellowship of the Ancient Mind" in the 1960s. I believe it was just a research body, researching for televi-

---

133 Montgomery (1976). This is a large volume from specialists in various disciplines in interaction.
134 One from Thomas Williams, the other from Lorimer Fison. Although their interpretations differ, their description as data is very similar. See file of papers on spirit possession at St. Mark's. Also "The Continuity of Sorcery and Magic in Fiji" (Tippett 1971c). Demon possession as a phenomenon on the mission field (China) was researched by the well-known missionary J. L. Nevius, a remarkably scientific work for the times (1880s). He used Chinese assistants for data collecting (1968 facsimile). For his basic findings see Tippett (1976b, 151–55).
135 Ibid., 167–68.

sion and film presentations. The businessman, head of the body, revealed that never a day passed but he got at least two phone calls from some unknown individual asking "if his business bought souls." What is there here of social malaise or anomie that would so lead individuals to want to market their souls?[136]

Yet out of that same Los Angeles context there began to emerge all over the area corporate groups in a fellowship of some spirit or other.[137] Whatever their despair and desolation, they formed a sodality. The idea was right, if the direction was wrong. Paul saw them this way in Corinth—a "fellowship of devils." They got some power from the very corporateness. It should have been easier now for the church to win them to Christ—but on the whole it was impotent.

Yet huge numbers of them did actually come to Christ. They left the LSD cults as corporate groups and turned to Christ; but it was not the work of the Christian church that won them.

They ceased sacrificing cats and dogs for blood to mix with LSD in their magical communion. They ceased their black masses with sexual excesses in ritual magic. They turned from their self-indulgence and symbolic animal lust in which they had thought to handle their identity crises. They achieved a new life by finding Jesus as a Person and a fellowship round Him rather than looking for something in their carnal worship structures and drug cults.

But how did this happen? How did they get from drug cult to Person, and find their identity in Him? How? Church history will probably simply report that "the drug cult craze died down in time." This will be a gross injustice and a half truth. Most of them were brought to the Lord by a similar company, really a nameless company, variously known as the Jesus People, the Jesus Kooks, the Jesus Freaks, and the "Jesus Trip."[138]

---

136 This mental set, or state of "anomie" was introduced into sociology by Emile Durkheim in his social analysis of Suicide (1897 [1951]).
137 On one occasion, because a graduate student of mine was researching migrations over a decade along road developments in Brazil and using computer material over micro-regions for identifying church growth potential, we became involved in certain aspects of spacial diffusion. It took us to the Professor of Geography at Cal State. This researcher had a huge map of Los Angeles spread over a whole wall of his office. It was dotted with coloured-headed pins marking the location of the LSD and other cults across the megalopolis. The map disclosed their clusters in Venice, along Hollywood Boulevard, and Sunset Strip. In a moment one saw the wide sweep of drug cults and satanist covens by the pin-head colours, and the general intensity of the movement.
138 A number of books describe the movement fairly well: Streiker (1971), Enroth, Ericson and Peters (1971). These presentations reveal the conservative theology (almost fundamentalist), but if the theology was old time, their presentation was certainly not. The message of "One Way" still met the felt-needs of our erratic world, but it was acceptable because of its radical identification with the people it wanted to win. The evangelists, and that they all were, looked like hippies and dropouts. Most of them had themselves turned from the drug-cult scene where LSD was mixed with the sacrificial blood of cats and dogs (and by the way that information actually came from the Venice Police who had to dispose of the increase of mutilated animals found in the streets). The negative of it all was that the Jesus People, although they had good fellowship among themselves, never really worked out a theology of Κοινωνια (Koinonia) to be the body of Christ in the world.

They worked the streets. They talked the same language. They wore the same clothes and looked like dropouts. They went to the simple basics of the Bible. They had Bible raps. Their art styles were familiar. There was meaningful communication, and there was the Person of Jesus. Unfortunately the distance between the regular churches and these dropouts was hard to bridge, and having left Los Angeles about that time, I never really got the end of the story. But the matter did show two things. Jesus Himself was the Way. But the church had shut herself off from the world of dropouts and drugs. The problem is with us still: how do we find a fellowship group in the church where they can feel they belong: having Christ and having beaten the drugs?

Dropouts and drug cults and black masses are not likely to introduce syncretism into the church. Many of them may be church dropouts, but they are not likely to return to the fold as it is, or respond to the message as it is. That in itself should give us food for thought, be it a different angle to the subject.

This related problem, namely, our youth drift into the drug scene and cultic satanism, is probably stimulated by the presence of ouija boards, tarot cards, astrology, and similar devices thought to be "only a game" or dismissed with the question "what is wrong with it?" In some specific cases, they may have been the actual cause of the drift, in others they opened doors that led to the drift. They certainly do lead to the development of tendencies which expose them to magical manipulation should it happen to come their way. A scientific study of this would take us beyond youth, even to the place of witchcraft in the break-up of mid-life marriages, but this is difficult research because one cannot set up experimental situations. One cannot play with human lives; one can only work from unhappy case studies. From the evidence which has come my way, limited but quite clear, the subject is frightening, especially when it involves possession, and a backsliding Christian, once deeply committed, now possessed by a vulgar spirit is a truly heart-breaking tragedy. This I have met.[139]

Research done on the wife-swapping clubs of the 1960s showed that their experimental indulgence created a vulnerability to satanic religion. So often the club did not really satisfy those involved and led to ennui, and the "search" turned to religion, but it was satanic, even the black mass. The real tragedy was that some of those wife-swappers were actually Christian backsliders. The next question for scientific investigation is surely—"what stimulated their backsliding in the first place?" This is tough research. It can only really be done by one who has been "through the club" and turned to Christ instead of Satan. And there are not many, if any, of them with training in the sociology of religion, and none of them who could examine the matter objectively. That is why one case study, one clear repentant testimony, is worth a whole file of statistical research.

---

[139] Tippett (1988, 40–42).

I have specified that one gap in my data base is the English portion, and what I have is documentary, not interview or experience. It all seems to go back to the shift in Britain's legal attitude to witchcraft in 1951, which, although it served humanity in its main intent, more or less legitimatized any type of supposed witchcraft thereafter. Other forms and practises, not in any way the medieval witchcraft, came out into the open. It was then that a "witch" could hold her head high and practise her craft openly, even if that craft be not medieval witchcraft but in point of fact, straight sorcery. This unintended "spin-off" came with the aftermath of war, homeward migrations of troops, and magical innovations galore—a real cross-fertilization of magical culture. What material came my way from Britain was more rural than urban. The 1960s featured a spate of black masses, grave robbing, animal mutilation, and a wave of church vandalism.

A church would be vandalised and magical symbols painted on the porch. In one case, the rector actually pronounced a curse on the vandalisers. There was a ruined monastery where an altar had been roughly restored, and two sheep hearts were discovered pierced by wooden pins in satanic fashion. A church cemetery was desecrated, the remains of a female had been removed from a grave and placed as a sacrifice on the church altar. A Presbyterian minister reported satanic masses being held in a ruined 17th century church in his neighbourhood. Investigation revealed evidential items—a mutilated Bible, a broken chalice, and an inverted cross over the altar. Remains of burnt holy wafers were found before an inverted image of Christ.[140]

Across the Channel, English tourists could witness a black mass sacrifice of a black cockerel performed in a Paris cellar. This was apparently a kind of satanic promotional scheme. It was offered also to English visitors to Switzerland and America, as it was to American visitors to Britain. This was all going on at the same time as a church of Satan wedding in San Francisco hit the headlines in the press because of the Hollywood personalities involved and the bride being the daughter of a prominent lawyer and a government figurehead, and just shortly before the famous Charles Manson case.[141]

We might recall that Anton La Vey, head of the satanic church, had declared in 1966, when "God was proclaimed dead," the "Sexual League came into prominence," the hippies developed as a free sex culture, and "The Satanic Age has commenced."

Much data has been collected about this kind of thing and much speculation about it. Christian writing has tended to confine it to the "radical fringes" of society, and not doing that much harm to the core of social life. One writer who came out of it and knows the

---

140 This picture of satanism in Britain comes mainly from newspaper and other reports at the time. It could be quantitatively extended but would be repetitious. Some preachers commented on the scene from the pulpit. I saw one sermon (from a distance) in the Expository Times.
141 We were in Los Angeles at the time of the Manson case and shared the public horror over the whole episode. Manson appropriated symbolism from the Bible, the book of Revelation. The story from the legal point of view has been written up since.

people personally, defines this church attitude as their "selective intention." Visser't Hooft called it their "rationalization." I quote my source: "Western man, inculcated as he is from birth with pragmatic rational concepts and modes of thinking, has a tendency to pick out the rational, logical processes of society and nature, and deny the existence of the illogical and irrational"[142] i.e., deny their reality.

This source for what is really going on explains the view of the church of Satan as: Christianity is utterly irrelevant, and they want nothing to do with the Christian God.

Churches and dusty pews are not needed, but "temples of indulgence" and "houses of prostitution" for people to release their hostilities and tensions by indulging in the so-called "seven deadly sins." Individuals need to be themselves and not worry about feeling guilty.

However, there is a satanic ritual, hymns, vestments, opening invocation to Satan, a naked woman as symbol of lust and self-indulgence as an altar. The congregation is sprinkled with a mixture of semen and water, symbolic of creative force, a priestly drink and libation to Satan, occasional psychodramas, and ritual curses.[143]

As for the "radical fringe," it is revealed that the congregation includes doctors, lawyers, teachers, policemen, IBM executives, a sociology professor, although they are mostly middle class disaffected Protestants, Catholics, and Jews, mostly under thirty-five, realists, materialists, degreed persons, and intellectuals. They search for emotional fulfillment and power within themselves. The church of Satan is flexible in that it is ready to change direction and steer a new course in satanism if it elects to do so. (This means that descriptions like the above should be dated. This was dated 1970). So much for the rationalized "radical fringe."

In passing the informant just cited has prepared a long list of names and addresses for disclosure only in the event of his "accidental" death. The bearing of the church of Satan on the Christian church is subtle and venomous; witness the disaffected Christian backsliders in their congregation, and the satanic church's organized prayer to Satan and fasting for the moral downfall of Christian pastors and evangelists.[144]

---

142 Visser't Hooft (1973).
143 These and other details are assembled in Lyons (1970). The earlier shape of the black mass with its sexual excess in ritual performance, the concept of communion with godhead through sexual ecstasy (a reaction against Victorian morality) has shifted. The processes of rationalization within the church has weakened it. There is now stronger operation against the "Grey Forces"/ the Affluent Establishment. Satan is savage and carnal, self-indulgent and active against the leadership of the weakened church. Satanists want to be master of someone. One, asked why he embraced Satanism, replied "Because I never felt so much power before!" This often works through money or through lust.
144 A number of satanist leaders have formed a band to fast and pray for the moral downfall of Christian pastors and evangelists. The secretary of the church leader Clark Taylor travelling recently by air sat with a man who took no food. The secretary asked if he was a Christian fasting. He disclosed that he was a satanist bonded to fast and pray for the satanic destruction of effective Christian evangelists. Apparently the satanic traveller was as discomforted as Peter about being associated with Jesus. In any case Taylor circulated a warning. Link this with Anton La Vey's diabolical perceptions (1971) and we have a truly frightening situation.

So satanic spiritual force penetrates into the church through seemingly innocent devices ("only games" and "What is wrong with it?") or subtly and spiritually by prayer and fasting in the name of Satan. Truly are we wrestling not against flesh and blood but against spiritual wickedness in high places. All this makes our spiritual relationship with the Lord so utterly vital.

There is still another area very difficult to assess scientifically or discern spiritually, namely the whole question of healing.

Alternative Medicine

Jesus built a healing ministry into His program and commissioned us to do likewise. Moreover there is possibly hardly an area in Christian mission where we have made more mistakes, intellectually, anthropologically, and spiritually than this one. Sure, the church has spent a fortune in medical work, and I am not critical here. We have researched at the scientific level, and have many blessings as a result. Yet in many ways the healing ministry of the church has hardly been just what the teachings of Jesus seem to have implied.

The desire for healing is one of the basic felt-needs of mankind.[145] Tribal societies have developed healing arts, and segregated persons as specialists in the art of healing—curers, shamans, et al. Time after time, when a tribal community breaks away from the organized church in a prophetic movement, one of the main features is its new healing ministry to meet a felt-need that had not been satisfied.[146] So often a conference on this matter leads merely to a new program or a new hospital, which may have a great deal of good in itself. But the problem is still there. It can never be solved round a conference table or rationalized. If the church is to be the body of Christ in the world, it must perform His healing ministry in all its dimensions. It must be a way of life, not a program to be supported.

The human need for healing in the absence of a continuing and effective ministry demands attention, even inside the church itself. Mental, physical, or spiritual, people want to be healed. This being obvious, one should not need to have to point out that every kind of religious kook will have some way of exploiting this need. If a need is not met in a wholesome way in the church or hospital, there are plenty of practitioners—some genuine, some deluded, some rogues in the world around us. Any person needing to be healed is a potential target for every kind of magical "medicine." There may be a genuine program which provides some physical benefit—if it ends there. Lots of these things, in point of fact, are package deals, which may or may not have been in the small type of the advertisement.

---

145 The Consultation on independent church movements in Africa, run by the C.W.M.E. at Kitwe, Northern Rhodesia in 1962 made a statement on Christian healing, from the African perception of healing and recognized the frequent rejection of Western medicine because it was not meeting the felt needs of the people.

146 See Sundkler (1961), Welbourn (in Hayward 1963), Survey Statement (ibid., 74–75), Welbourn (1961), Baëta (1962), etc.

After what I have written about ouija boards, astrological charts, and crystal balls, perhaps we should look at some of these herbs and cosmic healing programs, because of the number of church people with a desire for health who get involved with them.

One day (in July 1988) my wife drew my attention to a centrefold in a Canberra newspaper—four pages entirely given to what was designated "The Healthy Alternative." There was enough material in copy and advertisements for it to run over onto other pages.

If we allow for the health food advertisements and claims, osteopaths and therapists, which may or may not have been genuine, the advertisements and articles covered meditation systems, cosmic connections, Mahikari, tarot cards, astrology, acupuncture, harmony programs, power control, magnetic health, Shiatsu, Yoga, past life explorations, divination, hypnotherapy and mysterious names quite meaningless to me. Some were classified as "Counselling," some as "Alternate Medicine." One said specifically "nothing religious." Others frankly admitted the opposite. Some operated through an identified "locus of power," others had a mystical energy, the Eastern name of which was supplied. Most gave a phone number for appointments. Others invited folk to lectures, workshops, and the like. A New Age movie documentary promised to evaluate all these things. Some were apparently able to support offices or shop. Others held meetings in public halls and theatres. Twenty such items were advertised in one Canberra newspaper on that day. On the surface some were innocuous enough, but the small print of some showed "package deals"—astrological predictions, divination, tarot.

Some advertisements had the backing of news items and paragraphs of text about the practitioners, support of their claims, intended plans and writing. In some cases, the places booked for regular meetings suggested at least that business was booming.

Quite apart from what this all suggests about the trade (for that is what one has to call it I think), what does it reveal about our society, its hurts, its suffering, its mental and social felt needs that lonely people have to seek their own solutions to this kind of advertising? Moreover apparently they think they find something in these new beliefs and panaceas. What does it tell us, really? What lurks behind these extravagant claims? Even if we suppose there is some mental relaxation there, what else is there?

In the first place, most of these panaceas have a deep-level religious base, an Eastern religion, a theology of some other kind, a spirit force. The simple economics of that centrefold in a city our size, suggests a widespread people involvement that statistically must include a large portion of church people. Of course, when you meet them "It is not religious," or "We only do it for exercise or mental relaxation." Sure, I give them credit for being sincere, but I question their rationalization. And in some cases, I know there are deep-level religious roots, set for an unhappy discovery when it is too late. And those "package deal" or "fine type bottom line" advertisements ought to warn us.

Let me take a case from the centrefold, mentioning nothing but what is buried in the advertisement and accompanying news-item. A leading teacher of Sahaja Yoga whose full honourific religious name is given and her local name of endearment, "The Mother," runs meetings twice monthly, and explains the name is Sanskrit for "union with the divine." The process relates the spirit of the person with the all-pervading spirit by awakening the residual spirit energy within us (known as Kundalini). Her portrait shows her forehead adorned with a Hindu symbolic mark. On the surface, it all sounds pretty religious to me. And I leave it there. I merely report her statement. For any Christian considering this form of Yoga, I would ask a couple of questions.

Remember these are not quiz questions or addressed to anyone at random. They are specific questions to a professing Christian and presume his/her prior commitment to Christ.

(1) What does this offer that cannot be found in Christ? (2) Can I expect to share that religious affiliation without some injury to my covenant relation with the Lord? As an anthropologist I would anticipate that at a deep level somewhere, there is a cohesive cultural cluster that will show up at some time and land that Christian in a crisis situation that he/she might not be able to handle. Ultimately he will have to decide just where his loyalty lies.

There is in anthropology a theoretical construct spoken of as "the continuity of the cults" which recognizes how these cohesive cultural clusters survive. Administrations and churches have thought problems solved once and for all, only to find a resurgence in one generation after another after dormant periods. It reappears with the same form and character, even if contextually modified. These dynamics lie behind nativistic resurrection cults. The package deal and fine print are often a sign of the presence of a cluster of some kind. There are what we might call "pointers." "Union with the divine" and "relating the spirit of the person with the all pervading Spirit" are so intensely theological that a judgement "I only do it for relaxation" is just not anthropologically credible to me.[147]

We also have in the same centrefold an article (with accompanying advertisement) about a person whose business supports a shop. She writes as an astrologist for two national publications, appears on television and radio, has published a book for the international market, and is working on another relating "star signs to sex attraction." She sells crystals for healing, psychic symbols, subliminal tapes, incense (one presumes for sacrificing). Here is an advertisement loaded with cohesive cultural clusters. Maybe it is just an advertising coverage of things to sell so the business can support a shop, but it is loaded nevertheless with deep-level clusters that could come to the surface at any propitious set of circumstances. I can work out, diagram, and expound the possibilities in the anthropological

---

147 For cases of the "Continuity of Cults" see Worsley (1968, 114–22); and Tippett (1967b, 216, 371).

cultural dynamics round that shop advertisement.[148] Remember it is not secret information. It is meant by the astrological vendor for Canberra young people to read and buy. It would make a lovely article for a secular anthropological journal. It is as a Christian that I find myself shuddering. I think the church has to come to terms with reality. This is a new era of power encounter. Was the world's most conspicuous satanist right when he announced, "The Satanic Age has commenced!"?

Here we shall have to leave the Spirits and Related Powers (Type II). They are all found to be either spirit phenomena, religious, and a direct encounter with the first commandment, or spirit related, i.e. they can be operated to activate spirit forces or open the door for the entry of spirit forces.

We have a really great missionary theologian writing a book in the spiritual situation of the 1960s on *The Challenge of the World Religions*. It was a book heavy in German data and reflective of the situation in that country, dealing with invading Eastern thought on quite a different wavelength from my treatment. But he elected to discuss Yoga as a religion, and perhaps would have put it in my Type I. He wrote, "It appears harmless, a mere series of exercises but it leads people, without their noticing it, into a new spiritual world . . . yoga is a religion and is developing itself into one of the largest ersatz religions in the Christian sphere. It already recommends itself as a means toward the solution of all problems of life. . . . It is a religion and has an avowed religious goal."[149]

Beside that I put the statement of a person who had worked his way through satanism and knew it through and through: "Satanism is primarily a religion, for it seeks as a goal the surrender of self in the most extreme tradition of religion. As an organized religion, it displays a specified body of ritual and belief, and has an official and organized priesthood. The primary difference between satanism and most other religions is the source, the godhead."[150]

Whenever a Christian "plays around" with anything satanic or related to some ersatz religion, he introduces syncretism into his personal life and through him as a church person, into the church, and must be held responsible for fracturing the covenant relationship.

Jean Daniélou, in a small book directed basically to good Catholics but surely for all good Christians, says that "there is in history a furrow made by God" of which "we catch a first glimpse when He made the first covenant." This distinguishes the people of God from all the other religions as far as the inner life is concerned. Daniélou points out that the

---

148 Following Barnett's theory of cultural dynamics (1953) and bringing my focus to bear on the equation "c" in the recombination thesis model.
149 Vicedom (1963, 103–06) on "Yoga." Remember this was written in the 1960s. It is from an academic approach to the philosophical superstructure of Hinduism along the lines of its own missionary attack on the West. He has the support of a number of similar scientific and philosophical scholars and comes at the subject from a different angle from this paper, but with very much the same result: that whatever the manifest form may be it is ultimately religious.
150 View expressed in Lyons (1970).

essential difference is that "the other religions start with man." To the Christian, God has heard man's cry, and He has answered with grace. In the non-Christian religions, "grace is not present, nor is Christ." Turning to religious syncretism, of the allowance of non-Christians to shape Christian belief he says, "The vanity and illusion of syncretism lies in its belief that universality is a common denominator" (1962, 7, 8).

As we move on from Type II, having really hardly touched the surface, those assessments we should carry with us in our minds, and a fourth from the anthropology of primal religion. An artifact or natural formation stands always as it is—an artifact, or stone, or whatever—until someone presents a sacrifice before it or says a prayer to the spirit it enshrines for the purpose of adoration or worship. Then it becomes an idol, and a competitor with the Lord; the first commandment is bypassed, and the covenant relation is fractured.

And finally, all these matters we have discussed under Type II, show that the organized religion we have known in the church has met with widespread rejection by a large section of the community. Not only that, but the church itself has generally refused to accept that sad reality. Attacks on the Jesus Movement as "sentimental and emotional anti-rationality" that makes it "suspect to those who believe that the whole man must be engaged in the religious commitment" and demonstrate "the poverty of its rational thought," are clearly a case of "physician, heal thyself"—the "emotional" being also part of the whole man, and a failure to differentiate between the non-rational and anti-rational. In spite of the contextual differences in the forms of this movement around the world, the one real universal is an honest cry from a real felt-need, "Jesus, if you exist, come into my heart." This is true missionary, not "indiscreet proselytism" and "disconcerting to human reason," as Zimmerman points out.[151]

---

151 The references cited in this paragraph come from Marie Zimmerman (1973) on "The Jesus Movement." She found in her survey "Introduction" the missionary activity of the movement based on the Book of Acts. Although this was criticised by a number of Christian writers for a literalist use of a source that belonged far back in history and did not allow for nineteen centuries of Christian experience in the institutional church. Over against this we need to see the general rejection of a church which has segregated Jesus from the world. If the Jesus People want to build a society "in which money doesn't count much, and success and power are dirty words," what does this mean to normal Christians? What does it mean for us? Zimmerman's "Introduction" ends by regretting that "our theological efforts are often too exclusively directed to dogmatics" and raises the question of whether or not this stifles our very spiritual sense and prevents the spontaneity of faith Jesus recognized outside Israel (Matt 8:10) "a theology not found in most university curricula."

With reference to the view of "the whole man" as based on the full use of the human intellect, I myself take issue unless the wholeness also include the dimensions of sentiment, emotion, and faith. I was involved in a symposium integrating psychology and religion in which the major speaker argued these poles of rational and non-rational as both essential to human wholeness. He distinguished this non-rational (emotional etc.) from anti-rational and pressed for the greater recognition of this non-rational part of mankind as essential to his wholeness. The liberal critics of the Jesus Movement missed this completely. My basic contention of course is that the Jesus Movement rather than the Christian church had an answer for the drug cult scene and obtained a hearing. I ask the church to confront that fact and recognize why (Clark, Malony, Daane, and Tippett 1973, 8, 21ff, 93).

The Deifications

A.D. 40: The Emperor, Caligula, ordered that his statue be set up in the temple in Jerusalem. The following year, before his command had been carried out, he was assassinated. Even so the order shocked the Jewish world, which saw in Caligula the climax of pagan antagonism to the sovereignty of God—the desecrating horror prophesied in Daniel as precursor of the Judgement (Caird 1956, 26). A decade later the feeling was still in the mind of Paul (2 Thess 2:3–4).

These two verses have a packet of strong terminology which I translate literally to bring out the stress of the terms:

> Let no man in any way deceive you . . . the apostasy . . . is revealed . . . the one who sets himself against, and exalts himself over everything, and being called God, or the object of worship, sitting in the Temple of God, and showing himself to be God. . .

This intended manifest demonstration of godhead, after the earlier enactment of Augustus to establish emperor worship as a system over the Empire nearly a century before, for political reasons rather than religious reasons perhaps, had horrified the Jews and Christians alike because of its religious implications. Caligula's open revolt against God was not for atheistic reasons, for emperor worship was polytheistic and syncretistic. It subordinated God, as Satan had attempted in the third wilderness temptation (Matt 4:8–10).

Greece and Rome also deified the state, the city, and the human pursuits and indulgences, which may still be said in the manner of analogy, and of which I shall make a few comments nearer the end of this paper. There are numerous ways in which mankind has deified himself, made himself a god, as it were. Because it seems to me that we are brought to this idea in many of the religio-philosophical confrontations of our Christian life today I cannot avoid it. I want to take a hard look at the personality cults which impose themselves on us out of Asia, but before I can deal with this, I need to look at the biblical view of the prophets, and perhaps compare it with, say, China before dealing with personality cults.

One of the really great Christian scholars of my generation has been H. H. Rowley, who spent many years in the East and understood Eastern history, philosophy, and religion from face to face dialogue and research. As an Old Testament scholar also, he is top of his field. A professor of Semitic languages and literature, he left some fourteen or fifteen works—every one essential and authoritative. He was president of the Society for Old Testament Study and brought many perspectives from the non-Western world to bear on his Old Testament studies. He also mastered studies in French and German.

Rowley's work (1956) is a comparative study of the Hebrew prophets—Amos, Hosea, Isaiah, Jeremiah, Micah, and Ezekiel—over against their contemporaries, Confucius, Mencius and Motzu. He analysed their roles as reformers, statesmen, and religious thinkers. In statesmanship and reforms, he found remarkable similarities and much relevance for us today. Of course, their cultural heritages differed, but it was in their attitudes towards the relationship of mankind and his god(s) he found them poles apart.

His hundreds of documentary references show an equal familiarity with the Chinese classics as with the Old Testament, and it is therefore worth quoting him in this matter:

> The Chinese teachers as statesmen and reformers ... were worthy to stand beside the Israelite prophets.... In the setting of their times ... we may see them in deep moral earnestness and a burning desire to lead men into a finer world. In relation to worship, however, the prophets of Israel and the sages of China are in two different worlds. It is not merely the setting of their times but of the conception of worship.... The prophets of Israel desired to make the ritual of worship more meaningful, not merely more correct. It was the spirit that concerned them. They wanted to carry the spirit from the shrine into life and make the service of God in daily life part of the worship.[152]

Moreover, he went on, though the gods are reverenced in the remote Chinese sages, the prophets, despite their different levels, relate to a living personality—the intimate relationship (Comfort ye my people, etc.), the sense of communion, and the prophetic heritage (Elijah, Nathan, Moses) who prepared the way, and the concept of the people of God.

I mention this to demonstrate what comes down from them to me as I study our subject. The covenant relation of the people of God is so central and important that it be not fractured. It was in this heritage that Jesus placed Himself.

What happens when the philosophical religious superstructures of the East, as we know them today, are injected into our Judeo/Christian experience of the covenant relation with the Lord—and more particularly since World War II? This bears on the question of the life of the Κοινωνια (Koinonia), and how the avatars relate to Christ. Is it right to accept the prophet, sage, or guru in such a way as we substitute him for Christ, or equate him with Christ, or make them identical manifestations of the same spirit as co-equal? To what extent is this just a philosophical analogy, or is it the deification of man as God? When we introduce an Eastern religious exercise into our lives as Christians, is it merely a form, or does it imply our acceptance of a basic theology behind it? Are we—and this is the crucial question—are we jeopardising the covenant relation by deifying a guru, who thereby claims our loyalty which rightly belongs to Christ alone?

Or again, am I deifying mankind? Am I making him God? Or is he God as part of everything else—the pantheistic view? Am I a modern kind of Gnostic? Just how literally can I take the Eastern theology thrown at me by the pundits and gurus, especially those who

---

152 H. H. Rowley (1956, 120).

claim my adoration and homage? When this invades the university, how long does it take to invade the fellowship of believers?

There is no doubt about the process going on apace since World War II, although the beginnings go back before that; but we have really not done much thinking about its scope or its meaning. The first phenomenology I shall examine under this Type III then is the Eastern "personality cult."

Eastern Personality Cults

In a previous generation from ours, when the Christian missionary thrust in India was at the level of the pundits and scholars rather than at the people level, C. F. Andrews gave us a brilliant analysis of the renaissance in Hinduism under the impact of the teachings and ethics of Jesus, which stimulated the Bhakti reforms. Hinduism accepted Jesus the Teacher and His ethics, but not the total Christ. In the course of time, they perceived that those actually won from Hinduism to Christ, came to Him for deeper reasons and found Him the way to the Father. Out of this realization came opposition to the notion of the particularity of the gospel, the uniqueness of the Way. Many saw this as Western arrogance. Well, it wasn't Western, the incarnation having taken place in the form and fashion of a Galilean Jew. And the claim had been His own as in John 14:6 (Andrews 1912).

Now it seems to me that many of the contemporary thrusts from Hinduism and Buddhism, the Eastern movements currently making inroads into Christianity, are claiming their own form of particularity, and some are certainly aggressively missionary.

To the Christian who really takes his Bible seriously, Jesus was either precisely who and what He claimed to be (for if that be not true, the whole message falls apart, and He is an imposter) or He was a deluded enthusiast. Jesus claimed to have come from the Father, be the only way to the Father, and to have predated Abraham; and John claimed Him to have been involved in the creation, to have been incarnated. Neither was Peter silent on these matters. These passages of Scripture make a body of theology with very specific claims, so that the authority of Scripture also is at stake (John 4:26; 14:6; 1:1-2; 8:58; Matt11:27; Acts 4:12; Phil 2:5-11 etc.).

Thus there comes out of Hinduism a body of philosophical theology to be set over against that of the Scriptures we use in the church. Great teachers emerge and are either deified, or at least claim veneration as divine. Validation comes from Hindu sacred literature. The incarnation is claimed to be theirs (be it in poetry and myth and not in history). Bands of disciples are gathered and sent forth to proclaim the word of the guru, to plant missions, and to win the world. It is only round the period of World War II that that missionary thrust becomes really aggressive. The time depth of this general movement goes back a very short time. The oldest of these gurus was only born about the same time as my own father. Their methods of mission either copy those of Christian colonial mission or correct some of its faults. The period of the Bhakti saints is replaced by the period of personality cults. In so many ways, they are an answer to the Christian movement, either by doing the same kind of thing strategically, or countering it by bringing Christ down to the guru level of divinity.

There is one thing essentially their own. It springs from the idea of the all inclusiveness of Hinduism; symbolized as it has been as a huge lake into which everything flows, so that Hinduism is big enough to absorb everything religious, including Christianity. The personality cultists, or at least some of them, think to absorb Christianity. I speak from experience at this point. Likewise they expect Christianity to be able to absorb their own ideas and, of course, they come up against the particularity of Christianity. These dynamics come to light in a study of the modern personality cults.

While most of the gurus work from their own sacred books, they were always ready to twist the Christian Scriptures to suit their purposes. Some even started from the Bible to win Christians, using the old techniques of Valentinus and Marcion (Irenaeus 1953).

One general theological principle that comes up from time to time is the diametric opposite of biblical teaching. Many gurus have mankind aspiring to self-realization and thence to God-realization. The Son of God, of course. came down and assumed the human role. Mankind may be sanctified thus and prepared for the life eternal with God. He may receive the Spirit as a pledge and foretaste of more to come, but he does not become God. It doesn't work that way—not in the Scriptures.

Let me now examine some of these personality cults, inasmuch as it can be done in a few pages. I confine myself to a few which I know to have expanded into the Western world. For the moment, I keep to Hindu-based movements and their gurus, swamis and avatars—said to be god-men, , divine incarnations of the absolute—and something of their ashrams or retreat centres.

Absolute reality is Brahman. Man is really identical with Brahman: body, mind, and self, but body and mind are merely appearances. Self is Brahman. The task of the guru is to get to self-realization, and thence to god-realization. Were the cult founders superhuman? Many of their devotees certainly believe them to be so. There is an Indian devotional song, bhajan, which repeats over and over again that "Sai Baba is the Lord himself." Let me start with him.

Sai Baba of Shirdi: A popular local song sung in the streets of his locality many times a day runs,

> God dwells here in the form of Sai Baba. Devotees forget themselves at the very sound of his name (Harper 1972, 28).

Devotees hunger after him, and surrender themselves to him. It is a religion of miracles and a growing mythology. Those who knew him regarded him as God incarnate. The guru is avatar of the supreme being and usually announces this fact to his disciples. Sri

Baba told his followers: "Place me in the temple and I will stay there." (Presumably deified.) I have an outline of the worship service. A bhajan has a repetition line, "Sai is the Lord Himself!"

Meher Baba: The chant "Victory to Meher Baba" is common on many university campuses as students bow before the picture of their newfound saviour. These are the Baba Lovers, followers of Meher Baba who had declared himself as "Avatar for the Age, the Eternal One." He did not become divine because God descended, but achieved his divinity through his own sadhana. Now he is "The Highest of the High." His team of followers are "god-intoxicated souls" and his movement, the New Life Movement, was launched in 1949, when he declared,

> My old life places me on the altar of Absolute Godhead and Divine Perfection. My new life . . . perfect divinity is linked with perfect humanity." . . . My new life is "eternal" (Purdom 1964, 189).

This movement has a centre in Queensland, with some fifty resident devotees from Victoria, New South Wales, and Queensland. They are spoken of as Baba Lovers and cite passages from the Hindu sacred books continually.

Sri Aurobindo and the Life Divine: Their pilgrimage centre is at Pondicherry. Sri Aurobindo's father was a medical doctor, trained in England. His philosophy grew from a syncretism of Hindu thought and evolutionary theory. Physical evolution brought mankind to a level of mental consciousness which distinguished him from other animals. He is now on the verge of a still higher stage of evolution. Here is the link between the processes of ascent and descent in divine realization, where mind and supermind meet with a veil between them. With the rending of the veil, the mind receives the divine life and light in supermind, and the soul realizes its divine nature (Aurobindo 1955, 313–23).

In the evolution of consciousness, the "gnostic being" emerges (i.e. our divine being) in which man is alone with God and one with the eternal-self, plunged into the depths of the infinite in communion. From such achievement of "gnostic being," small gnostic communities will emerge and increase in anticipation of a further stage in the evolution in eternity—the divine life (ibid., 916).

In this way, the physical limitations of humanity are conquered, including the conquest of death and the experience of earthly immortality. The means for bringing this about is Yoga. For Sri Aurobindo, the detail of life is so organized as to be consciously directed towards divine evolution.

Sri Aurobindo's use of Yoga: "Integral Yoga" combines traditional Hindu Yoga (deeds, knowledge, devotion, spiritual discipline). Beyond this he has a "subtle metaphysical psychology." The higher self-spirit, psychic being, mental and vital, enclose the physical body, the egoistic self. The liberated being means the psychic level controls the physical:

> The psychic being is formed by the soul to support the mind and body. To grow aware of the psychic being and to bring it forward so that it controls all the levels of the individual, is one of the principal purposes of the Yoga (Donnelly 1956, 71).

The seven "subtle centres" of the body serve to open up higher forces of consciousness. "The object of Yoga is to enter into and to be possessed by the Divine Presence and Consciousness" to the end that "our will and works and life be the instrument of the Divine." (This is an over-simplification but I think it is an accurate summary of what the guru says.)

The divine life theology of Sri Aurobindo has claimed some prominent and scholarly westerners, who turned from Christianity and took up residence at his ashram, having converted to Hinduism. One American devotee acquired an island nearby, built a temple, and lived under the discipline. We have a record of a number of pilgrimages of Western devotees.

The worldwide influence of Sri Aurobindo is known as his "Force." He influenced many political events about the world from his ashram—even to Spain, Turkey, Ireland, and (less powerfully) to Egypt, including events in World War II, according to his biographer, Narayan Prasad.

Sathya Sai Baba: In 1950 an impressive shrine, "The Abode of Eternal Peace," was built and dedicated for Sathya Sai Baba to instruct his disciples and devotees. He was widely known as a miracle-worker. I cite one of his Western disciples on the point (abbreviated):

> Baba heals the sick, the blind, the insane, and casts out evil spirits, converts one type of matter to another ... travels from one place to another ... vanishing at will.... He is there unseen, bringing protection, blessings, help in problems.... He pierces barriers of physical space and time ... reads minds, moves and moulds them in the right direction, bringing as much influence to bear on a person as individual freedom and considerations of karma warrant

(Sai Baba 1968, 100).

In July 1963 Sathya Sai Baba suffered from a stroke, was paralyzed and in a coma for a short time. Eventually after a miraculous recovery, he revealed that the Hindu gods, Siva and Shakti had incarnated themselves in him and that he was now the lord in human form (Kasturi 1968, 74–84).

Many of his devotees lived at Prasanthi Nilayam (Home of Supreme Peace) where he had an auditorium to seat five thousand people, and a settlement where every component has a symbolic designation and regular worship services are held. In 1958 the translation of his messages and discourses had been commenced, and publication of the five volumes in English were begun. He cited frequently from Hindu, Buddhist, and even Christian texts and proclaimed,

> When someone asks you in great earnestness where the Lord is to be found,
> do not dodge the question.... Tell them he is here (Sai Baba 1981, 2:269).

The way to self-realization and god-realization is possible only to him who accepts this authority. His devotees said "Sathya Sai Baba is indeed God, with the three qualities of omnipotence, omniscience, and omnipresence ... the Guru of Gurus, the Vid (Wisdom) of the Vedas, the goal of man, the Supreme Power, and God in all his manifestations" (Suryanarayana 1967, xiii). (That is clearly modeled on Western theology, the creeds and the catechism, and a rather specific attempt to make the guru God.)

Ramkrishna Vedanta teaches the following fundamental beliefs. (1) Mankind, by nature, is divine. The omnipresent godhead is in each of us. Man therefore is God. (2) Man's aim in life is to manifest this godhead, even though it is hidden. Every creature is you yourself. Every soul is your soul. (3) Truth is universal. All religions have the same divine inspiration. They suit different temperaments, but they are the same. (4) Vedanta is impersonal. All prophets and great teachers are accepted, and likewise all personal aspects of godhead that are worshipped in the different religions, for they are all manifestations of the same God.[153] Vedanta really does not seek to make converts, but clarifies thought by appreciation of religion per se.

This is a widespread religion. In America they have major centres in New York, Chicago, Boston, St. Louis, Seattle, Providence, Washington, Portland (Oregon), Hollywood, and Lake Tahoe. They are highly influential in the universities, in the church, and in Western literature. They have over one hundred centres in India and more than fifty in the outside world. In my time, they had an active centre in Fiji. Their main advocacy is that people should know and practise their own form of religion better. Their universalism breaks down however whenever it confronts a religion with a claim of uniqueness and will not accept their notion of pantheism.[154] They have a heavy engagement in social welfare programs.

Swami Sivananda and the Divine Life Society: The headquarters of this movement were established at Rishikesh, an ashram on the banks of the sacred river Ganges. Swami Sivananda was educated in a Christian college and subsequently at the medical college at

---

153 Following Christopher Isherwood, American disciple (1945, 1–15).
154 For the notion of pantheism, see Walt Whitman (1959):

> I respect Assyria, China, Teutonia and the Hebrews,
> I adopt each theory, myth, god and demi-god,
> I see that the old accounts, bibles, genealogies,
> are true without exception.

or again,

> Thee in thy all-supplying, all-enclosing worship,
> Thee in no single bible saviour, merely.
> Thy saviours countless, latent within thyself,
> Thy bibles incessant within thyself, equal to any, divine as any.

Tanjore. He served as a doctor in Malaya, eventually returning to India to live as a pilgrim and ascetic. He came under the influence of Swami Tiswanandi Saraswati, who admitted him to the Sunyasa Order and gave him the name by which he is known, Swami Sivananda Saraswati (The bliss of Siva of the Order which worships Saraswati, the goddess of learning).

He utilised his medical knowledge for the benefit of needy pilgrims, and in a program of strenuous discipline, came to the state of self-realization and then god-realization. He became a writer on spiritual matters, a great traveller and lecturer, conducting congregational chanting, sankirtana. He founded the Divine Life Society in 1936, ran a monthly journal by 1938, constructed a temple in 1943, and a pharmacy in 1945. About the same time, he organized the All World Religious Federation for encouraging dialogue between the religions and sects. In 1948, he founded the Yoga-Vedanta Forest Academy to bring together his disciples and his foreign "seekers." An All-India and Ceylon tour in 1950 enlarged his influence and increased the demand for his writings. He opened an eye hospital in 1957. A worldwide mission was set in operation in 1961. His extensive writings have been interpreted by his successor Swami Chidananda.

One of the movement's major activities concerned the guidance of seekers, sadhakas—foreigners converting to his belief system. Swami Sivananda had advised moderation in this. The foundation of their spiritual development was laid in ethics and rules of health and hygiene. He did not press for complete withdrawal from the world and extended his message to all, whatever their status, although it was still to be a spiritual discipline for a spiritual goal. His message was serve, love, meditate, and realize. First service, as it purifies the earth, but it should be done in the spirit of worship. The goal is "bliss," transcending the physical to realize oneness with Brahman. Love requires practise, non-violence, self-giving. One cannot love in anger. Remove it with discipline. (Even the idea of love has overtones of pantheism.) Meditation is the only royal road to salvation. This is not wrestling in the mind but controlling the mind to let divine thoughts flow (Sivananda 1974, 420).

Realization, Samadhi, is union with the absolute. "The mind melts into Brahman.... Individual personality disappears. There remains Existence alone." The worshipper and the worshipped become one or identical. This is god-consciousness—not just inertia—but a condition of perfect awareness, perfect mental balance, which can be used in the service of humanity. Ignorance disappears. One can know the unknowable, see the unseen, and have access to the inaccessible. This is salvation, moksha.

The path to self-realization and salvation is Yoga, a practical system of self-culture, not a turning from life, but a spiritualization of it. According to Swami Sivananda, it is not itself a religion, but is an aid to religion. Swami Sivananda saw it as being used by all religions (which is in accord with the supposed all-inclusiveness of Hinduism). It implies the development of a spiritual and ethical attitude to life. It does not demand asceticism, but it does require the union of the individual soul with the supreme soul, and the surrender of the individual will to the cosmic will. This is the Yoga of Synthesis. The four traditional yoga, already mentioned, are ultimately all religious.

This attempt to accommodate to different modes of approach might compare with what the Christian sees as his diversity of spiritual gifts and is not a serious problem for the Christian; but for the acceptance of the whole body of yoga theology and its theological underpinnings, one must really view Christianity as one of many valid ways to God—equal with the ways of Vishnu and Siva, for example. There are hidden implications here. One might use yoga as a cultural artifact in finding a way of approach, but the basic theological contention, it seems to me, will always bring one up against the particularity of the gospel. Even if we presume this is not part of the Swami's "moderation" with foreign "seekers," one is still left with a way of salvation as an exercise and not the Person of Christ and His work on our behalf: "the full benefits of His passion" as our communion service expresses it. I might express my objection: there may be many disciplines and ways of coming to Christ; but there is only one way to the Father—namely, through a Person, not a system or exercise.

Swami Chidananda, the successor, was also the product of a Christian college where he was influenced by Christ; but as I read the record, rather than turning to Christ as Lord, he saw "Jesus in Krishna, not Jesus instead of Krishna." The Society promotional material puts it that way (Divine Life Society 1967, 16).

With this orientation, he toured the world. At the time of my source, in North and South America, in Europe, South Africa, and Australia, there were some thirty odd branches quite apart from 137 in India. The Divine Life Society, when it commenced missionary activity in Fiji, came my way as I have described above. Their goals were quite definitely religious, and I did not see any possibility of our respective theology being in the least degree compatible. Nor were our respective sacred literatures on the same "wavelength." Neither did I see where there could even be a dialogue at all, our paradigms were so different. Now I wish to leave these summaries and consider the place of the Eastern personality cult in the Western world and ascertain the extent of the invasion and its significance.

Indian Personality Cults in the Christian Community: The above examples of the Eastern personality cult, in which the guru or holy man becomes the focal point and maybe even deified—either by his own claim or by the declaration of his followers—as they spread through the universities, must eventually impinge on the life of the churches.

This opens up two areas for consideration: (1) the interfaith dialogue, and (2) that of syncretism within the Christian fellowship of believers. I am not concerned directly with the first in this paper, but rather with the second. The former would commence from the Great Commission and the mandate for world mission. The second concerns the nature and continuity of the covenant relationship of the people of God. They are quite different issues and should not be confused.

The common modes of diffusion have been through lecture tours and seminars, retreats, rap sessions on university campuses, the sale and circulation of literature, and the advocacy of certain apparently harmless routines for physical and mental health. Apart from the more direct lectures, most of these may be seen as back doors for entry into the thoughtful communities of the West—and that includes the Christian fellowships.

The secularization of education and the necessity for most Christian young people to pass through the schools and universities means the inevitable exposure of them all to university activities, visiting lectures, campus advocates, and the moral and theological attitudes of teachers. It is inevitable that these new ideas and movements will penetrate into the church fellowship groups, maybe without the parents and pastoral leaders even knowing about them. Thus the growth of syncretism within the Christian fellowships by a kind of spiritual osmosis is a practical problem.

Moreover our political strategy of ever-increasing Asian migration into Australia must only increase this encroachment of Asian theology, and more and more are we being pushed to view our traditional beliefs from a position of minority in our own land. I don't develop these points; I merely make the observation of the inevitable increase of the Asian theological presence in our church life.

The Vedenta Societies, under the Ramakrishna Order say they are not missionaries but "guest teachers," but they are structured after the pattern of colonial missions, and their lectures and seminars are available. They study the Upanishads and the Bhagavad-Gita mainly and use Hindu aphorisms and other literature. They have monasteries and convents, work through ordained monks, circulate journals and publish testimonies, especially those of prominent Western scholars who have adopted their movement. On the social level, they are reasonably easy to work with. They are certainly very like the liberal Christian missions of the 1950s, and would fit their semantic redefinitions of "mission" of that period.

The Sri Aurobindo ashrams have been similar. In particular they have pushed Western converts into their literary activities. They have a graduate school in California giving the MA and PhD, and scholarships for post-graduate work at a Hindu university for students specializing in comparative religions from a Hindu perspective. They run East-West culture centres (one in Los Angeles for example) where they promote "progressive spiritual activity in fields of education, the living arts, philosophy, and religion, and the teachings of Sri Aurobindo, the Integrator of East and West."[155]

---

155 East West Centre Newsletter, 1971.

The Radhasoami Satsang, founded in Delhi (1951) has western supporters in Canada, USA, and Mexico, and when the master travels, his supporters gather in audiences of two hundred to fifteen thousand. He found Christians so shaky in their beliefs that he could safely expound the Bible with his own mystical meanings. (Shades of Valentinus and Marcion at Lyons.) The master, Maharaj Charan Singh, has published a work, St. John, The Great Mystic, with the idea of winning Christians to his cause.[156]

Maher Baba Lovers have retreat centres in England, New York, and other places. They train their leaders in both India and England or wherever. Their metaphysical centres have accompanying bookshops facing the nearby university. They have considerable financial support from prominent supporters in the West, have acquired some nice land holdings including an old mansion. In 1958 he assembled 225 of his foreign "Baba Lovers" from round the world for special instruction. One of his famous presentations to this leadership team was entitled, "I am the Son of God the Father, and God the Mother in One" (Harper 1972, 213–19). In 1962 he brought some forty of his lovers from Europe, Australia, and New Zealand together with three thousand from the East for interaction. After he had "dropped his body," 186 American lovers made a pilgrimage to his shrine in India.

The Divine Life Society is established in many university cities in Canada, the USA, France, Germany, Holland, England, and through Africa and other regions. It stresses the Bhagavad-Gita, the Upanishads, and Patanjali's Yoga Sutras, runs regular seminars in the big cities, and thrusts at political, social, and economic leaders, as well as the religious. It runs an international journal.

In 1972 one statistician in America disclosed that over one thousand university graduates discarded their new caps and gowns and the ordinary pursuits of life and entered the temple disciplines.

ISKCON centres exist in England, Holland, Germany, France, Australia, and Japan. The divine command to the leader was to "spread Krishna Consciousness to the West through the English language." At first he did not take the command seriously, but he was challenged by a commentary on the Bhagavad-Gita which said "A disciple cannot separate the commands of a spiritual master from his life." He was immediately initiated into the Order of Sanuyasa and founded the International Society of Krishna Consciousness. They work through literatureand public chanting. The public display is said to develop their "ecstatic absorption in God-consciousness." They claim to be non-sectarian, that both Hindu and Christian will benefit by chanting the holy name "Krishna," for this is devotion. This was given to the world that mankind may remember God. In worship, the temple, altar, images,

---

156 Citing "Greetings," 1970, in East West Centre Newsletter: "In order to love God with body, mind and soul, we have to concentrate all the attention from the body to the eye centre, which is the seat of the mind and soul knotted together.... It is only when the energies are concentrated at the eye centre that we can love with all our entire being—that of the body, mind and soul." This is really not what the Bible says, but rather what Singh makes it say.

candles, and other adjuncts of worship are used. The question for a Christian with them is whether or not "Krishna" is adequate for God, or whether it carries with it any undesirable Hindu connotations (Harper 1972, 229–35, 243).

The important point is made. Everywhere around the world Hinduism is on the move and the rationalistic Christian community which knows not its biblical heritage is the main target. This is a considerable movement at various levels of faith and practise and through many forms of expression—lectures, chanting, literature, testimonies, retreats, and yoga, any of which could penetrate the Christian fellowship. Not only are we concerned that so many of our adherents have drifted out of the Christian fellowship into the personality cults, but we need to consider why they have left us and what they thought they had found in their new affiliations.

More important still, perhaps, is the nature of the faith shift itself. What do we mean by the fuzzy term "God-realization"? Are we engaging in self-deification? The whole theological and philosophical jargon is abstruse and open to interpretation. Like much Western theology of the period it emerged, it can be made to mean what one wants it to mean. It is "Humpty Dumpty Theology," as Humpty Dumpty said to Alice, "When I use a word it means just what I choose it to mean—neither more nor less" (Carroll 1958). To me it is deification.

Non-Eastern Personality Cults

I do not want that last section to be regarded in any way as anti-Indian. Personally I have high respect for Indians. Were I preparing a list of, say, one hundred great subjects for a bibliography of world figures, there would certainly be some Indians in it, Gandhi and Sadu Sundar Singh among them and possibly Tagore. I owe a debt to Indian thinkers, and I do not exclude the mystics from that list. My own understanding of the concept of "Sacrifice" has been enriched by the poetry of Tilak, but, of course, it was the Tilak whose life had been committed to Christ and knew of the sacrifice of Christ (Winslow 1923). I have many Indian friends from the north and south for whom the covenant relationship is precious, as with me.

On the other hand, there are persons from my own background whom, it seems to me, have jeopardised that covenant relationship and opened themselves to what I have called "self-deification." There are Western personality cults, which are perilously close to the same kind of critical theological exposure. Some of them have large followings. They have absorbed the same kind of people—disillusioned, lonely, spiritually hungry people—with the same felt-needs, and the same spiritual search. Moreover they raise the identical issues for the church which has failed to meet those felt-needs.

On the mission fields which I have visited, the same thing applies to some of the cargo cults, as also to certain Afro/American cults of the big American cities. So this is a worldwide crisis, and we are all in this together. Let it not be taken as affecting cults and personalities of one group of people alone.[157]

Every one of these is a subject for study in itself, and in many cases, the documentation is available. It may be that when a typology for their classification is eventually developed, it will reveal some cultural aspects of differentiation; but it may not—it may turn out to be entirely theological or based on some human universal relating to forms of rationalization. Rationalization and reinterpretation of the Bible to suit the mental attitudes of the expositors may turn out to be the major determinant. It would not surprise me. In any case, inasmuch as I can anticipate it now, I think that Indian mystics will not stand alone but have Afro-Americans, Melanesian messiahs, and Western scholars all in the melting pot together.[158]

Unfortunately I have never set out to research this, but such evidence that has come my way does suggest this to be so. Someone will have to research it soon from the angle of its bearing on the nature of the communion in the fellowship of believers and the covenant relationship.

A number of very unpleasant cults run by westerners have been written up either by journalists or by some escapee from their clutches. In these more often than not, a central person acquires great power, which he uses for his own glorification, even to the use of mind-programming techniques, Swiss bank accounts, and even ritualistic suicide, in one well-known case. There have been cases in which some exhausted victim or person whose home life has been torn apart by their unscrupulous methods has had the courage to write up the story as a warning for others. These make pathetic reading.[159]

Mrs. K—-, "Spiritual Reader and Advisor," had a notice placed in my letter box. Was I tired and sick of being mistreated? Was someone far away making me unhappy? Was I in love but not understood? Was I a hard-working person tired of getting nowhere? Did my husband, wife, or sweetheart mistreat me? Was I having trouble with my family? Did I want to get someone out of my life? And so on; that was only part of it. The notice had an Eastern symbol pictured on it.

I never responded, just put the paper in my file of items on animism. Shortly afterwards, she solicited my interest again, with precisely the same jargon. However the Eastern

---

157 Every cargo cult has its prophet, many of whom become messiahs and eventually are deified. This also happens with white prophets. Some, like Noble Drew Ali, are said to be reincarnations of earlier prophets, Muhammad in this case. According to Fauset, who researched the Afro/American cults, Father Divine's Peace Mission in New York, later Philadelphia, used its own sacred book New Day and regarded Father Divine as God (Father Divine). The United House of Prayer, Washington, used the Bible as its sacred book. Bishop Grace was co-equal with Jesus. (See Table, p. 120.) These need to be distinguished from the normal black denominational congregations.

158 Examples of biblical reinterpretation to suit nativistic movement, see "Hauhau" and "Ringatu" in Tippett (1971b, 68, 70–72).

159 See McCary (1985) for a good but tragic account of the operations of an American personality cult, how its influence and methods ramified through still further cults (e.g., the Jones Expedition to South America) and the struggles of one of their victims to save his family from separation and destruction.

symbol had been replaced by a cross—a Latin cross. Apparently her business (computer or card reading, I'm not sure what divination she used) showed more responses from church people than easterners.[160]

Sybil Leek, in her recent book (1975) on the history of curses and her typology of these things which is on sale in USA, Britain, Canada, India, Japan, and Australia, cites a sample letter, which she says is almost a carbon copy of a huge number.

> For years I have hated my husband, and now I want something done about it. I want you to put a hex on him. I do not care, but get him out of my life.

I merely cite her reference. You can make what you like of it.

And by the way, her own fortunes are so influenced by the planets that she has changed the colour scheme of her dresses. She is going through a planetary change and is more aggressive than she used to be.

What is the theology involved in this kind of thing? They all throw the emphasis on the self. *Do your own thing. Be free. Conquer everything. Be financially successful. Be powerful.* So one thoughtful writer puts it; astrology becomes idolatry when we allow the stars to determine our lives. It is a competitor to faith in God. Astral support is selfish—humans calling on outside powers to master their own destiny and gain power. This is egocentric, the sin of pride, self-fulfillment to personal advantage. Whether it be astrology or sorcery, it cannot come to terms with the Christian life of loving one's enemies or taking up a cross. This also goes for the ouija board and other forms of divination.

Another theological shortcoming about all these things, methods of self-mastery and self-fulfillment, even if they were true or justified, have a wrong time-span. They assume the past is bad and one must escape it. There is little place for all the fine and beautiful things which God gave me through my devout parents, the traditions of my Christian history, and the biblical bases of my faith. They assume things are all bad, that one needs escape, and a new kind of "trip." At the other end, they have no hope for the life to come. Their satisfactions are all in the here and now (if they do indeed satisfy). They are the "empty cup theology" of Omar Khayyam. Ultimately I "turn down an empty glass." This must be set over against the cup of the Lord and the promise of the feast above (Tippett 1973d, 29–30). Remember I am writing for the people of God in the covenant relation; and I am asking what these divinatory practises mean when introduced into the fellowship in syncretism. Even if one comes my way who cannot share my faith how can I help the poor fellow over that last dark river? I never heard of anyone finding his way into eternal life by a ouija board.

Without a past and without a future, without a heart reaching out to those in need, without a willingness to bear a cross—just a selfish hunger for success and money and

---

160 See Animism Clippings Carton, the Tippett Collection, St. Mark's.

power and sex in this present moment—how can anything be more ghastly and more misdirected and ultimately hopelessly unsatisfying than this "Casino Theology," this rationalization of the god of greed?

The Eastern personality cults are at least one point up on this. At least their search for salvation is in more than the selfish present, and they struggle with the time problem and speak in a sense to eternity. At least they are aware of the dimension. Second, they seek a personal solution even if it be the wrong person.

When the Apostle Paul came to Athens—the seat of Greek learning—and found the Athenians worshipping a multitude of religious objects (which is what the Greek says); he found the altar to the Unknown God and proceeded from that evidence of searching faith to expound the truth which went beyond their knowledge.[161]

But Hinduism has been offered the gospel, and the personality cults are evidence of refusal to accept, indeed even to establish other "world missions" in opposition to the Lord. They wanted a gospel on their own terms on a basis of Christian assimilation in Hinduism. That is not on offer. The covenant, is a διαθήκη (diathēkē) of grace, not a business contract on equal terms, συνθήκη (synthēkē), which is not a New Testament term.

Ultimately then all this religious paraphernalia fails to glorify Christ or to bring people to Christ or hold them spiritually united in Christ, and if they were Christian rituals that I should expect. At best they are useless pastimes, but they may be positively evil. Therefore I am disturbed when Christian people turn to them and especially when they rationalize about them in the presence of their children. The covenant relationship is too precious.

It is possible for a Christian experimenting with religious forms outside his known faith to involve himself in syncretism unwittingly, even, for example, in the use of the cross, which we normally regard as a Christian symbol. But this is not always so, and a Christian should always make it his business to understand the symbolism he uses.

I witnessed a ceremony in Guatemala in which several converts surrendered their fetishes before the Christian congregation—ancient Mayan fertility figurines and the like. One man handed over a cross. To me it was a Latin cross, but in discussion afterwards, I learned it was Mayan. It was not the cross of Christ at all. Nor is it generally known that the symbol used by the Peace Movement is a cross with a terrible history, which is as far from the idea of peace as we can get.[162] Moreover its satanic meaning is well-known to those people, yet it has even been used by a Christian priest in a folk mass. It is always dangerous to use paraphernalia and symbols we do not understand, partly because some who witness our actions may understand; but even worse, Christians seeing the symbol in use may take

---

161 Acts 17:23 "beheld your devotions" is actually to be translated literally "looking up at your objects of worship I found also the altar etc . . ." (τὰ σεβάσματα ὑμῶν) [ta sebasmata hymōn].
162 This record from Nero to the Nazi religion has been written up at length. See "How Peaceful is the Peace Symbol," Uplook, and "If you are for Peace Don't Use this Symbol," Christian Life Publications in Animism Clippings Carton, St. Mark's.

a satanic ceremony to be Christian and become involved unwittingly. I have noticed that syncretistic non-Christian crosses are even used by some groups to deliberately misguide Christians. We should never underestimate the subtlety of Satan. Movements claiming to be universalist often incorporate the cross in their symbolism, but there is only one cross of Christ that draws all men unto Him.

Scientology

Somewhere in this study we need to look at Scientology, and perhaps it is best dealt with under the Western personality cults, as everything seems to emanate from, or point to one L. Ron Hubbard. As a boy, he travelled widely in India and China and had contact with Buddhism and Hinduism, with fakirs and yogas—to which some elements of his theology would seem to point (Victoria 1965, 40). A good biographical study of Hubbard is found in chapter 6 of the official Government (Victoria) Report of the Board of Inquiry into Scientology, a major source for this unit. That report suggested similarities with early Gnosticism in the foundation period of Christian history (ibid., 68).

Much of the information we have of the changing emphases and methods of this movement comes from persons who have escaped from its clutches, but on the whole, they are very much intimidated, and he or she is a brave soul who will openly counter them, which is almost as terrifying as being its captive, according to their accounts. One of these courageous persons is Paulette Cooper who has given us The Scandal of Scientology which emerged in the same period as the material reported above (1975, 82–84). These are the main two sources of this unit.

Cooper makes the point that the movement has been subject to changes; that civil action in Britain and Australia have led to shifts in procedure, so investigation needs to set the time of documentation as before or after such and such an act, for example (ibid., 22 25). The shift from its scientific claims to religion is an example of this. The Scientologists' faith in "The Book" (Hubbard's) as a functional substitute for the Bible and other sacred books, the notion of Confessionals, the pattern of witness as mission, tithing, and the worship service are currently all religious acts, although they are all modified to meet the circumstances (ibid., 21, 28, 43).

To go back to the beginning, the movement claimed to meet the felt-needs of people by correcting their problems of mental health, social discord, etc., by bringing them into the world of the "totally free."[163] This was a salvation message—the "only way to salvation" (Cooper 1975, 188). It cut them off from the old life, gave them a new company of friends all occupied with one goal—the world mission of the cause (ibid., 22, 24).

---

163   The subway advertisement read, "Step into the exciting world of the totally free."

Being a secret organization, they were subject to auditions, confessional checks, by which those turning to the movements were exposed—socially, financially, morally (ibid., 27ff.). These intensive interviews utilised lie-detectors (E-metres), a psychological pressure ploy which the Bureau of Standards evaluated negatively (ibid., 145ff.). Persons advanced in levels and the organization operated "Sea Orgs," luxurious yachts where select persons were trained for leadership (ibid., chapter 7).

Hubbard, once a science fiction writer, has described his visits to heaven, Venus, and the Van Allen Radiation Belt (ibid., 21, 161). He restructured time in terms of A.D. (i.e. After Dianetics) and at one time had practised "witchcraft" with the sorcerer and mystic, John Parsons of the Aleister Crowley Cult (ibid., 161).

Most of the persons incorporated into the movement had emotional, social, and domestic problems and were redirected to a new company of persons with mainly the one concern of Scientology (ibid., 187). This "family" construct of "children" under Hubbard's paternalism was smooth enough until the "children" grew up and wanted to leave home (ibid., 187). Only then was the captivity manifest and the significance of the auditing sessions apparent. In some cases, it was discovered that reports of these were annotated "We can use this!" (ibid., 82–83). There was even a prison, known as "The Dungeon" in the basement of the London office for "children" who were too disobedient (ibid., 97). When relatives were antagonistic towards Scientology, they were designated suppressing persons, and listed as "outside protection" and "fair game" in Scientology ethics (ibid., 78). The participant was designated as PTS (Potential Trouble Source) and was commanded to "disconnect" even with a spouse, lover, parent, or child (ibid., 86). Crimes or indiscretions indicated in the security check were used as pressure here to effect the disconnection.

A theological extension of this kind of pressure was achieved by means of their doctrine of time depth not unlike the cyclical view of the soul among certain Asian faiths (ibid., 22). The "thetan," or spirit had lived through many lives, and crimes from previous lives were all recorded. This became manipulative in Scientology. To cite Hubbard himself on the doctrine: "It isn't a matter of believing or not believing that you have lived before. It is a matter of remembering or not remembering." It may be you were a cannibal once (ibid., 37, 91). In any case, the problems you encounter today are many of them due to evil committed in a previous existence by the thetan. Hubbard wrote a whole book on this subject. Thus a person troublesome to the movement might find himself pressured for crimes he never committed at all, which is precisely the error of medieval witchcraft.

That is the way it was down to the 1965 investigation, which found that it was extremely damaging to mental health, that the credentials of its practitioners were invalid, and that its practises were perverted and dangerous (Victoria 1965, 169). Moreover the report had an appendix on brainwashing techniques (ibid., 198–99). Although the case continued for many months, cost a huge sum of money, and involved an appeal which was rejected, within twelve years, this body, discredited as a medical, scientific, and psychological concern, was at work restructuring itself as a religion—not any religion, but as a denomination. A minister of the church of Scientology was appointed in the same state of Victoria, running services, and registered by the government[164] to conduct marriages, etc. A Melbourne newspaper reporter interviewed the minister of the "church" and apparently thought it "fun" to be interrogated with the discredited E-metre lie detector.[165]

According to another newspaper, that minister had formerly been a Sunday school teacher.[166] Outlawed under the Psychological Practises Act, which still applied, the whole thing was possible because the Commonwealth Marriage Act took precedence to the Psychological Practises Act of the State.[167] The new minister said it was a great triumph, insisted they were still "a modern science of mental health," and that someday the world would recognize Hubbard. The minister suggested the old Act had been passed in a "feeling of hysteria" and now the government had "turned a blind eye."[168] The accompanying newspaper photograph shows the Scientology minister wearing a pectoral cross—not quite an orthodox form—but still a cross. Such is the modus operandi of syncretism.[169]

Let us now return to the report of the original investigation. The official statement is abbreviated hereunder (but not altered by the abbreviations):

> Many of the theories and teachings of Scientology are so fanciful that the reaction of the normal individual ... is generally one of amusement and incredulity ... the impression may exist ... that Scientology is just harmless nonsense ... (that) not much harm is done by allowing silly people to have their silly beliefs and carry on their silly practises. Such an attitude is welcomed by the scientologists, for it serves to obscure the real nature of Scientology.
>
> A tolerant "live and let live" attitude is what scientologists fervently desire, for it is on the inertia of the community, generated by tolerance and polite disinterest, that Scientology thrives. (Victoria 1965, 14–15)

---

164 Melbourne Herald report, 19/5/77. (Filed with Report).
165 Ibid. See also Cooper (1975,110–11), "with an air of respectability. Jews, Catholics and Protestants join."
166 Report in morning newspaper. (Filed with Report).
167 Melbourne Herald, 19/5/77.
168 Report in morning newspaper, as footnote 111.
169 Ibid. Cf. Reference on Japanese Cross, footnote 27 in this chapter. This modus operandi of incorporating the cross into the vestments of the Scientologist minister of religion still calls for considerable investigation because of its syncretistic shift from times when it was striving for medical and psychological recognition. In this case I cite from one of their Bulletins (18/7/59):

> The whole Christian movement is based on the victim. Compulsion of the over-act motivator sequence. They won by appealing to victims. We can win by converting victims. They succeeded by making people into victims. We can succeed by making victims into people. (Victoria 1965, 150).

Yet now it is appropriate to gain respectability from Christianity, a new form of attracting converts from the Christian faith by the symbolic suggestion of affinity. This is quite different from Hubbard's earlier statement that Scientology was "first cousin to the Buddhist, a distant relative to the Taoist, a feudal enemy of the enslaving priest" (ibid., 16).

Side by side with this, the Q.C. commissioned to handle the enquiry now set the words of Hubbard himself in which he claimed to his supporters that "incredulity" was "our data and validity . . . and gives us more protection than any other asset." He went on "without a public incredulity we would never have gotten as far as we have . . ."

What have we now on our hands: a personality cult, led by a man with a background relating originally to Asian faiths, a science-fiction writer, discredited as a scientist and mental healer, but now the head of a syncretistic religious movement using familiar forms of religious practise and calling itself a denomination and a church?

This validation of Scientology as a denomination and its claim for religious practise on that basis is, in a way, similar to the action policy of the Navaho Peyote Eaters after years of prohibition under the drug laws. They changed their name to the Native American Church, described the peyote ceremony as their form of sacramental service, and claimed their validity under rights of religious freedom. At the same time, they came to terms with the acceptance of Christ as one of the holy people side by side with Pionyo, the peyote spirit. He was, of course, a holy person "for the white man." The modus operandi for validation was the same, but neither recognized the "one way" claim of Christ.

The study of personality cults through history and across the world, if they have sufficient time depth, tend to show up one of two possible alternatives. Either the personality nominates a successor and we get a prophetic hierarchy, rather authoritarian and despotic, or the movement gets a constitution and becomes an organization—a bureaucracy or an ecclesiastical system. We have numerous examples of each. The former may lead to a kind of deification, the latter to a kind of church, perhaps quite heretical, and normally in-growing. It will be interesting to see what happens to Scientology when Hubbard drops out of the picture. We need to remember however that any cultic movement which has fluctuating fortunes can burst forth into new life again in a later generation. This is what anthropologists call "the continuity of cults." In that case, Hubbard may well be deified. [L. Ron Hubbard died on Jan. 24, 1986—ed.]

As we leave the personality cults, whether they be Eastern, Western, or tribal, none of them lead us to Christ crucified, risen, and glorified. They may all claim to be "the only way to salvation," but none can demonstrate it with credibility. None lead ultimately to the Father of love. If they have a sacred book, it is surely the wrong book. None of them can really establish me in a sure and certain hope for what lies beyond or really transform my life here in the world of my mission. To none of them can I say with confidence what Peter said to the Lord Jesus Christ: "To whom shall we go? Thou hast the words of eternal life." There is surely no other way to the Father!

In what book do I find this word? Whose claim is it? Where can I place my faith? Whose is the grace which responds to it? To whom is the praise and glory given when I worship? No personality cult leads me in these paths. Completely do I agree with Peter, "There is no other name under heaven whereby we may be saved." On this conviction the Bible hangs together. No other personality can fill the bill.

Allegorical Deifications

One aspect of "deification" that cannot be bypassed is, in a way, somewhat allegorical; but it was real enough in Greece and Rome, where human emotions were actually set up for worship in the form of idols. These included the gods and goddesses of power and wealth, war, wine, and sexual love. The New Testament does not deify these but condemns them in terms of the vice deified in the outside society, because each was associated with some appropriate (or inappropriate) behaviour.

Many New Testament passages describing idolatry throw these behaviour descriptives into the passage, so that idolatry and sacrificing to idols are linked with fornication (1 Cor 5:11; 6:9; Eph 5:5), covetousness (Col 3:5; Eph 5:5), lying (Rev 21:8), murder (Rev 22:15), drunken revelry (Gal 5:19–21), extortion (1 Cor 5:10), and so on.

In our present-day world, these are still deified. We may not (with a few diabolic exceptions) set up altars to them, but we worship with intense devotion and relish the gods of power, money, sex, greed, pride, and a little subtly perhaps, even science.

This is possible (it is really more than just allegorical) when the human heart is set on these things to the exclusion of God—when they become the main objects of life's pursuits, our great desires which take us over and possess us. Actually the deep striving for money or power or sex or greed are manifest incarnations of our self-worship. We deify ourselves. We use our skills to subject others, to exploit, to dominate, to control the lives of other people. We enjoy the selfishness of our acquisitions and let the other person go and fend for himself. The stock exchange, the betting ring, the countless manipulations of daily life are the altars for self-worship and self-glorification. I really do not think this is just allegorical.

In the case of science, or any philosophical ideology, social or political, (even if it is by chance good in itself and fitted to serve humanity, improve the social life, and create happiness) can become deified when it dominates our souls, enslaves us, makes us the victim of computer control, and destroys our personalities. Even science, once we commit ourselves wholly to it, can become a god, and not a very nice god at that.

If God gave us scientific skills, it was for service, not enslavement. From the human side, God gives us skills to be His co-workers, συνεργοί (synergoi) or to be His house-managers, οικονομοι (oikonomoi). He expects it to be done responsibly.[170] That is the New Testament view. But scientific knowledge, like money or power, may be used to destroy or enslave. That is to deify it. The scientist or politician or business manager has it within himself to

---

170 For the exegesis of these terms, see Tippett (1988).

make himself falsely into a god, or to be a responsible servant of the Lord God Himself.[171] We have chosen a false "way of salvation," and it is the way of destruction.

This is a situation for theological evaluation. We have deified ourselves. Our avatars are power, money, learning, technical skill, and it is easy to rationalize their value. We are like the astrologer who sells his astrological wares to shape the lives of people who hope thereby to improve their luck, and forget that the Creator God who set the stars in their courses is available "without money and without price." So they "make cakes to the Queen of Heaven" as Jeremiah put it. This is a poor mixed up world which tells not the difference between Creator and the thing created. It is all man-worship in the last analysis. Let us know ourselves, our skills, our mental powers, our scientific know-how, but not treat them as the avatars of our man-worship. Let us enjoy the Lord God and glorify Him, not ourselves.

One thing which comes through to me in so many scientific autobiographies is the way in which they so seldom say, "This was my greatest creation: what a smart fellow I am!" (Journalists, biographers and cyclopedias may put it that way sometimes.) They tell how they "discovered" it. They may have had a feeling it was there somewhere. They searched. They experimented, and then they found. Invariably it was a sudden discovery. Most commonly they come back to the same word, "revelation." They tell of the excitement of that moment of truth. Someone had put it there, and they had found it. They never thought of themselves as creators. Like the great botanist Linnaeus when he first came upon an English heath brilliant with golden gorse, he fell on his knees and glorified God.[172]

What all this says to me is that we need to keep it straight. God creates. We discover. It is God who should have the glory, and we praise. We can deify science, which comes down to man-worship, but that leads to greed, not to praise.

Moreover we lose our sense of responsible management when we lose respect for the Creator Himself. And that is just why this old world is in such a tragic mess.

One of the most powerful presentations I have ever heard, came from an English professor of mathematics on the subject "Nuclear Power and Christian Responsibility." Five thousand Christians stood to applaud a man when it finished. But no one did anything about it. The world leaders went on their old way. Sure, we have to recognize that in the time of necessity God disclosed these secrets to us, that the world of tomorrow be saved from starvation and destruction. But we have seen it as power, and explored it most in the direction of human self-destruction. That is surely human self-deification.[173]

The subject matter of this section really needs a whole book in itself. The first part of the book would need to be biblical, and the third part, after the data base in the sec-

---

171 Ibid., for exposition of "Responsibility under God."
172 For "scientific discovery" as "revelation," see Coulson (1981).
173 See address at World Methodist Conference, Lake Junaluska, 1956. Proceedings (World Methodist Council, 244ff.).

ond, would test the syncretism of this self-worship in the life of the church itself, with its avatars of money and power, as we look at our organizations, our church boards, our investment policies, and the value system that has taken over our lifestyle. That is not to ignore all the good and wonderful experiences of discovering God Himself. It is rather to test our own stewardship of spiritual gifts, our management of church life with responsibility to the glory of God. The question for thought and prayer is, "To what extent does the place of pride, power and money fracture the covenant relationship by this syncretism of self-glorification. Just how humbly are we walking before the Lord?"

There was a day in the history of the church when a man was thrown into prison for his preaching Christ and faith-commitment. He utilised his time writing Christian literature using this allegorical format. He gave us Pilgrim's Progress, which in scores of third-world countries was the best seller next to the Bible in colonial times. He contextualized the gospel for those people. In one of his writings, he depicted the struggle for Mansoul, the city under the control of the devil.

Prince Emmanuel appeals to the bewitched city, "Oh! Unhappy town of Mansoul. Thou hast accepted Diabolus as thy King. Thy gates thou hast opened to him and shut against me." He appeals to Mansoul for their return to him: the same kind of appeal of Yahweh to Israel under a very different figure as Hosea the prophet had appealed to the faithless Gomer. (Two superb cases of message contextualization.) Bunyan lived in a day of holy war and black magic; Hosea in a day of moral domestic degradation.[174]

Sometimes I think the best contemporary effort at this kind of symbolic writing was Lewis' Screwtape Letters. I wonder why one never hears it quoted these days? Perhaps it came too close to home for our rationalizing generation. It hit the mark. And we couldn't take it. I think that both Hosea and Bunyan would have understood.[175]

The Deification of Ghosts

One type of deification which is met in many urban centres to which tribal people migrate must be mentioned, however briefly. This god is really a ghost, more often than not an ancestor. However whether an ancestor or not, it is the spirit of a person highly respected in his lifetime for some skill or remarkable competence. Maybe he was a great priest, a magic-man, a fisherman, a warrior, a house builder, a dancer, a hunter, an orator or storyteller, a poet, or a gardener.

Upon his death he is deified, and becomes a god of the craftsmen concerned. The expert, once renowned in his day, is now deified with a special craft ritual, sometimes just for his son and heir, sometimes for the whole class of craftsmen. The craft cult preserves the

---

174 In Bunyan's most ambitious and last work, The Holy War (1948) in which the forces of the universe battle for Mansoul.
175 Lewis' The Screwtape Letters (1961), a fine sustained metaphor; letters from the Undersecretary of the Father Below to a junior devil on earth, whose job is to confuse Christians.

technical skill and understands the selection and production of quality craft materials. The living and the dead share the common concern. The god receives the worship of those who follow, and they receive his blessing and protection (Tippett 1968, 68–76).

With urban migration, this rural worship is transplanted, and in some countries where medieval patron saints have survived, the animist's craft god may coalesce with a patron saint, in which case the bush worship forms and beliefs may actually take over the veneration of the saints.

In other cases, the bush cult disappears with Christianization, but the occupation, craft, and some of the ritual survive in a modified form. Christian dancing masters tend to come from the dancing master clan. In my time in Fiji, a large percentage of the native ministers had actually come down from the priest clan.[176]

This is important information in distinguishing between Christopaganism or syncretism in conversion movements on the one hand, and truly indigenous Christianity on the other.

When, in the former, the craftsman's ghost is deified and worshipped, his shrine or "locus of power" is normally a tool of trade or one of his finest crafted artifacts. If Christianization has been effective, this disappears. However when large communities—work gangs for example—migrate, the cult may survive to give the migrant craft group identity. This is not rare in the emerging cities of the third world.

When tribal people migrate from rural to town or urban contexts, a meaningful Christian contextualization is called for—work songs, Christian dedications, services of blessing, first fruits, thanksgivings, and festivals of praise to God; but alas, in many centres of third-world migration, the migrants are left to re-establish their old pre-Christian sub-cults to lesser deities and patron saints; maybe even magical more than religious, with no recognition whatever to the Lord God, as Creator, Provider, and Preserver.

Outside a small market town, I walked past a field of rice one day. It had been planted to supply the market gardener with produce for sale in the town. I stopped suddenly staring in amazement at the crop, abundant enough, but completely overgrown with prickly mimosa so that it was utterly impossible for anyone to harvest it. My national companion noticed and felt an explanation was called for. Sheepishly he confessed the gardener had performed an ancient pre-Christian ritual there at the planting. Rather than seeking the blessing of the Lord, he used a fertility ritual, set up a protective magical stone, poured out a libation before the ancestral tree, and placed sacrificial rice puddings before a rustic altar, and called on his gardener ancestor to deliver the goods. He got a good harvest, but never did harvest it.

As I went on my way, the words of Solomon came to me:

---

176 It is surprising how frequently this came up. I found that one could virtually identify a Christian minister in Fiji who had come from the priestly line by his style of public prayer and the way he went about his liturgy.

> I went by the field of the slothful, and the vineyard of the man void of understanding; and lo it was all grown over with thorns, and nettles had covered the face thereof, and the stone wall thereof was broken down. Then I saw and considered it, I looked and received instruction. (Prov 24:30)

As I recall the incident, my companion pointed out that the gardener was not slothful, but his industry was certainly devoid of understanding and misdirected. Our discussion went on to consider Christian functional substitutes for planting, cultivating, and harvesting, giving recognition to God the Provider.

Here were people rural in spirit despite their modernization in the town market—still feeling the need of bringing the supernatural into their agriculture. The church had neglected this in its nurture of converts, and cultivators on the urban fringe felt the void. To meet this, they were returning to the pre-Christian way, and my national friend did not fail to expose the problem.

What goes for the market gardener, also goes for the craftsman, the fisherman, the peanut seller at the bus exchange, the vendor of sweetmeats, and maker of shoes. And as I saw in Ethiopia, it goes for the little blacksmith mending broken pocketknives as he stokes up his tiny fire and asks the fire-spirit for protection in his labour. If God be not honoured in mankind's means of livelihood, the ancestral patron will surely receive the homage and be deified. Maybe his name will actually be associated with that of a Christian saint, and the syncretism be mistaken for Christianity.

Was not Jesus looking at this same problem from another angle in the passage recorded by Luke (11:24–26)?

Conclusion

When Gerald Anderson tried to get yet another article from Hendrik Kraemer on syncretism for his symposium on Christian mission, he was met with a flat refusal, and all he could do was publish Kraemer's letter under the title "Syncretism as a Theological Problem for Mission" (Anderson 1961, 179–82). Kraemer had given years of study to the subject, had probed its theological and practical depths, and had given his work to the world. The Christian world had read it, and accepted Kraemer as the great authority on the subject. Hoekendijk said at Milligan, "Surely he had said it all!" Now he was being pressed to speak again. He argued that another theological statement in itself was "not theology in full, but an amputated specimen of theology" that needed "expression in action and new forms of life." He could only go on pointing out "the creeping dangers of syncretism" and "subtle temptation that will continuously try to eat away the heart of Christian truth." He could go on appealing to the responsible Christian agencies as he had in 1938, and although they had read, they had not responded even three decades later. In frustration and disappointment, he wrote "One more article on syncretism as a theological problem . . . will not cause the least change, because theology and spiritual strategy are usually kept separate."

Like Kraemer, I have tried to break new ground in confrontation of this unwillingness of the Christian church to bring together its knowledge of truth and its strategy in the world. What then can I hope to achieve in a paper like this? It seems to me that preparing a typology of forms of syncretism and its link-up with the religions and spirits should at least demand a consideration of its widespread nature. An awareness of what surrounds us at least demands our intellectual acceptance or rejection of this truth. Or, on the other hand we can "thrust it aside," "refuse to face the facts," "sweep it under the carpet," "pigeon-hole it," "bypass it" (whatever figure of speech we like); in any case our theological belief and Christian strategy are to be utterly segregated from each other. Like Kraemer, I am sick and tired of being told by my religious superiors and boards "not to rock the boat."

The Australian Scene

Anyone with any doubt about the depth of occultism in Australia (the new forms of witchcraft in particular) and its expansion during the 1960s and 70s should read Drury and Tillett Other Temples, Other Gods: The Occult in Australia (1980). It is an exhaustive factual survey depicting the scene rather than taking up a particular position. The persons and parties, organizations, resource centres, and research in progress are all identified, together with occult art and writing. The book is an overview by two writers sympathetic to occultism, though not satanists or familiar with other untreated areas.

There is no doubt about the increasing interest in the occult over the period. Neither is there doubt about the exploratory nature and disagreements among them. That is, there are many processes at work. The book is of more value to occultists as a source reference than for documentation in articles like mine. The implication seems to be that our world is seeking occult "truth" and requires guidance to its reference material for the purpose of selective decision-making. The various networks of occultism are identified, together with their Australian connections. One is impressed with the great number of academic persons mentioned, the conference activities held at Australian universities, and the new dimensions of psychic research discussed. Something is certainly going on. Nothing is static. In passing, from time to time, one is made aware of prominent occultists who have come out of Christian educational institutions, even recruited from Christian clergy. So-and-so is said to have begun his occult pilgrimage by using a ouija board. Be it noted also that one is referred to a body that actually combines Christian and occult linkages.[177]

---

177 An Anglican Commission of Enquiry recognized that the church had ignored the biblical statements about the spirit world "because they were unfashionable," and there was need to get back to "the true basis of biblical supernaturalism." The Commission expressed concern about the paraphernalia of the occult and deplored the space given to horoscopes in the press. The reporters covered all this quite objectively but showed that for many churchmen these were not the real issues of great concern. Manifestly there was no agreement among them, and some were them-

A survey of high school students in Sydney revealed some 80 percent both believing in God and knowing their zodiac signs, some 50 percent firmly believing in Satan and the spirits, having tried to contact the spirits and taking part in séances. About a third have had their fortunes told and have consulted the stars (half of those do so regularly).[178]

We live in a dynamic situation, alive with experiment and decision-making—a kind of "missionary" situation which is possible surely only because the traditional churches are not meeting the felt-needs of their adherents.

The Tripartite Typology

A tripartite typology of syncretism in our midst is a convenient but temporary structure for the analysis of phenomenology in process. It is one way of surveying and listing the forms which exist. It permits our identification of forms and evaluation of their intensity (although as yet we have no tools for measuring this). At the simplest, but most important level, it makes us aware of the issues to be confronted, especially the theological issues. It demands a relating of our belief and action.

(1) The major confrontation of Christ and the religions is found to be a direct encounter, both an intellectual and a power encounter. An earlier generation of scholars has left a great body of comparative literature on the subject, and we are aware of the issues between, say, Hinduism and Christ, mythical incarnations over against the historical event, the linear and cyclical views of the soul, the theories of sickness and healing, the nature of salvation. These have all been tabulated by missionary scholars of the last century and are revived among us now in our homeland since the Asian religions have become missionary, especially in our academic centres.

The issues at stake for the Christian cause are: (a) whether or not the theological distinctives of the Christian faith are to be preserved or merely preserved as intellectual options; and (b) whether the authority of Scripture is still valid, whether Christ alone is the way to the Father. These issues are still relevant, indeed vital, and if this be so, then an awareness of direct syncretistic encounter of the religions is our concern.

(2) The indirect encounter of the religions (i.e. their penetration into Christian practises and processes, thought to be innocuous, but emanating from the religions and bringing an undergirding theology with them, with their intellectual value systems that differ from those of Scripture), not always perceived as religious, but relating to Buddhist, Taoist, and even Shinto values, are accepted for physical and mental reasons and widely practised by

---

selves somewhat Gnostic. After the temporary excitement died down there were few tangible results, and the church was as divided as it had been before. If ever one needed to justify Visser't Hooft's contention that these enquiries always failed through rationalization, here it was. The shouting died down, the "captains and kings departed," and things remained as they were (Church of England in Australia 1975, 154–66).

178   Ibid. The precise statistics are found on p. 160.

Christian people. This is tantamount to admitting that Christ has no answer for these felt-needs. This is in error.

(3) Possibly the most widespread encounters of syncretism in our present world scene (certainly the most pernicious in their threat to human happiness and stability) are demonic or satanic. These may be either organized, corporate Satanism or individually demonic, and prosper because the Christian rank and file refuse to take them seriously. This syncretistic encounter threatens to undermine the whole Christian fabric, destroys domestic bliss, and tears individuals and Christian groups apart. They are experimental or exploitative and receive a hearing because of the unmet spiritual felt-needs and religious voids left by our somewhat innocuous traditional patterns of Christian nurture and counselling and our unreadiness to take seriously either the Christian or satanic power dimensions at hand. The subtlety of the satanic invasion of our day and generation is penetrating and syncretistic.

(4) The tendency of both Eastern and Western personality cults to move from prophetism towards deification is a feature of our century, though not by any means confined to it. It marks a direct challenge of human power to the central and sole authority of Christ as Saviour and Lord, about which we are warned in both the Old and New Testaments. Asian religious mysticism and Western greed, and their acquisition of power over the lives of human society, are false religions which come to us by a slow and demanding syncretism.[179]

To this extent then, the Typology offers a frame of reference for our consideration of the character and extent of syncretism in the church of this current century. But we cannot leave it there. This is only the first stage of classification and description, and there must be many forms and practises not yet identified. It is all so extremely diverse. Moreover it is easier to observe effects and trends than to put one's finger on the precise point at issue. One thing is certain: they all in some way fracture the covenant relationship between the people of God and their Lord. That raises the basic question of what they are thought to offer the Christian that the Lord Jesus Himself cannot supply. It should be obvious that the closer we live to Christ, the less we shall feel the need of this kind of thing.

(5) The cultic presence in our midst highlights the dynamic character of the contemporary mind-set. Our world is ready for major religious change. The spiritual re-formulation of our times will shape the "battles" and blessings of the next half-century, and these are highly significant for Western Christianity. Western Christianity may well be so undermined by syncretism that it is absorbed by an unbiblical heritage and ceases even to understand any covenant relationship. In this case, the blessings and promises (which certainly will not perish from the earth) will pass to some non-Western communion that will accept Christ alone as Lord—if the movement has not already begun in that direction. It

---

179 Cf. Rom 1:20–25.

is not for me to prophesy, yet it is the word of Jeremiah that comes to mind: "The harvest is past, the summer is ended, and we are not saved." (Read the whole passage, Jer 8:18–22.)

Yet the contemporary readiness for religious experiment—the evident ease with which we abandon tradition and innovate with new forms—shows a world with fields "ripe unto harvest" with issues to be won or lost. Our responsibility as the people of God is highly significant. It behooves us to be faithful and discerning in our stewardship under God. One hopes the Typology may assist that discernment and thereby help the faithfulness.

Ultimately, of course, the whole issue resolves itself not purely in "knowing" but in "doing," on our readiness to act on the word of Scripture, and our conviction that Christ and Christ alone is Saviour, that He alone is the hope of the world and the only way to the Father. It was not by accident that the great sermon of Jesus, commonly called "The Sermon on the Mount," which demands maturity from His followers, should be drawn to its conclusion by a parable that differentiates the wise and foolish in terms of hearing and doing (Matt 7:24–27).

9

A SURVEY OF THE NEW SHAPE OF SYNCRETISM IN POSTCOLONIAL MISSION AND MINISTRY AT HOME AND ABROAD: CONTEMPORARY CONFRONTATIONS

Syncretism and Theological Thought

In one sense, this article comes at the end of a long road. The author has been concerned with syncretism in some way or other for the past fifty years, although he did not always designate it by that name. Were we living in a gerontocracy, one would have the right to speak on a basis of experience and hindsight.

However the problem actually goes back to the very beginning when God called forth a people from among all the peoples of the earth to be His own, and established them as His people in a covenant relationship with Him. If we go back far enough, we find Moses engaged in encounter in Egypt—and meet the phrase "My people." From the start, we are involved in a theological matter—a religious relationship. Israel became an entity.[180] Her first laws commence with the statement of this relationship. His people are to have one God and reject all others. At the same time, they were to take over His value system, to be "holy unto the Lord" because He Himself is holy (Lev 11:44; Deut 7:6–9; 14:2).

Wherever and whenever there was a trouble spot for Israel it may be traced somehow to a fracture of that covenant relationship, a breaking of that first commandment in some way or other. This lay behind the episode of the golden calf. It necessitated the confrontation with Baal at Mt. Carmel. It explains the dynamics of Josiah's reformation. It was the cause of the captivity in Babylon and the warnings of the prophets. Its shadow falls over the cross of Christ and explains why thousands of Christian martyrs went to their death before the beasts.[181] It showed up in Christian times in every era of history, in the period of heresies, in the persecutions, and down through the Reformation and the Evangelical Revival. (Rev 2:13; 17:6).

---

180   See Tippett (1979); Ex 20:3–4; 22:18, 20; etc.
181   The point of encounter was their refusal to offer sacrifice to the emperor and confess him as "Lord and Saviour." No polytheism. No coexistence.

To our own day, we may never bypass that covenant relationship and the priority of the first commandment. With the transmission of the faith[182] to the Christian church and its inheritance of the promises, we are ourselves in this stream of covenant relationship. As Peter put it, we are "a chosen generation, a royal priesthood, a holy nation, a peculiar people . . . a people of God" (1 Pet 2: 9–10).

Nor have we escaped it in our own relatively short lifetime. Those in my own age group began the Christian encounter in the days of the Social Gospel, when the person of Christ was "on the line" as it were. On the mission field, it showed up in issues of Christopaganism which still threatens the indigenization of the third-world churches. Always it has called for theological faithfulness and Christian vigilance.

The matter of syncretism as a concept and a specific theological issue was really articulated by Hendrik Kraemer, author of The Christian Message in a Non-Christian World (1938) and other writings.[183] It was published by the International Missionary Council and had widespread coverage at the time. It was widely read and greatly applauded by the right people in the right places—but the missionary cause at large did little about it. This was in the eleventh hour for colonial missions. With any scholar who fights passionately for a cause, what usually happens is that he becomes known as the great authority on the subject. He was cited in PhD dissertations, scholarly research, conference presentations, and sermons. His ideas were accepted as the latest academic statement, but no leader, activist, or movement put his ideas into practical application. Missionary-vested interests swept them under the carpet. Decision-making authorities said, "Yes, some day we will have to deal with this, but not yet. The time is not convenient," and they filed it away for future reference.[184]

Meantime there was a war, and then a period of rehabilitation, with a new body of leaders and their new ideas and a new set of goals. A great deal of strong missionary thinking had come in the eleventh hour of colonial missions—Sidney Clark, David Paton, a revival of Roland Allen, and of course Kraemer.[185] With the war and post-war rehabilitation, they were swept aside and left for some new set of circumstances to bring them to light again. Syncretism was not the only consideration in this position, but it is the one before us.

Now, one must admit that there is indeed a great gulf between a good theological idea and its practical application. It is all very well for the theologian to indicate what ought to be done when the administrator has to implement it in a rather earthly world, especially if the theologian has no administrative "clout," and the administrator is in no way a theo-

---

182 Phillips (1946) shows the continuity through church history. See also Irenaeus (1953).
183 See also H. Kraemer's articles in International Review of Missions, but especially Kraemer (1938).
184 This was exactly the same with such issues as the indigenization of mission field churches, and again with their independence. See Tippett (1967b, 92).
185 Forward thought on Group Conversion fell into this period, especially in China, which today is enjoying the benefits of this policy: e.g. Three-Selfs growth.

logian. In dialogue, one will idealize and the other rationalize, and the issue is bound to be shelved over and over again.

To return to Kraemer then, he confronted the missionary world with the theological truth about syncretism in 1938. Three decades later, he was disillusioned about the effects and the inaction regarding its implementation. Nor was he alone in this. When Hoekendijk was asked to participate in the Milligan Consultation on Syncretism his response was "Do we need another? Hasn't Kraemer said it all?"

Even so, something new was injected at Milligan. The four participants came from four different Christian denominations, four different nations (i.e. four patterns of education), and four different disciplines. At least it was an attempted synthesis of theology, mission strategy, history, and anthropology. So there was a clear drawing together of major differences and methods to move toward new perspectives. Even though the observer-reporting failed to rise above the liberal/conservative theological dichotomy, the synthesis bore good fruit in the missiological exchanges that followed.

Just before this, Kraemer had been approached to write on syncretism as a missionary problem in a theological symposium and had declined to do so. The editor had to be satisfied with publishing his letter of refusal so that we know how he felt about it.

After Kraemer's passionate efforts at the theological level had brought no material results, the reflections in his letter are significant.

"A sound theological idea," said Kraemer, "is not only an intellectual delight," but it is also "the most practical thing in the world. This indissoluble oneness of clear thought with vigorous action belongs to the essence of true theology." He went on to relate this to syncretism, which he considered the major issue of the East/West encounter. He insisted that it was "not merely theoretical" but "eminently practical because it decides the whole attitude of life and its directive ultimates." And again, theology in itself (i.e. what the isolated treatment of syncretism as a theological problem for mission often amounts to) is not theology in full, but an amputated specimen of theology. Full theology includes expression in action in new forms of life. From this, he expanded into the idea of "the necessity and inevitability of clear-sighted, Christian confrontation with the creeping danger of Syncretism," and eventually he said, "one more article on Syncretism as a theological problem for mission will not cause the least change, because theology and spiritual strategy are usually kept neatly separate" (Anderson 1961).

So he declined the invitation to write the article, but his response on his choice not to do so is an insight on the subject. Moreover he ended his letter with a hope and prayer for "the awakening of the responsible agencies to the fundamental necessities."

Personally I feel that such symposia do keep the fundamental issues before us, educate the rising generation of missionaries and strategists, and open new avenues for synthesis.

One might add that Visser't Hooft, who left us another fine work on syncretism, No Other Name, was also disgusted by the way our dialogue so often led to rationalization and inaction. He pinpointed this in each period in which he assembled data for analysis.[186]

Several things are now apparent in all this. First "creeping danger" suggests a situation which is certainly not static. We may always be confronted with syncretism in some form or other, but it may be expected to vary from one historical context to another and from one culture to another. It is never adequate to be just academic about this. Some form of action in the world situation is always called for.

A diachronic study of the precise forms of syncretism met through Scripture history, considering each historico-cultural level, shows both the basic continuity of syncretism and the fact of its ever-changing forms. Syncretism was one thing in the wilderness, another in the oriental kingdom, again something different in the Babylonian captivity and still different in the Graeco-Roman urban churches. I have examined this elsewhere, as indeed did Visser't Hooft also.

If this were true for the people of God in scriptural times, it must also have some significance for us, for example, as we pass from the colonial to the postcolonial eras, from competitive empires to world computer technology and atomic power. True, many of the old colonial problems are with us still, but others we have not met before. To this end, then, I speak as a person with one foot in yesterday and another in tomorrow. The lessons my generation had to learn still have to be learned today, but their shapes are different.

The Changed Face of the Postcolonial World

Many of the old imperial influences of British, French, Dutch, German, and American colonialism have either vanished from the scene with the emergence of independence and liberation movements, or are on the way out. In the process, responsibilities are passing to the liberated people themselves. They are finding a new set of problems of their own. On the other hand, there have been great migration movements from those countries to the homelands of their old paternal rulers.[187]

These migrations from the old colonies have changed the face of the countries to which they have migrated—the old homelands of the mission-sending churches. Britain and Australia suddenly find themselves multicultural, with their traditional values suddenly shattered. The West Indians in Britain and Asians in Australia, even more than the

---

186   See Visser't Hooft (1963) in which he examines syncretism at different periods and places as a sequence.
187   Migration is always a major factor in social and religious change. Witness the impact of slavery on the Americas—the establishment of spiritism which has over six hundred practising cults in America today; and the forms of Christo-paganism, peculiar to Spanish America, with the mixture of African gods and Catholic saints, a well-researched area (Herskovits, Metraux, Bastide, Johnson and many others).

Spanish-Americans in California and Cubans in the southeast of America, are re-shaping the countries concerned.[188]

Or to put it in another form: suddenly the fastest growing religion in Australia is Islam. Every here and there, a new mosque suddenly begins to take shape. A new body of Buddhist literature, written often by westerners, begins to appear. Indian personality cults circulate their literature in public places. Hare Krishna dances are often seen in the streets. An Asian missionary travels on my own bus with a bag of tracts. Yoga is practised in the church halls. Many of these are quite manifest, others are growing secretly by personal witness.

I have to send to Sydney for certain office equipment and items of special sizes; but I can obtain any kind of occult equipment by just going down the street. Horoscopes and tarot cards are at hand. Although 80 percent of our high school students still vaguely believe in God, there is not that percentage in the churches, and more than that number can tell you their zodiac sign. Over 50 percent believe in spirits, so the scientific agnostics have not won them all yet. About the same number have tried to get in touch with the spirits and participated in a séance somewhere. These figures were roughly the same in two Australian capital cities.[189] Sorcery, wrongly called witchcraft, is thereby legalized. One could go on and on for the whole article, but the point is made.[190]

Some of these items represent direct missionary invasion. Others are of the creeping syncretism type. Some of them win converts away from the churches. Others are practised within the church companies. Some are tolerated in coexistence. Many of them have specific targets. Many are bypassed by Christian leaders with a nonchalant "What's really wrong with them?" A gruesome book could be written about those who had started on the slippery trail with a ouija board. Worst of all, I do not see how we can even think of the covenant relation in this atmosphere. If there is nothing else wrong, the focus itself is certainly wrong.[191]

---

188 Multiculturalism is a major political and religious issue in Australia. Islam, Buddhism, Hinduism, Taoism, and a host of Asian cults, philosophies, alternative medicine, meditation, and self-realization programs are vended in every city. Their religious underpinning is often latent, and Christians as individuals and groups are exposed to syncretism without being aware of it.

189 Survey conducted for a commission of enquiry (Church of England in Australia 1975). Sydney and Adelaide are the two capital cities referred to here. See Drury and Tillett (1980, 160).

190 This legalization of the practise of sorcery because it is wrongly called witchcraft is due to the passing of laws aimed at solving the medieval witchcraft injustices. It is a case of relieving one error by creating another just as bad. Sorcerers now call themselves witches and practise openly, sell their wares, advertise, and are available for their evil purposes. Known as "white witches" they are disowned by the Satanists. They make, use, and supply voodoo dolls and coloured-headed pins for working evil, and are quite open about it, both on television and in their autobiographies. Leek (1968), etc.

191 Satan surely exploits the incredulity of the many church people who just will not believe how slippery this trail really is. This point was brought out by the official inquiry into Scientology, and a statement of its leader was cited on the matter. Hubbard told his followers that "without a public incredulity we would never have gotten as far as we have."

Many of these things start in our secondary school and higher educational institutions. I mean the exchange of ideas takes place there, and the readiness to experiment is there; the literature from astrology to satanism is circulated there, and although I have not researched it, most of the agnosticism I have met (vocal on the matter) is there.

To me this is the most open mission field in the world today. Moreover it is a field open for harvest, as Donald McGavran would say. Witness: more than 80 percent believe in God, but are vainly seeking Him in the occult and satanism. Here are the aggressive programs, the wild futile hopes, the seeking, the writing, the philosophical ideologies, the crack-pot experiments, the dangerous rituals, and the Eastern personality cults offering a human messiah as an alternative for Christ. This is not secularity. It is not irreligion; it is just plain wrong religion. It was the same in America in the 1960s in the drug cults when Anton La Vey declared the Satanic Age had begun.[192]

The point for this paper is that so many of these offer solutions that start by running alongside our faith. This coexistence is based on the idea that Hinduism, for example, is all-inclusive and big enough to absorb Christianity without injuring it. Even were that true (which it is not), it is not big enough to absorb Christ. We get into trouble by regarding Christianity as a religion among other religions. I do not offer anybody Christianity. I offer him Christ Himself as Saviour and Lord, the only way to the Father. So I come back again to the particularity of Christ, as the critics call it.[193]

The strange thing about it all is that here in Australia, Asian immigrants have freedom of religion, inasmuch as they can seek to missionize Christians. Conversely, since the independence of these Asian countries, an Australian often cannot exercise that same freedom in their homelands any more. They can be teachers or doctors maybe, but let them seek conversions to Christ, and that is another story; very quickly one will find a visa at stake (Tippett 1973c). So the postcolonial scene is completely changed, and the mission field is now often within our own land.

I would hope that somewhere your discussions would focus on the fact of the mission at home, within the churches themselves, because it is ultimately there that the syncretism begins and takes root. It is there in the covenant relationship for individuals and the corporate group of people of God that the first crack appears, and the covenant is fractured. I hope you will recognize how utterly theological this issue really is.[194]

---

192   Anton La Vey, founder of the satanic church in San Francisco made the proclamation. "The Satanic Age has commenced" in 1966, soon after God had been declared dead by a well-known churchman (Lyons, 1970). See also Harper (1972).
193   See Daniélou (1962, 17–18), Forsyth (1908, 32–33), Vicedom (1963) on Yoga, as the greatest ersatz religion in the Christian sphere.
194   Several researchers have gathered case studies of tragedies in the Christian context that have commenced with this type of "playing with fire." For a precise statement of the theology, see Daniélou, Forsyth, Vicedom, Visser't Hooft and others.

Here in Australia, we have come to see that Asian migration is more and more inevitable. The distribution of the world's population and the production of food being as they are, we have no option to challenge it. Moreover we know that this means some dramatic changes. Our own population balance will change. We Christians will become a minority in our own land. We will work from a position of certain man-power weaknesses. We have some grim possibilities to face as we look to the next century. The creeping danger of syncretism suddenly becomes a somewhat terrifying issue. Somehow we have to get back into the spiritual dynamics of the New Testament church which worked from a minority position. The cultural context will be peculiarly our own, but the vision has to be New Testament. What exactly does Peter's description of the people of God mean for us? Sure, the face of mission changes dramatically. Every land with a growing multicultural population is confronted with its own developing form of syncretism, and the responsibility on the inner ministries of the people of God becomes more and more significant.

The Western religious world now is confronted by the fact that the tide has begun to flow from East to West. Its spiritual panaceas are broad, absorbing, polytheistic or pantheistic, and always themselves syncretistic. Its sole monotheistic offer is itself quite syncretistic. In no way can it fit the first commandment. Its ideas of incarnation are mythological and not found in God's action in history. Its ideas of spirit, so often offered to us as a universal solution and ultimate absorption, is far removed from the Spirit witnessing with our spirits that we are sons of God and joint heirs with Christ.[195]

Offers of alternative medicine are many, and offers of physical relaxation have a lightly-veiled theology of a harmony and balance between good and evil quite incompatible with Scripture. Programs of self-realization are based on a focus which can only lead to the deification and worship of self. They solicit our support in letter box campaigns. They advertise seminars and courses. They rent offices and establish centres about our cities. Sometimes disclosures are suggested in the small type of their advertisements, but normally one advances through several levels before one confronts their ultimate doctrine. And often hidden in the background is a cyclical view of the soul.[196]

The tragic thing about all this is the way in which the missionary drive of the so-called great religions of Asia to win the West came just after Bultmann's demythologizing thrust, while the European world was reading that "God was dead," and the missionary was being told to "Go home," and we were starting to talk of the "secular city." Could it have been

---

195 The idea of the flow of religious thought from East to West was pointed out by the Eastern philosophers themselves. See Harper (1972). It is a feature of Eastern personality cults.

196 For the relationship of syncretism to the covenant relation of the people of God, see Chapter 7 in this volume where syncretism is seen in biblical terms as "making a covenant with other gods," as "playing the harlot," and as "sinning a great sin." The psychodynamics of biblical incidents are examined and the focus in the second temptation of Jesus was seen by Him as an attempt to challenge His authority as God and turn away the purpose of God for the salvation of the nations. The cults themselves are seen as rival κοινωνια (koinonia). See Tippett (1973d, 25–33).

that the West was so advertising its spiritual bankruptcy that we made the Asian thrust inevitable? The confluence of events was so startling that it could hardly be by accident that the East began specifying alternatives for so many distinctives of the Christian gospel at this point in time.[197] One could not really prove this, but the confluence is certainly remarkable enough for us to focus on our Christian responsibility for so advertising to the world that the covenant relation of the people of God was fractured. No doubt there was a letter from Screwtape to Wormwood on the subject at that time in the Satanic Archives.

What I will be more dogmatic about is that here is a great truth: Show to the world that the covenant relationship means little to the people of God, and you open the door to this creeping syncretism; Satan knows full well that before long he has you "hooked." One could produce scores of case studies of broken homes, broken lives, and broken church groups to demonstrate this. As we face the postcolonial era with the wind blowing from East to West, we had better understand the meaning of being a people called out and being holy unto the Lord.

Now, I recognize that I have been talking rather negatively, more or less as if the forces of Christ were in retreat. I know, of course, that even when the pressure is great against us, we are not literally in retreat. The prophets warned the people of God in this way. They did not listen and went into captivity. The message however always had that remnant that was saved. When one generation is faithless and pays the price, even from captivity, a new and faithful one is being born.[198]

The mission of God will go on to the end of the age, and He has promised to be with us. I have no doubt about that. But we have been asked to focus our thoughts on syncretism, and that is one of the most negative aspects in all of Christian mission. It is the point of our vulnerability and the point where our human frailty can be most easily exposed. Our training in the Christian warfare must prepare us to stand firm at that point, clad in the whole armour of God, for we wrestle not against flesh and blood but against principalities and powers (Eph 6:10–12).

If the casualties have been heavy, we need to ask ourselves honestly just why this has been so. When I run through the tragic list of apostates whose downward course began with seemingly innocuous experiments that were supposedly "just a game," and church leaders said "What's wrong with it?" and let it pass, I have one nagging question: What was wrong with the church itself? Why were they not led into a covenant relationship with Christ? Why did they have to experiment at all? How did we fail to make clear to them that Christ is all we need? I know of Christians who started out from ouija board games and

---

197 We note also that much of the writing on Eastern faiths which finds its market in university circles comes from western converts. This is especially so in Buddhism and Hinduism, e.g. Isherwood (1945) et al. See Tippett (1973a).
198 Some of the most severe prophetic oracles of judgement against Israel end up with the reassurance of God's determination to restore the covenant relation and His purpose of salvation. See Hosea and Jeremiah.

ended up as practising sorcerers, of a missionary who turned his back on God and took up with a spiritist medium, of more than one minister of religion who is currently an occult leader.[199]

I cannot answer my question, but it comes back every time I see a Christian home torn asunder by some creeping syncretism that started in an almost innocuous way. An utterly terrible book, The Compleat Witch (La Vey 1971), that aims at disrupting marriages by sexual bewitching, indicates the simplicity of the road into witchcraft via astrology. If I have only one sentence to say to you, let it be: Don't treat Satan lightly. He surely knows how to handle creeping syncretism.

Perhaps I have concentrated too much on this aspect of syncretism in our midst; if so, it is because of the shocking cases that have cast their shadows across my path. It does seem to me that some of the major confrontations of Christian mission and ministry in postcolonial times will involve these matters, and they are heavy on my heart. However this is really only part of the picture, and before I finish, I should like to list a brief Typology to help our focus on the issues at large.[200]

Causes of Syncretism in the Church Which Need Our Attention

(1) The first cause lies in our own life of faith and practise. In a way, we are ourselves partly responsible—I mean theologically responsible. There is this whole matter of relationship with Christ, and that is a personal matter. It is theological, but it is pastoral theology not just systematic reasoning. The more I cultivate my personal relating to Him, the less I want to experiment with questionable things. This is not to cut myself off from the world; it is rather to take Him with me wherever I go in the world. I do not seek to introduce people to a church system so much as to the Jesus who is all the world to me. I cannot even face the world without Him. The moment I get separated from Him, I feel the syncretism beginning to creep in. I see no other way to the Father's heart of love and His abundant grace but through Christ alone.

(2) The second cause of syncretism lies in our failure to translate our beliefs into action. We dialogue. We rationalize. We shelve the matter for a more convenient season. We fail to repair a defect in the covenant relation. Here we have a moral responsibility as the Lord's house-managers (stewards). How often one weeps for having left a word unsaid when it might have been said! Again the fault is with us ourselves.[201]

(3) There are direct and indirect satanic forces at work. They call for our alertness and vigilance. Again we might have said a word, a word of encouragement or caution, but we

---

199 See Tippett (1988), the first case study.
200 Anton La Vey (1971) told his followers that "Belief in astrology on the part of others (italics his) is one of the best magical weapons on which any witch can rely."
201 For the husbanding of our spiritual gifts and the meaning of our stewardship responsibility, see Tippett (1988), Chapter 7.

let it pass. It might have been received and helped someone make an important decision. Even if not received, it was rightly said—a prophetic ministry. The New Testament word is "Watch and pray." Each of us can witness in his own way. Some of us excel with apologetics. Some can be only vigilant, and watch and pray. The word comes hard from us, but it is never lost.

(4) The social structure of our academic, scientific, and often agnostic system, with its dogmatic supposedly scientific bias against religion, is something we need to combat actively. It tends to shape an intellectual climate especially among young "half-baked" academics. This agnostic intellectualism has suffered a few rebuffs in recent years. Several disciplines have reached out to data that is not measurable and hard to document, but recognized as reality. We have the academic equipment to deal with this quasi-scientific mental-set. We ought to be ready to present the faith in terms of our disciplines to our peers. There is a wide field for mission here, and its witness is urgent.[202]

(5) The experimental mood of the rising generation has its good points, but it also has its dangers. The sudden availability of the fantastic resources of wealth, power, technology, know-how, and sex can be appropriated by those who have not the maturity to handle them. It may lead to the self-glorification of human power and indeed the worship of self. This can become a most vicious form of syncretism.

(6) Finally there are the direct thrusts of the religions, especially those which are openly missionary, some at the level of their philosophical superstructures and others at the level of grassroots animism. With them we may place the magical systems, not that they are really religious, but because people wrongly classify them together. The theology of the religions is often latent rather than manifest. The magic is frequent and manifest in the syncretism we confront daily.[203]

This does not mean that the old colonial forms of syncretism spoken of as Christopaganism or spiritism have been disposed of. Indeed they are as active as ever. Moreover with the migration of rural people to urban centres, tribal religion and bush magic have taken root in the cities, and urban missionaries should see to it that their training provides a good course in animism which percolates into the new urban lifestyle, its trade, crafts, markets, sport, and personal relations.

A good example of this process at work is found in Solomon Islands Christianity, in which a plantation town complex where a new network of sorcery and counter-sorcery developed and invaded the lives of the Christian migrants (Tippett 1967b, 341–45). This

---

[202] See typescript paper at St Mark's on "Task and Method," bound in Vol. 198.
[203] Religion is the appeal to supernatural resources beyond the person himself—prayer, worship, sacrifice, etc. Magic is the manipulation of rituals to achieve specific ends. Both speak to a person's felt-needs, but the attitude of the practitioner and the source of power or skill are quite different. See Malinowski's contribution (1962, 256–67) to B.B.C. Symposium on Science and Religion, Sep/Dec 1930.

migration was linked with the economics of a recruiting labour system for plantations, people being recruited from different localities, some Christian and others not so.

Much migration was due also to the recent wars at and since mid-century. Returning troops brought magical practises from the war localities and established them in their urban homelands, many of them on the fringes of communities of long-standing Christian practise, so that the lifestyle of the people of God was very much disrupted by this syncretism.[204]

A rather irresponsible generation of Australians having sought their excitement in Asian holiday centres, like those who frequently seek adventure at or near Kuta, in Bali, for example, have returned to their homelands loaded with magical and satanic ideas and processes. Much of this, although only on the fringe of the church life, does enter into it with unfortunate results.[205]

Is There Any Difference in Colonial and Postcolonial Syncretism?

So we live in a day of dramatic change! What does it mean to pass from the colonial to the postcolonial age? Are the things you face today and tomorrow really any different from those I have faced in mine? Culturally, of course, the difference is tremendous. I saw the motorcar replace the horse. You see the launching of spaceships. But really, it is not so much that we move from one era to another, but rather that we are continually moving. I was confronting movement during World War I, just as you are today.

There always have been periods of going and coming, with caravans trading and armies moving from place to place. The movement of peoples has always meant the cross-fertilization of cultures, the confrontation of religions, and the mixture of ideas. The

---

204 There was a time in Fiji when the writer became aware of an extension of magical performances, new in type. At least they were not Fijian. Deeper examination brought to light the fact that the rituals had a Solomon Island pattern. They turned out to be innovations brought home by Fijian troops who had served in the Solomons. They were mostly identified in new suburban areas developed for increasing population—new housing areas.

   A feature of the changing shape of an Oceania missiological library is the new categories of Asian migration material: "Indians of the Dispersion," "Chinese of the Dispersion," etc. This has just as profound an influence as had African slavery in the New World of an earlier period of history, and a religious influence at that: spiritism in one case, Hinduism and Islam in another.

205 The Hinduized animism of Bali, which has every imaginable aspect of religious phenomena and power encounter, is worth a whole book in itself. I met with a Filipino Catholic priest who was deeply involved in power encounter with the spirits as an exorcist. He showed me a whole cupboard of fetish-type paraphernalia surrendered like votive offerings. He had charted the countryside and identified the power centres of the magical practitioners with whom he was dealing. I saw a huge mural painted by a man who had been healed, in which he tried to depict his demonic experiences and deliverance.

   From the same magical environment, I discovered a number of Australians of questionable responsibility holidaying in a locality nearby, more famous for nude beaches, but busy "looking for kicks" by dabbling in sorcery and other arts, and collecting cultic material for importation into Australia for magical business. They hung round the fringe of the surfing circuits and were a good example (or bad one) of how these magical arts are transferred from land to land. I saw enough of this to realize that it was a subject for study in itself. Some of the encounters were quite dramatic and I saw evidence of the Filipino priest's power which was always in the "name of Christ." The arts practised were no doubt very old; but the export into Australia was an innovation of our times. Syncretism is moving into the urban West. Sooner or later it must strike our Christian youth.

postcolonial era is really no different. Syncretism is no new thing, and that is why the Bible takes it so seriously.

We study the New Testament, and we find the apostles citing a version that is recognizably different from the ancient Hebrew form. There has been a movement, a transition, the development of new linguistic forms—the early forms of Hebrew and now in the Koine Greek. Change is an ongoing thing, a transition, not a sudden jump from one era to another.

Trade centres like Corinth were living proof of continuing cross-fertilization of culture, with two harbours, one pointing to Italy and the other to Asia, a route north to Macedonia, and one south to the Peloponessos, with trade, theatre, language, and religion mixing together in manifest syncretism, so that the literary characters speak of this ever changing vulgar syncretism by a new verb invented for the description—"to Corinthianize."[206] We do not wonder that it was to the Christian κοινωνια (koinonia) in this city that Paul gave an oratorical barrage of demands for holiness in the Lord.

Multiculturalism, international trade, sexual facilities at port cities, rising and falling warfare, organized tourism (and this there was in New Testament Greece), the technological increase of speed, and the greater simplicity for travel, virtually assure now, as then, that the postcolonial world, which is our own mission field will be multicultural and syncretistic. This is the world into which Christ is sending us in our day—our inescapable mission field.

Our front line κοινωνια (koinonia) will need to treasure and safeguard that covenant relationship with Him, if it is to be a front line centre for power renewal, and if we are to be good soldiers of Jesus Christ rightly dividing the word of truth. The group requires more than its own powers. The covenant relationship is precious and must be kept loyal to Him. So, time after time, the test falls back on ourselves, our loyalty to Him who alone is the way to the Father.

P. T. Forsyth said in his day, which was a lean time in missionary action, that "the recent decay of missionary faith has gone with a genial creed of much sensibility, but of no grandeur, and little power" (1908, 32-33). Visser't Hooft, who studied through several periods of religious syncretism in sequence and found each one culturally different but spiritually identical, found the way of compromise, or rationalization, and of syncretism powerless, because it had no fixed centre, and therefore no point of reference. It is this centralization of faith and values in Christ which proves to be all-important through every period. Cultures and times change, but the fixed central point of reference—never! (Visser't Hooft 1963, 89).[207]

---

206 The Greek word is κορινθιάζομαι (korinthiazomai). It was used by Aristophanes to describe a state of general whoredom.
207 See also Daniélou, Vicedom et. al.

In another paper, I have researched the changing cultural pattern through the Scriptures—confronting a golden calf in the wilderness, the worship of Baals on Mt. Carmel, the reformation under Josiah, the urban multiculturalism of Corinth, and so on (all entirely different contexts), yet the first commandment and the covenant relationship of the people of God are a continuity running through the whole diachrony of culture change. Thus the changes of the postcolonial era may be expected to change our new confrontations culturally and intellectually, but the spiritual battle will be identical.

As I listen to a great many church groups in our time, here are some of the voices I hear:

> Man is sufficient. He has the capacity to save himself.
> This is the hour for drawing together all races and religions,
> remembering that as God is One everywhere, mankind is one; all
> religions are one, indeed we ourselves are part of God. Make your prostrations
> before the Supreme Brahman; develop the
> Atman within you. Realize yourself, and know your godhead.
> Let yourself go, and let this spirit possess you.
> God is all around you, and you are part of God.
> There is nothing wrong with it. It does nothing to harm your relations with
> Christ.
> I do it purely for health and exercise—it isn't spiritual.
> I felt a cone of power above me.
> Step into the exciting world of the totally free.

That is a sample only. Everyone has a context of its own, which I have studied enough, at least, to recognize. Each one I know can fracture the covenant relationship. Does the apostle speak to us still:

> Ye cannot drink the cup of the Lord and the cup of devils
> (1 Cor 10:21).
>
> What fellowship has righteousness with unrighteousness?
> What communion has light with darkness?
> What concord has Christ with Belial?
> What part hath he that believeth with an infidel?
> What agreement hath the temple of God with idols?
> (2 Cor 6:14–18).

There was a way, it is true, in which the apostle related to people out in the world and in cultural situations. He had a good standing with the church at Corinth—otherwise he could never have addressed them so firmly as this. But Paul saw people as bonded together by their value system. This is something not conditioned by the culture as different from that in another culture; but as fellowships within a given culture. He speaks of the cup of the Lord as over against the cup of devils, of the fellowship of the righteous as over against the fellowship of the unrighteous. These are value-system communions within the same culture—the fellowship in Christ as over against the fellowship in Buddha. It is not the culture that is on trial here, but the bonding of people within any given culture. We are in the area of spiritual values, of spiritual attitudes, of the spiritual quality of our lifestyle—in other words, how we walk with Christ, how we relate to Him as covenant people.

At the area of cultural interplay and interaction, there will always be some mixing. Without that, communication itself is difficult. Witness itself will be defective. But whatever the cultural form of my witness, it is in the relationship with Christ that one's witness is ultimately evaluated. It is certainly bad if we plant foreign churches that never grow, and do so in a language foreign to the worshippers; but it is infinitely worse if we give them a foreign social philosophy or intellectual theology that never brings them into a real relationship with Christ. That is syncretism. And this is always our battle and will be through the postcolonial era.

And this is why both Paul and John formed the habit of warning Christians to keep clear of idols (1 Cor 6; 1 John1:21).

The Fixed Centre and Point of Reference

One is continually being made aware by Christians who obstruct the point of view I take on these matters that I make things difficult for any interfaith dialogue. Of course it is a difficult matter, but I didn't make it difficult. There is nothing I have said that is not Scripture-based. It is the theology of Peter, Paul, John, and Jesus that they find hard to handle. Moreover there are two issues that the Christian cause will be confronting continually throughout this postcolonial age: syncretism within the fellowship and the Christian mission in the world. I do not want to deal with these issues in this paper; they are subjects for their own research. However they are the "bone of contention" because they "make it difficult for interfaith dialogue." When Visser't Hooft says syncretism is always accompanied by rationalization that holds up Christian action, this is what he means: Time after time, we refuse to deal with syncretism at all because we cannot separate it in our minds from interfaith dialogue and the Christian mission.[208]

I have tried to look at syncretism as a "thing in itself" and to evaluate it in terms of biblical values and directives. I look for a "universal," i.e. a value that is not pinned to one

---

208 Many critics who line up with the cause of interfaith dialogue do so in opposition to the idea of Christian mission itself, in spite of the fact that the Christian regards it as a mandate from Christ. At the same time they fail to recognize the equal (and sometimes greater) aggression of the non-Christian religions to win over Christians. It was built into Islam from the beginning (e.g. Jannisaries). It is programmed by the Eastern personality cults, from Ceylon World Fellowship and many of the modernist movements. I myself have met eight or nine movements face to face in my lifetime, Divine Life Society, Arya Samaj, Sōka Gakkai, and several Buddhist academic movements. I have space here to document only one example, but can supply others. Here is a quotation from a Muslim book, "The task of shattering the cross to pieces demanded that, just as Christian missionaries had been penetrating to the nooks and corners of the earth, Admani missionaries should roll the tide back, and carry the fight into the homelands of the Christians themselves. The wind is now beginning to flow from East to West" (Ahmad, 1965).

time only, maybe back in early Old Testament history and its cultural setting. I have found such a universal in the covenant relation of the people of God. I know that to isolate syncretism from the whole world situation and to look at it as "a thing in itself," whatever the context, is a recognized method in science: to study a thing as an entity without context to learn about it and then look at it again in specific contexts. This is academic because in reality it takes the context to give the meaning.

By this method, I learn the fundamental importance of the covenant relation. Then by looking at a diachronic sequence of biblical situations, they all assume new meaning, and I see just how universal this concept really is.

At the same time, when folk gather to discuss syncretism and they refuse to do so academically, but insist on interpreting everything in terms of interfaith dialogue, (which is another subject to be discussed as "a thing in itself" sometime), we have what the man in the street calls a "red herring." The subject is confused. The rationalization defeats the whole purpose of the research. When we have discovered just what syncretism is, and after that, just what interfaith dialogue is, then—but not till then—should we bring them together and take a hard look at the real life situation. This is the scientific method of synthesis. One could talk for a long time on this scientific method, but that too is "a thing in itself."[209]

Some time ago I was invited to make a presentation on the nature of syncretism for a commission to investigate its growth in the church. I drew many illustrations from other denominations and other places around the world to help them look at syncretism itself as objectively as possible. All I can say was that I was strictly biblical wherever I made an evaluation. I mentioned no denomination in my presentation for the same reason of objectivity. (In any case I was speaking to a denomination not my own.) Many of the participants (who went to work on their own after I had left) apparently supported the presentation, and the report was passed. I was not surprised to hear that a couple had submitted a minority report, for it had been quite manifest on the occasion of my visit that the interfaith dialogue viewpoint was represented among the participants.

When I read it, I expected to read about "the well-being of society" in a "wider ecumenism," and a "vision of the unity of humankind under God" which had to be rather hard-pushed by my validity tests. It was interesting to learn that Paul and John "had a hint of this vision" when both Paul and John were so dogmatic about idolatry in the κοινωνια (koinonia). Of course we were supposed to be dealing with things "in the church" (which I take to be at least supposedly the people of God in a covenant relation) and not interfaith dialogue in the outside world. I mention that because the minority report went directly to "The Theology of the Interfaith Dialogue," a preparatory document for an entirely

---

[209] For a discussion of synthesis in scientific method in missiology, see Tippett (1987b, xi–xx).

different consultation by a different body. This became their basis for discussion—and misunderstanding.

This document presupposed three categories of people, or three attitudes in the debate. They were (a) exclusivism, (b) inclusivism, and (c) pluralism. The first is the most extreme and finds "no salvation outside the church" (an inaccurate definition surely). The second "retains the uniqueness and supremacy of Christ and affirms the presence of God in all creation." God's saving power is in Christ but not confined to Him. He works through the Spirit and non-Christian peoples and cultures who may not even know the name of Jesus. Pluralism holds that religious differences are due to different interpretations of revelation and cultural limitations. God may reveal Himself in different traditions, myths, symbols, and texts. They are not necessarily equal; one may be better than the other. Most pluralists regard Christ as the most perfect of many revelations.

The second and third are said to be open for religious dialogue—the second probably the most suitable for present use, the first "makes interfaith dialogue difficult."[210]

The rationalization just oozes out of this pathetic statement. One can see theological problems being avoided or compromised. Syncretism is avoided as a subject, and in the Christian mission, there is no place for the authority of Scripture (just a text beside the Ramayana and Koran, etc.); and, whatever comes later in the report, this is the platform from which it is written. How bankrupt can our theology become!

As a piece of research analysis, it is also sociologically terrible. It specifies three categories in the mind of the person who formulated the basis for discussion report. They are quite inadequate categories into which the really good missiological writers of the world just cannot be forced. The presuppositions are wrong. Very few of the "extremists" say "no salvation outside the church." Most who are worth reading say "no way but through Christ," which is very different, and it is said on the word of Christ himself. One presumes that Visser't Hooft, Vicedom, and others would be classed as "extremists"—and Daniélou, to include a lucid Catholic writer. These men all deny the treatment of the Christian faith as "Christianity" placing it among the religions and getting bogged down in comparative religion. Christ stands out as Lord and Saviour. Here is the most significant point—soteriologically and ecclesiologically, and it has no category. If ever a typology for analysis betrayed the finding a researcher intended to force his data to say, we have it here.

If Paul says anything on the unity of humanity, it is not on the basis of a low-level religious dialogue, but has to be unity in Christ, and in Christ alone. The Pauline doctrine of the cosmic Christ is poles apart from the interfaith use of the term. The ultimate realization of the unity of all things in Christ has a forward projection. It is in the fellowship of believers that we have the pledge and foretaste of that to come. Likewise in the com-

---

210   Much abbreviated, but retaining the terminology of the minority report, and I believe an accurate reduction.

munion of the Lord's table and the Holy Spirit, all have their existential awareness and experience, the earnest ἀρραβών (arrabon) of the eschatological and the Christian eternal hope, which is as far as we could possibly get from the Hindu cyclical view of the soul (Eph 1:3–23).

There is no unity possible. The Hindu and Buddhist have to abandon their view of the soul, or the Christian does. Christ, and Christ alone, can bring any cosmic unity. If this be not so, then we must completely abandon the Scriptures as our way for faith and practise, and it has no authority. That, of course, would relieve us of the need for believing Jesus Himself when He said "No man cometh unto the Father but by me" (John 14:6 and Eph 1:1–14 go together).

I have read a great deal of Eastern religious literature. There are many fine and beautiful ideas. Some of their saints have drawn close. I observe that some of the good theological and ethical points have similarity with the Christian Scriptures, and there are values where their running is parallel. There are points where their picture of Indian lifestyle actually leads into the gospel narrative.[211] There are stepping stones into the Christian faith. There are also a number of poetical constructs, which are like a stretching forth into the unknown to grasp something that seems to be there. Much of that material can actually find its answer in Christ (cf. Pickett 1938). I know there is a way of Christ into the heart of India. I know that ideas the poets conceived can be realized in Christ, because He was a real Person and an historical event. There is hope there for unity in Christ; but there is no hope if the historicity of God's revelation in Christ is jeopardised or surrendered, or if the salvation of the human soul is sacrificed to a cyclical view which is incompatible with Scripture. My own view of sacrifice, say, has drawn from India, but of course that came from Tilak, the Christian poet, whose own Indian views had been sanctified by Christ (Winslow 1923).

I remember, of course, that the most successful of all Christian missionaries did not tear down the pagan paraphernalia in Athens, but starting with the altar to the Unknown God, he went on to tell them about Him. He proceeded from the known to the Unknown. This is what a missionary is trying to do by translating the Bible and working from the felt needs of a tribal people, say, through their own typology to Christian functional substitutes within a Christianized orientation. If this is not interfaith dialogue—what is it? If it isn't empathetic, then what is it? It is not quite fair to dismiss such a witness as an exclusivist who makes interfaith difficult (Acts 17:22ff).

It is not at this point where interfaith dialogue has to begin, but in a self-examination of our own kind. As far as I am concerned, I start with my Lord and Saviour and the holy Scriptures. This is bigger than Christianity as a religion and bigger than any historical denomination and helps me fix my sight on a covenant relationship that is not bound

---

211 For example, see T. C. Carne (1944a and 1944b), small books from a biblically oriented missionary.

by one culture, but can emerge in any culture. I can work in terms of a Christ who is not culture-bound. But to do this, I have to recognize the truth of Christ and the integrity of the Scriptures. Here is my fixed centre and frame of reference.

When it comes to syncretism, which has no fixed centre or reference point, except when it is openly hostile, as in satanism, the Asian religions are by no means the only false gods before us. The whole area of sorcery, of worship of the spirits, of spiritism, of personality cults (some leading to deification), of drug cults and the like, comes under our purview. We are also concerned with the devices and mechanisms by which Christian people get "hooked" on these religions. This has little, if anything, to do with "interfaith dialogue" for example. A person does not worship a ouija board, but the thing can lead him into a satanic cult, and immediately he has broken the first commandment.

Now, a builder needs to know and have confidence in the reliability of his measuring tools—square, rule, calipers, spirit-level, and plumb-bob. I understand that for the Christian these are Christ and the Scriptures. They stand or fall together, those two. If we do not agree there, then we have another discussion before we can even start to deal with syncretism.

In my own experience and reading, I can assemble a sad record of folk known to have been once good, active Christians, who have been sadly led off into witchcraft, the drug scene, and family discord by reliance on astrology. Astrology, ouija boards, tarot cards, and other forms of divination make poor measuring tools. They interfere with the nurture of the fellowship of believers and turn the attention away from Christ and the Scriptures. As Jeremiah pointed out centuries before Christ,

> My people have committed two evils:
> They have forsaken Me, the Fountain of Living Waters,
> And hewn out for themselves,
> Broken cisterns which hold no water (Jer 2:13)

Even physical and meditative programs can misguide spiritually if they shift the focus from Christ to self, by accepting the balance of good and evil as harmonious interplay, which is far removed from the Pauline recognition of this as a problem which he can only face in Christ. Ultimately this is a conflict of views of salvation.[212]

To sum up, then, if our subject is syncretism in the fellowship of believers, and we are not here discussing encounter in the world (i.e., we are examining the inner life in the fellowship with Christ), Christ and the Scriptures must be the terms of reference within which we do our measuring and testing. Then the issue is quite plain. It is a case of either:

---

212 Paul did not say "How may I integrate these opposites into a harmony of the universe" which would have been to concede the point of their manifest incompatibility. He recognized the true nature of the problem and his dependence on divine resources from outside himself to find his deliverance (Rom 7:21; 8:1). This is Paul's reply to the supposed balance of Yin and Yang.

> I respect Assyria, China, Teutonia and the Hebrews,
> I adopt each theory, myth, god and demi-god,
> I see that the old accounts, bibles, genealogies, are true without exception.

or again,

> Thee in thy all-supplying, all-enclosing worship—
> thee in no single bible saviour, merely,
> Thy saviours countless, latent within thyself,
> thy bibles incessant within thyself,
> equal to any, divine as any (Whitman).[213]

Or, on the other hand,

> I am persuaded that neither death nor life, nor angels, nor principalities, nor powers, nor things present, nor things to come, nor height, nor depth, nor any other creature, shall be able to separate us from the love of God which is in Christ Jesus, our Lord. (Romans 8: 38–39).

The human situation under postcolonial multiculturalism may have changed dramatically; but the human predicament is the same. The testing tools remain the same. The frame of reference and the fixed centre stand firm. The people of God must still stand true in the covenant relationship.

---

[213] The first quote comes from "Birds of Passage," the second from "Thou Mother with My Equal Brood." These are typical. One might cite "Song of Myself" to include the animist domain of fetishes and cultic possession, which have now invaded our urban jungles.

AFTERTHOUGHT AND DECLARATION

This is probably the last of my writing on this subject, not only because I know I am going down hill physically and think I have said most that I can say, and other things have to be pulled together before I go hence, but because the battle has to be carried on now by others.

I have given a quarter-century to this subject—the best of my years, the best of my Bible studies, the best of my anthropology—and I have done so for one reason alone: that His name be glorified. Now that Australia is becoming an Asian country, the battle will need to be fought on different terms, and I am sure that God will raise the men to do it.

If the rising generation should prove disposed to listen to an old man as he lays down his tools, I would say just two things.

(1) There is no let-up in this war until the end of the age. As the world situation changes, each of us in his day and generation has to face the continuing problem in his own peculiar situation. I cannot face tomorrow's human situation; I only know it has to be faced until the end.

(2) As I look back on the last twenty-five years, I find that biblical history and revelation always have spoken to those human situations, and show to us of other eras and cultures just what is continually at stake through them all. I find I have drawn from the wilderness experience of Israel, the episode on Mt. Carmel, the reformation under Josiah, and so on from Old Testament times and from the early church in Acts, from the prophetic messages of Jeremiah and Isaiah, from the letters of Paul, the unique claims of Jesus Himself and especially His high priestly prayer, and the general strong agreement of Peter, Paul, and John on the matter of creeping idolatry. The spiritual cohesion between these portions of Scripture is so strong that I must say with Paul, "Woe unto me if I preach not the gospel." I must stand by the Book as I stand by the Lord Himself. To reject this cohesive cluster of revealed truth is unthinkable. In no way may I allow any rationalization to jeopardise it. If the Lord should spare me long enough to write on the new interfaith dialogue in Australia, with Christians in the minority position, it will have to allow for the cohesion of the first commandment and the Great Commission, the prophetic warnings, and the exclusive claims of Christ. Underneath it all lies the theology of the people of God called to

communicate Him to the nations, the demand for holiness unto the Lord, and the protection of the covenant relationship. In all ages, the people of God have tended to fracture that covenant relationship by rationalizing about it.

The people of God are called to an ultimate purpose, depicted in the city of the consummation of all things. The features are the glory of God, the Lamb as the Light thereof, and the nations which are saved bringing their glory into it (Rev 21:23–27). Our critical path in the divine pert chart leads there. If we are in the purposes of God, there is to be no human rationalization.

REFERENCES

Ahmad, Mirza Mubarak
1965   *Our Foreign Missions.* Rabwah: Ahmadiyya Muslim Foreign Missions.

Anderson, Gerald H., ed.
1961   *The Theology of the Christian Mission.* Nashville: Abingdon Press.

Anderson, Robert T. and Barbara G. Anderson
1965   *Bus Stop for Paris: The Transformation of a French Village.* Garden City: Doubleday.

Andrews, C. F.
1912   *The Renaissance in India: Its Missionary Aspect.* London: Church Missionary Society.

Aurobindo, Sri
1955   *The Life Divine.* Pondicherry: Sri Aurobindo Ashram.

Ayer, Joseph Cullen
1952   *A Source Book for Ancient Church History: From the Apostolic Age to the Close of the Conciliar Period.* New York: Charles Scribner's Sons.

Babbage, Stuart Barton.
1937   *Hauhauism: An Episode in the Maori Wars, 1863–1866.* Dunedin: A. H. and A.W. Reed.

Baëta, C. G.
1962   *Prophetism in Ghana: A Study of Some "Spiritual" Churches.* London: SCM Press.

Barnett, Homer G
1942   "Culture Growth by Substitution." *Research Studies in the State College of Washington* 10: 26–30.
1953   *Innovation: The Basis of Cultural Change.* New York: McGraw-Hill.

Bastide, Roger
1978   *The African Religions of Brazil: Toward a Sociology of the Interpenetration of Civilizations.* Translated by Helen Sebba. Baltimore: Johns Hopkins University Press.

Bavinck, Johann. H.
1964 *An Introduction to the Science of Missions.* Translated by David H. Freeman. Philadelphia: Presbyterian and Reformed Publishing.

Belshaw, Cyril S.
1964 *Under the Ivi Tree: Society and Economic Growth in Rural Fiji.* London: Routledge and Kegan Paul.

Blatty, William Peter
1971 *The Exorcist.* New York: Harper and Row.

Bourguignon, Erika, ed.
1973 *Religion, Altered States of Consciousness, and Social Change.* Columbus: Ohio State University Press.

Brannen, Noah S.
1968 *Sōka Gakkai: Japan's Militant Buddhists.* Richmond: John Knox Press.

Bromiley, Geoffrey W., et al.
1979 *International Standard Bible Encyclopedia.* Vol. 3. Grand Rapids: Wm B. Eerdman's.

Bunyan, John
1948 *The Holy War.* Chicago: Moody Press.

Carey, William
1792 *An Enquiry into the Obligations of Christians to Use Means for the Conversion of the Heathens.* London: Hodder and Stoughton.

Carne, T. C.
1944a *Galilee by the Ganges.* Melbourne: Book Depot.
1944b *The Lily and the Lotus.* Melbourne: Book Depot.

Cave, Hugh B.
1959 *The Cross on the Drum.* Garden City: Doubleday.

Caird, G. B.
1956 *Principalities and Powers: A Study in Pauline Theology.* Oxford: Clarendon Press.

Carroll, Lewis
1958 *Alice Through the Looking Glass.* London: Mellifont Press.

Charan Singh, Satguru
1970 "Greetings." *East West Centre Newsletter.*
1974 *St. John, the Great Mystic.* Beas: Radha Soami Satsang.

Church of England in Australia
1975 *The Occult: Report of an Anglican Commission of Enquiry.* Sydney: Aio Publishing.

Clark, Thomas Curtis and Esther A. Gillespie
1937 *1000 Quotable Poems: An Anthology of Modern Verse.* New York: Harper and Brothers.

Clark, Walter Houston, H. Newton Malony, James Daane, and Alan R. Tippett
1973 *Religious Experience: Its Nature and Function in the Human Psyche.* Springfield: Charles C. Clark.

Cooper, Paulette
1975 *The Scandal of Scientology.* New York: Tower Publications.

Coulson, John
1981 *Religion and Imagination.* Oxford: Clarendon Press.

Courlander, Harold
1960 *The Drum and the Hoe: Life and Lore of the Haitian People.* Berkeley: University of California Press.

Courlander, Harold and Remy Bastien
1966 *Religion and Politics in Haiti.* Washington D.C.: Institute for Cross-Cultural Research.

Cox, Harvey
1966 *The Secular City: Secularization and Urbanization in Theological Perspective.* New York: Macmillan.

Cross, Frank Leslie and Elizabeth Livingstone, eds.
1974 *Oxford Dictionary of the Christian Church.* New York: Oxford University Press.

Daniélou, Jean
1962 *The Salvation of the Nations.* South Bend: University of Notre Dame Press.
1964 "Christianity in the Non-Christian Religions." In *Introduction to the Great Religions,* edited by Jean Daniélou. Notre Dame: Fides Publications.

Deissmann, G. Adolf
1927 *Light from the Ancient East.* New York: George H. Doran Co.

Deren, Maya
1953 *Divine Horsemen: The Living Gods of Haiti.* London: Thames and Hudson.
1973 *The Voodoo Gods.* St. Albans: Paladin.

Divine Life Society
1967 *The Divine Life Society: Handbook of Information.* Sivandanagar: Divine Life Society.

Donnelly, Morwenna
1956 *Founding the Life Divine: An Introduction to the Integral Yoga of Sri Aurobindo.* New York: Hawthorn Books.

Drury, Nevill and Gregory Tillett
1980 *Other Temples, Other Gods: The Occult in Australia.* Sydney: Methuen.

Dryden, John and Arthur Clough
1932 *The Lives of the Noble Grecians and Romans, by Plutarch.* New York: The Modern Library.

Durkheim, Emile
1951 *Suicide: A Study in Sociology.* New York: The Free Press.

Ellwood, Robert S
1974 *The Eagle and the Rising Sun: Americans and the New Religions of Japan.* Philadelphia: Westminster Press.

Encyclopædia Brittanica
1984 S.v. "Taoism." *Encyclopædia Brittanica*, 5: 797.

Enroth, Ronald M., Edward C. Erickson, and C. Breckenridge Peters
1972 *The Jesus People: Old Time Religion in an Age of Aquarius.* Grand Rapids: Wm B. Eerdman's.

Fairweather, William
1908 *The Background of the Gospels Or Judaism in the Period between the Old and New Testaments.* Edinburgh: T. and T. Clark.

Father Divine
1936–1989   *New Day*, various issues. Philadelphia: New Day Publishing Co.

Fauset, Arthur Huff
1971 *Black Gods of the Metropolis: Negro Religious Cults of the Urban North* Philadelphia: University of Pennsylvania Press.

Firth, Raymond
1963 *We, the Tikopia* Boston: Beacon Press.

Fisher, G. P.
1945 *History of the Christian Church.* New York: Charles Scribner's Sons.

Forsyth, P. T.
1908 *Missions in State and Church.* New York: A. C. Armstrong.

Giddens, Anthony
1972 *Emile Durkheim: Selected Writings.* Cambridge: Cambridge University Press.

Guiart, Jean
1956 *Culture Contact and the "John Frum" Movement of Tanna, New Hebrides.* Albuquerque: University of New Mexico.

Harper, Marvin Henry
1972 *Gurus, Swamis, and Avataras: Spritual Masters and Their American Disciples*. Philadelphia: Westminster Press.

Hawaii Children's Mission Society
1967 *"Hawaii": Fact and Fiction*. Honolulu: Hawaii Children's Mission Society.

Hayward, Victor
1963 *African Independent Church Movements*. Edinburgh: Edinburgh House Press.

Herskovits, Melville. J.
1937 "African Gods and Catholic Saints in New World Religious Belief." *American Anthropologist* 39 (4): 635–43.
1937 *Life in a Haitian Valley*. New York: Alfred A. Knopf.
1951 *Man and His Works: The Science of Cultural Anthropology*. New York: Alfred A. Knopf.
1958 *The Myth of the Negro Past*. Boston: Beacon Press.

Howe, Reuel L.
1963 *The Miracle of Dialogue*. Greenwich: Seabury Press.

Howson, John S.
1872 *The Metaphors of St. Paul and Companions of St. Paul*. Boston: American Tract Society.

Irenaeus
1953 "Selections from the Work *Against Heresies* by Irenaeus, Bishop of Lyons." Edited and translated by E. R. Hardy. In *Early Christian Fathers,* edited by C. C. Richardson. Philadelphia: Westminster Press.

Isherwood, Christopher
1945 *Vedanta for the Western World*. Hollywood: Marcel Rodd Co.

Johnson, Harmon A.
1969 "Authority Over the Spirits: Brazilian Spiritism and Evangelical Church Growth." MA thesis, Fuller Theological Seminary School of World Mission.

Kasturi, Narayana
1968 *The Life of Bhagavan Sri Sathya Sai Baba*. Prasanthinilayam: Sanathana Sarathi.

Kidd, B. J.
1922 *A History of the Christian Church to A.D. 461*. Vol. 2, *A.D. 313–408*. Oxford: Clarendon Press.

Kirk, John R. and G. D. Talbot
1966 "The Distortion of Information." In *Communication and Culture*, edited by Alfred E. Smith, 308–21. New York: Holt, Rinehart and Winston.

Kraemer, H.
1938 *The Christian Message in a Non-Christian World*. London: The Edinburgh House Press.
1961 "Syncretism as a Theological Problem for Missions." In *The Theology of the Christian Mission*, edited by Gerald H. Anderson, 179–82. Nashville: Abingdon Press.

Kraft, Charles H.
1973a "Towards a Christian Ethnotheology." In *God, Man and Church Growth*, edited by A. R. Tippett, 109–26. Grand Rapids: Wm B. Eerdman's.
1973b "Church Planters and Ethnolinguistics." In *God, Man and Church Growth*, edited by A. R. Tippett, 226–49. Grand Rapids: Wm B. Eerdman's.
1973c "Dynamic Equivalence Churches" *Missiology* 1 (1): 39–57.
1979 *Christianity in Culture: A Study in Dynamic Biblical Theologizing in Cross-Cultural Perspective*. Maryknoll: Orbis Books.

Latourette, Kenneth Scott
1938 *The History of Expansion of Christianity*. Vol. 2, *The Thousand Years of Uncertainty*. New York: Harper and Brothers.

La Vey, Anton S.
1969 *The Satanic Bible*. New York: Avon Books.
1971 *The Compleat Witch*. New York: Dodd, Mead.

Leek, Sybil
1968 *Diary of a Witch*. Englewood Cliffs: Prentice-Hall.
1975 *Sybil Leek's Book of Curses*. Englewood Cliffs: Prentice-Hall.

Lewis, C. S.
1961 *The Screwtape Letters*. New York: Macmillan.

Liddell, Henry George and Robert Scott
1929 *A Greek-English Lexicon*. Oxford. Clarendon Press.

Linton, Ralph
1936 *The Study of Man: An Introduction*. New York: D. Appleton-Century.

Lofland, John
1966 *Doomsday Cult: A Study of Conversion, Proselytization and Maintenance of Faith*. Englewood Cliffs: Prentice-Hall.

Loomis, Albertine
1967 *Grapes of Canaan: Hawaii 1820*. Honolulu: Hawaii Mission Children's Society.

Lowie, Robert H.
1970 *Primitive Religion*, rev. ed. London: Liveright Publishing Co.

Luzbetak, Louis J.
1963 *The Church and Cultures: An Applied Anthropology for Religious Workers.* Techny: Divine Word Publications.

Lyons, Arthur
1970 *The Second Coming: Satanism in America.* New York: Dodd, Mead.

Madsen, William
1957 *Christo-Paganism: A Study of Mexican Religious Syncretism.* New Orleans: Tulane University.

Malinowski, Bronislaw
1945 *The Dynamics of Culture Change: An Inquiry into Race Relations in Africa.* New Haven: Yale University Press.
1946 "The Problem of Meaning in Primitive Languages." In *The Meaning of Meaning: A Study of the Influence of Language Upon Thought and of the Science of Symbolism*, edited by C. K. Ogden and I. A. Richards, 296–336. New York: Harcourt, Brace and World.
1954 *Magic, Science and Religion.* New York: Doubleday and Co.
1962 *Sex, Culture, and Myth.* New York: Harcourt, Brace and World.
1965 "The Anthropology of Changing African Cultures." In *Methods of Study of Culture Contact in Africa*, edited by B. Malinowski. Oxford: University Press for International African Institute.

Marris, Peter
1961 *Family and Social Change in an African City: A Study of Rehousing in Lagos.* Evanston: Northwestern University Press.

Maslow, Abraham H.
1943 "A Theory of Human Motivation." *Psychological Review* 50 (4):370–96.

Maurier, Henri
1968 *The Other Covenant: A Theology of Paganism.* Translated by Charles McGrath. Glen Rock: Newman Press.

May, L. Carlyle
1956 "A Survey of Glossolalia and Related Phenomena in Non-Christian Religions." *American Anthropologist* 58 (1): 75–96.

Mbiti, John S.
1969 *African Religions and Philosophy.* New York: Anchor Books.
1969 "Eschatology." In *Biblical Revelation and African Beliefs*, edited by Kwesi Dickson and Paul Ellingworth, 159–84. Maryknoll: Orbis Books.
1971 *New Testament Eschatology in an African Background.* London: Oxford University Press.

McCary, Richard
1985   *Invasion of the Oneness People: The True Story of a Religious Cult.* Hollywood: Global-Tel Publishers.

McFarland, H. Neill
1967   *The Rush Hour of the Gods: A Study of New Religious Movements in Japan.* New York: Macmillan.

McGavran, Donald A., ed.
1972   *Eye of the Storm: The Great Debate in Mission.* Waco: Word Books.

McGregor, Pedro and T. Stratton Smith
1966   *Jesus of the Spirits.* New York: Stein and Day.

Métraux, Alfred
1959   *Voodoo in Haiti.* Translated by H. Charteris. New York: Oxford University Press.
1960   *Haiti: Black Peasants and Voodoo.* New York: Universe Books.

Möeller, Wilhelm
1893   *History of the Christian Church in the Middle Ages.* London: Swan, Sonnenscheim and Co.

Montgomery, John Warwick, ed.
1976   *Demon Possession.* Minneapolis: Bethany Fellowship.

Neill, Stephen
1970   *Call to Mission.* Philadelphia: Fortress Press.

Nettleton, Joseph
1906   *John Hunt: Pioneer Missionary and Saint.* London: Charles H. Kelly.

Nevius, John L.
1968   *Demon Possession.* Grand Rapids: Kregel Publications.

Nida, Eugene A.
1952   *God's Word in Man's Language.* New York: Harper and Row.
1959   "The Role of Cultural Anthropology in Christian Missions." *Practical Anthropology* 6 (3):110–16.
1960   *Message and Mission: The Communication of the Christian Faith.* New York, Harper and Brothers.
1968   *Religion Across Cultures: A Study in the Communication of Christian Faith.* New York: Harper and Row.

Opler, Morris E.
1945   "Themes as Dynamic Forces in Culture." *American Journal of Sociology* 51 (3): 198–206.

Parrinder, Geoffrey
1958   *Witchcraft*. Harmondsworth: Penguin Books.

Pfitzner, Victor C.
1967   *Paul and the Agon Motif*. Leiden: E. J. Brill.

Phillips, Godfrey E.
1946   *The Transmission of the Faith*. London: Lutterworth Press.

Pickett, J. Waskom
1938   *Christ's Way to India's Heart*. Lucknow: Lucknow Publishing House.

Pozas, Ricardo.
1962   *Juan the Chamula: An Ethnological Re-creation of the Life of a Mexican Indian*, trans. Lysander Kemp. Berkeley: University of California Press.

Prabhupāda, A. C. Bhaktivedanta
1970   *Krsna: The Supreme Personality of Godhead*. Boston: Iskcon Press.

Purdom, C. B.
1964   *The God-Man*. London: Allen and Unwin.

Radin, Paul
1937   *Primitive Religion*. New York: Viking Press.

Rattenbury, Harold B.
1949   *David Hill, Friend of China*. London: Epworth Press.

Reichelt, Karl L.
1951   *Religion in Chinese Garment*. London: Lutterworth Press.

Reyburn, William.
1957   "The Transformation of God and the Conversion of Man." *Practical Anthropology* 4 (5): 185–94.

Rivers. W. H. R.
1922   "The Psychological Factor." In *Essays on the Depopulation of Melanesia*, edited by W. H. R. Rivers, 84–113. Cambridge: The University Press.

Rowley, H. H.
1956   *Prophesy and Religion in Ancient China and Israel*. New York: Harper.

Sai Baba, Sri Sathya
1968   *At the Lotus Feet*. Bombay: Sri Sathya Sai Seva Organisations.
1981   *Sathya Sai Speaks*. Prasanthinilayam: Sri Sathya Sai Educational and Publication Foundation.

Sapir, Edward
1949   *Language*. New York: Harcourt, Brace and Co.

Sherif, Mustafer
1936   *The Psychology of Social Norms*. New York: Harper and Brothers.

Sivananda, Swami
1974   *Bliss Divine: A Book of Spiritual Essays on the Purpose of Human Life*. Sivandanagar: Divine Life Society.

Smalley, William
1955   "Culture and Superculture." *Practical Anthropology* 2 (3):58–71.

Streiker, Lowell D.
1971   *The Jesus Trip: Advent of the Jesus Freaks*. Nashville: Abingdon Press.

Sumner, William G. and A. G. Keller
1927   *The Science of Society*. 4 vols. New Haven: Yale University Press.

Sundkler, Bengt
1961   *Bantu Prophets in South Africa*. London: Oxford University Press.

Suryanarayana, A. V.
1967   *Paradise Gained: The Divine Life of Bhagavan Sri Sri Satya Sai Baba*. Guntur: Modern Printers.

Tallant, Robert
1946   *Voodoo in New Orleans*. New York: The Macmillan Co.

Thauren, J.
1926   *Die Akkommodation im Katholischen Heidenapostolat*. Munster, Aschendorff.

Thomsen, Harry.
1963   *The New Religions of Japan*. Vermont: Charles E. Tuttle.

Tippett, Alan R.
1960   "Probing Missionary Inadequacies at the Popular Level." *International Review of Mission* 49: 411–19.
1963   "Initiation Rites and Functional Substitutes." *Practical Anthropology* 10 (2):66–70.
1967a   "Religious Group Conversion in Non-western Society." Research in Progress Pamphlet. Pasadena: Fuller Theological Seminary School of World Missions.
1967b   *Solomon Islands Christianity: A Study in Growth and Obstruction*. London: Lutterworth Press.
1968   *Fijian Material Culture: A Study of Cultural Context, Function, and Change*. Honolulu: Bishop Museum Press.
1970a   *Church Growth and the Word of God*. Grand Rapids: Wm. B. Eerdman's.

1970b	*Peoples of Southwest Ethiopia.* Pasadena: William Carey Library.
1971a	*Evaluation of the Novel Hawaii and the Film Version.* Unpublished manuscript.
1971b	*People Movements in Southern Polynesia: A Study in Church Growth.* Chicago: Moody Press.
1971c	"The Continuity of Sorcery and Magic in Fiji." In *Anthropological Writing, 1962-71.* Unpublished manuscript, 343–87. Tippett Collection, St. Mark's National Theological Centre.
1972	"Possessing the Philosophy of Animism for Christ." In *Crucial Issues in Missions Tomorrow,* edited by D. McGavran, 125–43. Chicago: Moody Press.
1973a	"A Not-So-Secular City." *Christianity Today*: 88–89.
1973b	*Aspects of Pacific Ethnohistory.* Pasadena: William Carey Library.
1973c.	Situational Givens in Frontier Missions." In *The Gospel and Frontier Peoples,* edited by R. Pierce Beaver, 58–76. Pasadena: William Carey Library.
1973d	*Verdict Theology in Missionary Theory.* Pasadena: William Carey Library.
1976a	"The Role of the Catalytic Individual in Group Conversion from Animism." In *Psychologist Pro Tem,* edited by Donald F. Tweedie and Paul W. Clement, 231–42. Los Angeles: University of Southern California Press.
1976b	"Spirit Possession as it Relates to Culture and Religion." In *Demon Possession,* edited by John W. Montgomery, 143–74. Minneapolis: Bethany Fellowship.
1979	"People of God." In *International Standard Bible Encyclopedia,* edited by Geoffrey W. Bromiley, et al. Vol. 3. Grand Rapids: Wm B. Eerdman's.
1987a	"Ethnic Cohesion and the Acceptance of Cultural Change: An Indonesian Case Study." In *Introduction to Missiology,* 285–301. Pasadena: William Carey Library.
1987b	*Introduction to Missiology.* Pasadena: William Carey Library.
1988	*Let the Church Be the Church.* Canberra: St. Mark's Theological College.

Turner, Harold W.

1960	"Searching and Syncretism: A West African Documentation." *International Review of Mission* 49: 189–94.

Vicedom, Georg F.

1963	*The Challenge of World Religions.* Philadelphia: Fortress Press.

Victoria

1965	*Report of the Board of Inquiry Into Scientology.* Melbourne: A. C. Brooks.

Visser't Hooft, W. A.

1937	*None Other Gods.* London: SCM Press.
1963	*No Other Name: The Choice Between Syncretism and Christian Universalism.*London: SCM Press.

Wallace, Anthony F. C.
1956 "Revitalization Movements." *American Anthropologist* 58 (2):264–81.
1966 *Religion: An Anthropological View.* New York: Random House.

Wand, J. W. C.
1937 *A History of the Early Church to A.D. 500.* London: Methuen and Co.

Welbourn, F. B.
1961 *East African Rebels: A Study of Some Independent Churches.* London: SCM Press.

Wells, Ann E
1971 *This Their Dreaming: Legends of the Panels of Aboriginal Art in the Yirrkala Church.* St. Lucia: University of Queensland Press.

Warneck, Gustav and John Mitchell
1901 *Outline of a History of Protestant Missions from the Reformation to the Present Time.* New York: Fleming H. Revell Co.

Whitman, Walt
1959 *Complete Poetry and Selected Prose,* edited by James Miller Jr. Boston: Houghton Mifflin Co.

Winslow, Jack C
1923 *Narayan Vaman Tilak, the Christian Poet of Maharashtra.* Calcutta: Association Press.

Winter, Roberta
1978 *Once More Around Jericho: The Story of the U.S. Center for World Mission.* Pasadena: William Carey Library.

World Methodist Council
1957 *Proceedings of the Ninth World Methodist Conference.* Nashville: Methodist Publishing House.

Worsley, Peter
1968 *The Trumpet Shall Sound: A Study of "Cargo" Cults in Melanesia.* New York: Schocken Books.

Wright, Fred H.
1953 *Manners and Customs of Bible Lands.* Chicago: Moody Press.

Yamamori, Tetsunao and Charles Taber, eds.
1975 *Christopaganism or Indigenous Christianity?* Pasadena: William Carey Library.

Yinger, John Milton
1964 "On Anomie." *Journal for Scientific Study of Religion* 3(2): 158–73.

Zimmermann, Marie and Raymond Facelina
1973 *Religious Life: International Bibliography.* Strasbourg: Cerdic-Publications.

INDEX

A

acceptor, 47–50, 53
advocate, 43–44, 46–48, 50, 53, 63, 114, 151
Aeons, 28
Africa, 29, 70, 106, 123, 152
   African, 44, 48, 122
      movements, 44
Afro-messianic movements, 44
Against Heresies, 27–30
Ahab, 89–90
Allen, Roland, 172
alternative medicine, 137–41
America(n). *See* United States of America.
Amos, 67
Anderson, Gerald, 165
animal sacrifice, 135
animism, 11, 16, 21, 30, 34, 36, 60, 70–72, 75, 104, 108, 180
anthropology, 10–12, 50, 59, 108, 119–20, 139, 141
   anthropologist, 11, 14, 17, 21, 33–36, 38, 45, 47–49, 59–61, 68, 70, 73, 77, 79, 87, 89, 91–92, 106–08, 110, 118, 122, 137, 139
Antioch, 67
Aphrodite, 5
apologist, 4, 27–28, 68–69
apostasy, 30, 32, 93–94, 142

Aquinas, 63
Arianism, 43
Aristophanes, 3
Asia, 3, 142, 182
   Asian, 174, 176, 178, 181
      faiths, 158
      migrants, 63, 109, 151, 177
      religions, 76, 109, 112, 167–68, 188
      theology, 151
Assyria, 31, 148, 189
   Assyrian dominance, 92
astrology, 61, 77, 79–80, 82, 91, 95, 97, 102, 127, 130, 138–40, 162, 179
Athens, 67, 156, 187
Augustine, 63
Aurobindo, Sri, 146, 151
Australia, 61, 72, 109, 150–52, 155, 157, 166, 174, 176–77
   Australian, 166, 176, 181
      Aboriginal, 25, 33–34
      totemism, 34
   North, 57

B

Baal, 67, 81, 105, 183
   Baalism, 91
Baba, Sathya Sai, 145–48
Babylon, 67, 103, 171
   Babylonian, 92, 102

Bacchus
  worship of, 3
Bali, 181
baptism, 4, 29, 35, 54, 69, 121
Barnett, 49, 53
Bau, 35
Bavinck, Johann, 14, 30
Beatitudes, 38
Bernard of Clairvaux, 6
Bethel, 92-93
Bethlehem, 16, 72
Beyerhaus, Dr., 44
Bhakti, 144-45
Bible, 11, 23, 31, 34, 36, 46, 80-81, 128, 132, 134-35, 144-45, 152, 154, 161, 163, 182, 187
  biblical, 29-30, 33, 56, 62, 69-70, 76, 81, 87, 89, 98-99, 103-04, 106-07, 116, 128, 153, 155, 162, 185
  characters, 32-33
  creedal statement, 28
  doctrine, 113
  languages, 65
  message, 55
  names, 28, 69
  narrative, 86
  perspective, 101
  reconstruction, 85
  stewardship, 66
  teaching, 66, 145
  values, 35, 184
  view, 44, 142
  world, 111
  gospel, 10, 13-14, 17, 21-22, 25-26, 31, 34, 37-40, 42-45, 47, 49-50, 54-55, 57, 59-60, 63-66, 96-97, 144, 150, 156, 187
  Social, 172
  Scripture, 10, 12-13, 29, 33, 37-39, 56-57, 65, 70, 76-78, 80, 85, 88, 97, 103, 105, 110, 114, 116-17, 144-45, 167, 169, 174, 177, 187-88
  study, 75, 131
Brahmins, 43
Brazil, 48, 77, 120
Buddha, 32, 184
Buddhism, 77, 113-14, 157
  Buddhist, 109, 114-16, 147, 167, 175, 187
Bunyan, 163

C

Cakobau, Ratu, 51
California, 129, 151, 175
Caligula, 142
Calvinist, 14
  theology, 13
Canada, 152, 155
Canberra, 64, 77, 116, 138, 140
cannibal, 16-17, 36, 51, 72, 158
Carey, William, 59
Caribbean, 120
catechism, 38
Celts, 27
Central America, 72, 75
ceremonialism, 48
Chidananda, Swami, 149-50
China, 31, 142, 157, 189
  Chinese, 64, 105, 115-16, 143
Christianity, 12-14, 16, 19-22, 24, 36-37, 43, 49, 54, 62, 68, 70-71, 74, 100-01, 103, 108, 110, 112, 114, 121, 128, 136, 144-45, 147, 150, 165, 180, 186-87
  indigenous, 9, 22, 25, 32, 35, 46, 59-60, 164
christocentric, 30, 35

Christopaganism, 9, 11, 13–15, 22, 24, 32, 40, 66, 164
church, 1–2, 4, 10–11, 13, 15, 21–30, 33–40, 44, 46, 49, 51, 54, 58–62, 64–69, 72–73, 75–77, 85, 88, 96–97, 99–102, 104, 100, 118–19, 121, 124–25, 128, 132–38, 140–41, 144, 150–51, 153, 159–60, 163, 165–68, 172, 174–79, 181, 183–86
  growth, 6, 185
  history, 28, 119, 133
  plant, 21, 26, 66
Clark, Sidney, 172
Colonial/colonialism, 51, 58, 62, 111, 120–21, 144, 151, 163, 172, 174, 180–81
Colossae, 39, 97–98
Commonwealth Marriage Act, 159
communication, 10–12, 17, 22, 33, 35, 36, 42, 44, 59, 63, 65, 78, 112, 118, 134
communion, 1, 3, 5–7, 32, 39–40, 46, 68, 143, 154, 168, 183
community, 1–2, 19, 23, 27, 29, 46, 50, 57, 63–64, 71, 96, 105, 125–26, 137, 141, 153, 159
Confucius, 142
contextualization, 6, 64–66, 78, 90, 163–64
conversion, 17–18, 26, 33, 35, 49, 54, 62, 70–73, 75, 164
convert, 1, 3, 17–19, 22, 27, 30, 33–34, 36–37, 43, 49, 54, 60, 68, 70–72, 75, 77–78, 96–98, 147, 149, 151, 156, 165, 175
Cooper, Paulette, 157
Corinth, 1–5, 67–68, 97, 133, 182–83
covenant relationship, 6, 67, 76, 80–81, 85–87, 89, 93–94, 99, 103, 140, 153–54, 156, 163, 168, 172, 176, 178, 182–83, 189
Crete, 62
  Cretan, 62

criticism, 11, 27, 76
cross-cultural, 12, 17, 21, 26, 31–32, 42, 46–50, 54, 56, 59–63, 86, 124
Cuba, 48
  Cuban, 175
culture, 10–11, 14, 25, 28, 33–34, 38, 42, 50–51, 60, 63, 65, 74, 103, 107–08, 118, 135, 149, 181–84, 186–188
  cultural, 14–16, 19, 21, 24, 26–27, 30–31, 33, 36–37, 40–41, 46–47, 49–50, 54, 56–57, 59, 63, 66, 71, 77, 80, 86, 89, 91–92, 103, 108, 118–19, 121, 124, 139–40, 177, 183–85
  cohesion, 50, 72
  ethos, 11
  form, 11, 13, 15, 22, 30, 35, 38, 42, 45–46, 54, 64
  heritage, 13
  relevance, 11
cults, 4, 39, 54, 57, 59–60, 68, 73, 75, 96–97, 99, 109, 112, 119–20, 129, 132, 134, 139, 142, 144–45, 150, 154, 160, 163–64, 175
  fertility, 67, 81
  LSD drug, 129, 133
  personality, 153, 156–57, 160
  Tanit, 4
  Tyche, 95

D

Dahomey, 48, 70, 122
  Dahomean, 48, 120
David, 37
Day of the Dead, 19, 21, 74
de Nobili, 43
deification, 107, 142, 163
  allegorical, 161
deism, 43
Deissmann, Adolf, 56
demon, 16–18, 72–73, 95

cannibal, 17
   demonic, 61, 70, 73, 75–77, 79–80, 132, 168
   possession, 131
demoralization, 51–52
devil. *See* Satan.
divination, 76, 80, 96, 102, 124, 131–32, 138, 188
doctrine, 16, 28, 30, 68, 70, 107, 113, 177, 186
Dravidian, 70
drug addiction, 75, 109–10, 112
dynamic equivalence, 54, 57–58

E

Eastern, 116, 138, 142–44, 154, 160
ecclesiology, 186
education, 16–17, 30–31, 37, 52, 54, 71, 151, 166, 176
Egypt, 17, 81, 89, 147, 171
enchantings, 102
England, 52, 152
English, 56, 102, 147, 162
Ephesus, 67
eschatology, 20, 34, 44, 71, 75
ethics, 144, 149, 158
ethnohistory, 86, 90, 119
ethnopsychology, 105, 107, 131
ethnotheology, 85–86, 92, 131
Europe, 101, 106, 150
   European, 177
    history, 62
evangelicalism, 49
evangelism, 26, 44, 46, 96
exorcism, 94, 107

F

faith, 7, 10, 13–14, 16, 21, 26–28, 30, 32–33, 35–40, 42, 45, 48–49, 57, 60–61, 65–66, 68, 70, 72–74, 76–77, 88, 98–99, 107, 109, 118, 130, 132, 153, 155–56, 158, 163, 167, 176, 180, 182, 186–87

distortion, 25–33, 37–38, 69, 71, 73
fellowship, 1–3, 5–7, 10, 21, 23, 33, 38, 54, 75, 87, 98, 103–05, 109, 132–33, 144, 150–51, 153–55, 183–84, 188
Forsyth, P. T., 182
France, 152
   French, 120–21, 142

G

Gakkai, Sōka, 29, 70, 77
Galilee, 11
   Galilean Aramaic, 11
Gamaliel, 106
Germany, 152
   German, 142
gerontocracy, 171
Gnosticism, 27–28, 30, 157
   Gnostic, 27–30, 143, 146
gods, 1, 3, 39, 67, 70, 81, 91, 95, 112, 116, 122, 143, 147, 161, 188
   rival, 106, 110
Goths, 10
   Gothic, 65
Graeco-Roman, 1, 88, 97, 99, 102, 105
Great Britain, 135, 155, 157, 174
   British, 120
Great Commission, 18, 40, 58–59, 76, 150
Greece, 161, 182
   Greek, 3, 10–11, 18, 29–30, 62–63, 76, 88, 95–96, 102, 156
Guatemala, 156

H

Haiti, 48, 122
Hauhau Movement, 29
Hebrew, 10–11, 18, 31, 58, 67, 89, 92, 182, 189
hermeneutics, 44
Herskovits, Melville, 48, 51, 70
Hindu, 4, 43, 68, 70, 108, 113, 139, 145–47, 151–52, 187

Hinduism, 61, 64, 70, 108, 113, 140, 144–45, 147, 149, 153, 156–57, 167, 176
Hoekendijk, Dr., 45
Holland, 152
Hollywood, 79, 135
Hosea, 163
Hubbard, L. Ron, 157–60
humanism, 3
Hunt, John, 65

I

Iberian, 48
iconoclasm, 38, 91
ideology, 48, 161
idolatry, 67, 80, 94, 101–03, 107, 161
India, 52, 70, 144, 152, 155, 157, 187
interfaith dialogue, 184–88
Irenaeus, 27–30, 32, 68–69
Isaiah, 24, 67, 81, 93–94, 103, 142
Israel, 67, 87–89, 92, 94, 143, 171
Italy, 3, 182
   Italian, 3

J

Japan, 152, 155
   Japanese, 115
Jeremiah, 81, 93, 142, 188
Jerusalem, 91, 93–94
   Council, 27
   New, 38
Jesus Movement, 141
Jew, 11, 16, 32, 72, 88
Jewish, 90, 95, 98, 142
John, 28, 97, 99, 102, 184–85
John Frum Movement, 29, 69
Josiah, 67, 81, 90–93, 183
Judea, 95

K

Khayyam, Omar, 155
koinonia, 44, 73, 101, 185
Korea
   Korean religion, 112
Kraemer, Hendrik, 165–66, 172–73
Kraft, Charles, 14
Krishna, 29, 70, 150, 152–53

L

La Vey, Anton, 130, 176
Latin, 63, 65, 155–56
Latin America, 14–15, 22, 106
legalism, 4–5, 98
Linton, Ralph, 46, 107–08
Los Angeles, 29, 112, 127, 133–34, 151
Lutheran, 116
Lyons, 27, 68
Lystra, 67, 96

M

Macedonia, 182
magic, 11, 32, 62, 71, 95, 102, 105–06, 112, 117–19, 128–29, 133, 135, 163, 180–81
   black magic, 124, 163
   chant, 32
   magical
     arts, 52
     equipment, 77
     manipulation, 134
     medicine, 137
     potions, 122
     stone, 164
     weapons, 80
   magician, 102, 129
   white magic, 125
Magus, Simon, 96
Mahikari, 116, 138
Maine, Sir Henry, 20
Malinowski, Bronislaw, 34, 55
Mansoul, 163

Maori Wars, 29
Marcion, 68, 70, 116
Mary, 4, 29, 32, 68–69
materialism, 3, 75
Maya tribe, 22, 71
  Mayan, 156
McGavran, Donald, 42–43
Mesoamerican, 48
Mexico, 4, 22, 152
Mezo-American Indian, 4
Micah, 67, 142
Milligan College, 58, 100, 108, 173
ministry, 1, 10, 19, 63, 66, 75, 93, 110, 171, 180
  healing, 73–74, 124, 137
missiological
  exchanges, 173
  literature, 9
  problems, 14
  research, 59
  theory, 60
  writers, 186
missiology, 12, 41, 52, 58, 66, 98
mission, 1, 11, 17, 26, 29, 32, 38–40, 44–46, 58, 60–62, 65, 73–74, 76, 86, 88, 93–94, 99, 103–04, 110–12, 128, 137, 150–51, 157, 173–74, 176–78, 184
  colonial, 58, 62, 111, 151, 172
  field, 70
  history of, 25
  policy, 43
  postcolonial, 58, 60, 111, 171
  world, 156
missionary, 12–13, 21, 25–26, 29, 33–34, 36, 40, 43, 45–47, 49–50, 52, 54–55, 57, 59–63, 70, 73, 75–76, 110, 122–23, 128, 132, 140, 144, 167, 172–73, 175, 177, 179–80, 182, 187

Moses, 80–81, 128
Mount Carmel, 67, 89, 105, 183
Mount Sinai, 88
multicultural, 40, 88, 95, 177, 182–83, 189
Muslim, 109, 116

N

nativistic movements, 29, 36, 44, 51–52, 70, 73
Navaho Indian, 33, 55
  Peyote Eaters, 160
Nazareth, 17
Neill, Stephen, 58
New Age, 138
New Guinea, 54, 60
New Hebrides, 29
New Orleans, 121
New South Wales, 146
New Testament, 2, 5, 9, 39, 44, 59, 67, 76, 86, 94, 96–97, 99, 102–04, 161, 168, 177, 180, 182
Nigeria, 48
Nilayam, Prasanthi, 147
Niles, D. T., 114
North America, 106, 150

O

Oceania, 14, 29, 106
Old Testament, 2, 9, 67, 82, 100, 102–03, 142, 168, 185
oral traditions, 33, 36–37
ouija board, 76, 79, 131–32

P

pagan, 1, 9–10, 13, 16, 19, 26, 36–38, 49, 55–57, 62, 67, 69, 80–81, 96, 142, 187
paganism, 2, 27–28, 30, 51
Palestine, 94–95
Pasadena, 116
passive qualities, 46–47

of a cultural element, 45, 47
   table, 47
Paton, David, 172
Paul, 2-3, 30, 39, 44, 57, 68, 82, 96-99, 102, 104-05, 107, 121, 133, 156, 184-86
   Pauline, 4, 56, 96, 107, 186, 188
Pentecostal, 77
Pergamos, 39
persecution, 171
Peter, 97, 99, 144, 160, 172
Peyote Spirit, 68, 160
Pharisee, 94
   Pharisaism, 94
Philistines, 81
Pionyio, 68
pneumatology, 44
Portugal
   Portuguese, 120
postcolonial world, 174
Prasad, Narayan, 147
preaching, 23, 29, 55, 58, 66, 69-70, 93, 163
prophesy, 93
Protestant, 121
Psychological Practises Act, 159

Q

Queen of Heaven, 4, 67-68, 93
Queensland, 146

R

Red Sea, 89
Reformation, 62, 92, 171
religion, 16, 19-20, 22-23, 25-26, 30-32, 34, 39-40, 48-49, 59, 61, 70-71, 75-76, 81, 88-90, 95-97, 100, 103-06, 109-10, 112-13, 116-17, 120, 128, 134, 138, 140-42, 145, 148-49, 151, 159, 166-68, 176, 179-83, 186-88
   pagan, 1, 9

Roman Catholic, 4, 9, 22, 48-49, 70-71, 116, 120-21, 186
Rome, 43, 56, 67, 95, 161
   Roman, 57, 95, 101
Rousseau, 101
Rowley, H. H., 142

S

salvation, 21, 30, 35, 39, 49, 97, 149-50, 157, 160, 162, 167, 186
Salvian, 4, 68
Samaria, 67, 96
San Francisco, 135
Sapir, Edward, 108
Saraswati, Swami Tiswanandi, 149
Satan/devil, 3-4, 7, 16, 68, 72, 77, 88, 107, 133, 136, 142, 157, 163, 183
   church of, 76
   satanic, 77, 134, 140, 168
      Age, 140, 176
      ceremony, 157
      fashion, 135
      ideas, 181
      invasion, 168
      magic, 129
      meaning, 156
      power, 168
      religion, 134
      ritual, 136
      spiritual force, 137
      wedding, 135
   satanism, 124, 128, 130, 134, 136, 140, 166, 168, 176, 188
schism, 36
Scientology, 157-60
Scripture. *See* Bible.
secular, 11, 24, 38, 49, 59, 65, 76-77, 85-86, 100, 104
   city, 77, 112, 177

secularism, 43, 151
Semitic, 95
Sermon on the Mount, 66, 87, 169
sex, 36, 107, 156, 161, 180, 182
  attraction, 139
  culture, 135
  sexual
    abuse, 36
    bewitching, 179
    excesses, 133
    love, 3, 161
    traps, 128
Shakers, 53
Shaphan, 90
sin, 63, 76, 89, 92–93, 97, 136
Siva, 147–48, 150
Solomon, 38
Solomon Islands, 180
sorcery, 77, 96, 102, 116, 118–19, 124–25, 127, 129, 135, 175, 180, 188
South Africa, 106, 150
South America, 150
Spain, 147
  Spaniard, 14
  Spanish, 9, 17, 21, 24, 49, 71
spiritism, 77, 120, 124, 180, 188
spiritualism, 120
syncretism, 6, 9–10, 13–15, 18, 21–22, 25–27, 30–32, 36, 38, 43, 45–48, 52, 55, 58 59, 64, 67–73, 75–77, 81, 86–87, 89–90, 92–105, 108, 110–11, 113, 117–19, 134, 140–41, 146, 150–51, 155–56, 159, 163, 165–68, 171–75, 177–85, 188
  dangers of, 66
  definition of, 62
  degree of, 65
  dynamics of, 61, 71
  problem of, 59, 62
  threat of, 1

T

Tai Chi, 116
Taoism, 108, 116, 167
Ten Commandments, 38
theology, 6, 13, 61–62, 64–65, 68, 74, 92, 103, 108, 110, 116, 121, 138, 143–44, 150–51, 153, 155, 157, 165–66, 173, 177, 179–80, 184, 186, 191
  incarnational, 10, 85
  indigenous, 45
  theological, 13, 27, 32, 44, 56, 61, 66–70, 75, 85–87, 89, 94, 103, 107, 109, 113, 118, 139, 145, 151, 153–55, 158, 165–67, 171–73, 176, 179, 187
  liberal/conservative dichotomy, 173
Timothy, 97, 107
totemism, 34
transformation, 13–14, 33
  formal, 25–27, 30–33, 36–37, 39
Trobriands, 55
Turner, Harold, 52
Tyche, 95
Typology, 58, 80, 101, 103–06, 166–67, 169, 186–87

U

United States of America, 52, 77, 122, 175
  American, 53, 59, 76, 114, 122, 135, 147, 153
universalism, 2, 63, 76, 113, 148, 157
urban, 1, 6, 75–76, 95, 99, 105–06, 118, 122, 164–65, 180–81, 183

V

Valentinus, 29, 68, 70, 116, 152
Vatican, 121
Venus, 3, 5
Victorian, 11

Vishnu, 150
Visigoths, 65
voodoo, 120–22, 127

W

Wallace, Anthony, 52
Wangaratta, 25
West Africa
West African, 52, 120
Western, 4, 10, 13, 21, 23, 34, 36, 44, 46, 49, 52, 54, 58, 62, 64, 73, 125–26, 142, 144, 147, 151, 153–54, 157, 160, 168, 175, 177
witch, 80, 125–30, 135
witchcraft, 124, 126–29, 135, 158, 166, 175, 179
Witchcraft Convention, 127
witchdoctor, 123
World War II, 143–44, 147
worldview, 10, 32, 34, 46, 48–50, 52–55, 58, 71, 90, 92

worship, 3–5, 11, 16, 21, 23–24, 29–34, 36–37, 47–48, 55, 58, 64–65, 67–69, 71–72, 80–82, 92, 95, 98, 117, 121, 129, 141, 143, 148–49, 152, 160–61, 164, 183, 189
  ancestor, 19
  astrological, 91
  carnal, 133
  emperor, 96, 99, 142
  man-worship, 162
  nature, 72, 83
  saint worship, 70
  self-worship, 86, 161, 163
  spirit worship, 118, 188
  sun worship, 4, 21, 32, 68
  temple, 91

Y

Yamamori, Tetsunao, 9
yoga, 52, 61, 115, 138–40, 146, 149–50, 153, 157, 175
Yoruban, 48